The Triumph and the Tragedy

*Biographies of Andrew Fisher,
Frank Tudor, Charlie Frazer,
Percy Coleman and Frank Anstey*

*to show some aspects of the
Australian Labor Party
1890 – 1934*

John Murdoch

Published by John Murdoch

Copyright © John Murdoch 2013

The National Library of Australia
Cataloguing-in-Publication Data

Murdoch, John R. M.
The Triumph and the Tragedy

ISBN 978-0-9871238-2-4 (pbk)

1. Australian Labor Party--History--19th century.
2. Australian Labor Party--History--20th century.
3. World War, 1914-1918--Political aspects--Australia.
4. Maritime strike, New South Wales, 1890.
5. Australia--Politics and government--19th century.
6. Australia--Politics and government--20th century.

324.29407

The Author of this book accepts all responsibility for the contents and absolves any other person or persons involved in its production from any responsibility or liability where the contents are concerned.

All rights reserved. No part of this publication may be reproduced, stored in a retrieval system, or transmitted, in any form, by any means, electronic, mechanical, photocopying, recording or otherwise, without prior permission from the author.

Typeset in Book Antiqua 12pt

Produced by **TB Books**
    P.O. Box 8138
    Seymour South Victoria 3880
    Email: info@tbbooks.com.au

Cover Design by TB Books

For Heidi

It is the future which counts with the Labor Party, and not the past. If it be not a party with promises, and with the promised land always in view, it is nothing.

> Sir Ronal Munro Ferguson to the Secretary
> Of the State for the Colonies, 18th March, 1917

Contents

INTRODUCTION 13

PART ONE
The Dream and the Destruction:
A Portrait of Andrew Fisher 19

> **Chapter I**
> 'I was not above ten years of age when I first went into the mine.' 23
>
> **Chapter II**
> 'Parliament was a great deal worse than I had imagined it would be.' 39
>
> **Chapter III**
> 'State enterprise through the whole of the Commonwealth has been most successful.' 57
>
> **Chapter IV**
> 'That this proposal will relieve misery, I have not the shadow of a doubt.' 73
>
> **Chapter V**
> 'I have decided to be an applicant for a position in the public service.' 93

PART TWO
The Leader Whom they Chose:
Frank Tudor and the Labor Party after Hughes 103

> **Chapter I**
> 'In a shop in which I worked in England, they turned out a thousand dozen hats a week.' 107

Contents

Chapter II
'I should go back to my trade if I left political life.' ... **116**

Chapter III
'I candidly admit that I cannot bring myself to send men out of Australia to fight.'.. **128**

Chapter IV
'I sometimes long for the old times when we were fighting together.' **143**

PART THREE
And Who Awakened When?
The Political Philosophy of W. G. Spence................... **153**

Chapter I   Three Score Years and Eight..................... **157**

Chapter II   Exploiters, Angels and 'Scum' **166**

Chapter III The Vision … **173**

Chapter IV … and the Void **182**

PART FOUR
The Leader Who Never Was:
The Short Life of Charlie Frazer................................. **187**

Chapter I
'In this country, 'tis "Youth must be served".' **191**

Chapter II
'He has improved out of sight since he bounded into Parliament.'.. **215**

Chapter III
'The bitterest of critics in the Labor ranks.' **238**

Chapter IV
'More importance attaches to the speech of one associated with the Ministry.' **251**

Chapter V   'I want to go on a trip.' **265**

PART FIVE
No New Ideas:
Percy Coleman and Post-war Labor 271

PART SIX
Reflection in Writing
Frank Anstey and the Literature of the Labor
Up-and-Down 285

PART SEVEN
Photos 301

REFERENCES 313

Abbreviations

AA — *Australia's Awakening,* W. G. Spence, 1909
ANL — The Australian National Library, Canberra
AWU — *The History of the Australian Workers' Union,* W. G. Spence, 1911
CO 418 — The Colonial Office files for Australia in the Public Record Office, London
CPD — Commonwealth Parliamentary Debates
CPP — Commonwealth Parliamentary papers
Crouch Memoirs — MS by Richard Crouch MHR in the Latrobe Library, Melbourne (MS 9599)
DT — The *Daily Telegraph*
Frazer's Scrapbook — MS 981 in the ANL
ML — The Mitchell Library, Sydney
QPD — Queensland Parliamentary Debates
SMH — The *Sydney Morning Herald*
The *Age* — The *Melbourne Age*

INTRODUCTION

The Great War brought about the ghastly and senseless deaths of millions of men, destroyed the social order in Europe, and prepared the way for the loathsome dictators who were to be responsible for a second and even more terrible conflict. As a side-effect, the murdering fields of France were to wreck a positive antipodean phenomenon, the rise of the Labor Party in Australia as a movement of democratic progress and equality. For longer than two decades before the war had started, this development in the whole of the southern continent had been considered, in most of the western world, to be taking place in what was often called "the land of social miracles."[1]

It had indeed all started so promisingly in the early 1890s, when Labor began to become a political force at a time of great social unrest. At first there was much discussion about the writing of such men as Henry George, Edward Bellamy and Karl Marx. Their tracts justified the working classes in banding together, since they provided an appropriate form of idealism to counter the liberal belief in the capitalist virtues of independence and individualism. The increasing success of Labor in some of the colonial parliaments made it less necessary for its politicians to make loud noises vindicating the writings of philosophers from far away. The leading Labor men became far more practical and hard-headed than the theorists. Although they had dreams of a glorious future, they had much less interest in generalised speculation than in specific measures to win democratic and social reforms for their movement.

It all led to the rapid development of Labor from next to nothing in 1890 to become, twenty years later, the most successful Australian parliamentary force of its time. The spectacular victory in the federal elections of 13th April, 1910 was made possible because the party won votes of many people from outside the narrower trade union movement which had given it birth. This flood-tide of Labor was not wholly due to the proposals for reform. The entire movement, as a result of its successes, had become permeated with a home-grown feeling of righteousness together with the anticipation of a democratic morality which transcended mere economic issues.

This positive development was not to be lasting. Although the newly-developed idealism seemed to be strong, and even invincible to many of those who believed in it, it was shattered by the war and Labor was transformed from being "an active party of initiative to a purely negative party of resistance."[2] The visitors from Europe had no reason to continue their interest in the workers' movement which had lost all its magnetism and drive. After the war was over, the wonder, felt and expressed by the academics and social observers, ceased to exist. The new books about Australia were either confined to travellers' tales or dry textbooks concerning conditions on the continent.³

The first of the following biographical essays seeks to portray some facets of this unhappy circumstance by considering the life experiences of the Labor Party's second leader and three times Prime Minister, Andrew Fisher. The intention is to make an analysis of his character and of the influences which helped to form it, in order to understand how he was able to take advantage for many years of the opportunities offered by the political situation of his time. Additionally, Fisher's leadership style has not always been fully appreciated,⁴ and this portrait of him attempts to redress unfavourable opinions by showing that he was by no means only a well-meaning figurehead, but instead a most important part of the Labour successes up to 1914. Finally, the analysis shows why he was incapable of mastering the challenge of leading Australia during the great crisis of war, thus destroying his own career and turning him into a disappointed exile from the land of his extraordinary achievements.

The second biography considers the wretched political events of this unhappy development, from the point of view of Frank Tudor, who was chosen in November 1916 to succeed W. M. Hughes as party leader. Although Tudor was a man of excellent and honourable character, he was hopelessly out of place in the political jungle of 1916, and outclassed in the following years by opponents of greater ability and far stronger and more ruthless ambition. He thus could do nothing more than reflect the miserable performance of his entire party during the final years of the war and in the time of reconstruction which followed. In this way Tudor, as well as Fisher before him,

Introduction

personified the dismal descent of Labor from being at the centre of the movement of thrusting progress into becoming little more than a grouping of narrow-minded complainers at the very edge of events.

The third biography concerns the history of the Australian trade union and Labor Party movement, as well as the dreams of its glorious future, as shown in the words of William Spence, who was far from being reticent in their expression. He set down his mature workers' philosophy on the past and future in two idealistic books published in 1909 and 1911. Spence did not, of course, express sentiments which were shared by all the Labor men and women. He had his own subjective opinions, and to state that each of these was in the mainstream of Labor thought would be a simplification.[5] Yet in his broad outlook and enthusiasm as well as in his ability to generalise, Spence expressed concepts which were shared by many of his co-workers and party friends. Such a collective attitude was one of the basic reasons why the Labor Party was able to hold together with increasing popular approval for over two decades. The essay goes on to show how Spence's career and idealism of Labor were suffocated by the war, leaving the party as little more than a one-sided pressure group on behalf of the insular interests of the workers.

The next two biographies have a different purpose. They are intended to personalise some aspects of the unfortunate changes which so rocked the Labor Party. The first one is concerned with Charlie Frazer before the war, when Labor was enjoying its triumphant surge, the second with Percy Coleman after it, when the party had sunk into stagnation. The essay on Frazer shows how, between 1904 and 1908, he was of great importance in tactical matters and in securing the acceptance of crucial policies, and also how his leaders between 1909 and 1913 were able to make use of his talents on behalf of the Labor movement in general, especially as he had an ability for organisation and administration which is not always possessed by those of cabinet rank. Frazer's life, therefore, shows how open his party was for new impulses and ideas before the war, a form of political creativity which made the most significant impact on the electorate.

The brief biography of Coleman shows the opposite, after the war had destroyed Labor's unity and idealistic purpose. The new development in the 1920s required strict conformity to unchanging ideas and rigid discipline, and the younger party members voluntarily subjected themselves to the will of narrow-minded men who could have been their fathers. Coleman's life demonstrates this change in party attitudes which caused Labor to be closed to most forms of positive initiative stemming from personal ability and ambition. He thus personified the differences between the Labor attitudes of before the war, the earlier kind which had enabled Frazer to be so successful, and the later sort, when Coleman's obedience to regulations made of him little more than a party hack.

Finally the sixth and last essay shows the miserable development in the Labor literature after the war had exploded into life. The productions of Frank Anstey were well-researched and put together, but in nothing were they redolent of the positivism as expressed by Spence; and the visitors from Europe found nothing to interest them in the doings of the post-war Labor Party.

Introduction

My thanks go to Jennifer Gowland for her help in uncovering the references which gave shape to Frazer's early life in Victoria; to Helene Charlesworth for those on his work for the Goldfields Trades and Labor Council and the Kalgoorlie Municipal Council; to Alison Pilger for the early dates of Tudor and his family; and to the Australian National Library for the kind permission to reproduce the illustrations from Frazer's scrapbook.

PART ONE

The Dream and Its Destruction

A Portrait of Andrew Fisher

Whether a man is a Lord or a scavenger, test him on his merits and actions and, if these things ring true, then 'let sense and worth o'er a' the earth bear the gree and a' that'. The great aim of Parliament and nations of all kinds has been summed up by Burns. This is all we are trying to do. If there is suffering which can be removed without deterioration to the race, it is the duty of a free country and a free Parliament to remove that disability, to give every man his place, not according to his money or position into which he may have been born.

Andrew Fisher in Kilmarnock
18th May, 1911

Chapter I

'I was not above ten years of age when I first went into the mine.'

To be a coalminer in Scotland in 1862 was, as always, a dirty, unhealthy, exploitative, and an unpleasant form of employment in every way. Twelve hours a day with a shortened Sunday, for breadline wages, was the rule.[6] The ever-present risks of explosion and injury and the long-term fate of lung disease were the rewards. The miners lived in wretched rows of terraced houses built by the owners, with the fear of instant ejection if the tenants could not work, and therefore be unable to pay their rent during times of illness or strikes. Drinking water came from the street pumps, and privies and washhouses were communal. The miners, filthy after the interminable shifts, enjoyed no bathing facilities at the pit heads. They had to scrub themselves clean at home whilst their wives washed their working clothes ready for the following day.

Yet these dismal conditions represented an enormous improvement from a hundred years earlier, when fifteen hour days had been the rule, and women as 'bearers' had carried up to a hundredweight of coal in each load from the depths of hell to swell the profits of those who owned them after a year and a day of toil. Now that there were trade unions, there were better drainage and safety measures, there were the shorter hours, and there were incentives for the miners to do something for themselves and the standard of living of their families. The miners of the eighteenth century had lived in sullen desperation that their lives could never change, but by 1862 each of them knew that improvement was a possibility.

Crosshouse near Kilmarnock in Ayrshire was a mining village like dozens of others. It consisted of grimy rows of tiny miners' dwellings with monotonous slate roofs, without front gardens, dominated by the twelve working pits which were the cause and reason for their existence. One of the miners was Robert Fisher, who was described by his neighbours as being 'like Carlyle, gey ill to put up with'.[7] He married Jane Garven, the daughter of a travelling greengrocer, in March 1859. In regular succession she gave birth to John, Andrew (born on 29th August, 1862), Robert, James, Jean, Janet, David, and William.

The growth of his family was the motive for the difficult but dutiful father to found the Crosshouse Co-operative Society in March 1863, in partnership with James Barrowman, John Murdoch and several other local men, with a capital of fifteen pounds.[8] Robert Fisher was far from being a man who laboured only to keep himself and his family alive, drinking away his few short hours of leisure. The Co-operative was his attempt to do something for the community, so that his children could grow up into a better world. It was a blow at the truck system, where the mine-owners had the right to pay their workers in vouchers to be redeemed in food or goods at their own shops at rates fixed by themselves. Fisher and his associates wanted wages and all transactions to be in cash, their initiative was an attempt to eradicate some of the advantages which unfettered capitalism demanded for itself. The slow success of the Cooperative showed that the miners were ready and able to make a serious attempt to improve the conditions in which they had to live.

Fisher's second son Andrew sucked this attitude into himself as he did his mother's milk. To unite against the forces of capital, that was the constant lesson of his earliest years. One person alone was nothing, to work together created the strength which could move the mountains of privilege, change the course of the stream of politics, and bend the decrees and laws of the possessors into a form which could be of benefit to the labourers of the world. No influence in his early years was to be more important for him than this. It was to be his greatest strength in later years when, in the times of his personal triumphs and success, he was and remained the man who, although chosen by his colleagues to speak for them, took no credit for himself except as the representative of all.

The slow development of the Crosshouse Co-operative was dependent upon the strictest trust and honesty with its funds. Andrew Fisher grew up in an atmosphere of the most painstaking bookkeeping. The morality of a struggling financial system became an integral part of his character. His personal affairs were always well ordered, and he became a keen and careful investor. In public matters, his belief was that using the power of money correctly was a blessing which created benefits for all. It was both the key and the solution to the problems of social justice. To misuse this power to one's personal advantage was a crime. All his life Fisher showed how vitally he had learnt this lesson. When in office, he kept the Treasury in his own hands, so that the final word of honest decision and distribution should be his alone. Never was a politician so scrupulously determined to bring about a financial system that would enable those who needed help to get it.

For Fisher, the mentality of the Co-operative was reinforced by the serious, unbending faith of Presbyterianism. He was regular in attendance at Sunday services characterised by an entire lack of pomp and colour. Although he was never a fanatically religious man like many in the kirk, he absorbed as a matter of course its teaching that the individual had the duty to act in the righteous ways demanded of him by the community, always according to the precepts of the Bible. A man's every deed was made in the knowledge that God was watching him and assessing whether his life would be considered worthy when the Day of Judgement came. Ambition was permitted, provided it was not merely a personal one, but was exercised on behalf of one's fellow-men. To strive for personal advantage against the interests of the group was to subvert the essentials of everything of ethical value, it was the suicide of character, it was to betray the living Christ. True fulfilment was in the opposite, to act on behalf of the good of all, to take the most leading part possible in standing up for righteousness, the virtue for which Jesus was crucified, and therefore for which He died.

The bedrock of Fisher's character was formed by these teachings. He was never to be one for subterfuge or any kind of trickery. 'Get right up against a man' was his principle in dealing with people, and he held to it all his life.[9] All that a human being possessed was the worth of his promise, the honesty of his word. Fisher's was the strict and serious refusal to compromise on matters which were of great importance to him. This was seen as obstinacy or stupidity by people who did not agree with him, and he could indeed be so single-minded as to ignore or postpone things which appeared to him to be side issues. But he was always acknowledged to be straightforward, filled with transparent sincerity, personally modest but utterly determined to fight for what he thought was right, and anchored in his tolerant but unbending certainty in the correctness of his morality. These were traits which those who knew him best learned to trust, appreciate, and admire. But there were other sides to his personality as well. From the style of life of the Elders of the kirk stemmed Fisher's lack of humour as the lowland Scot. Jesting, fun, and reckless laughter were seen as dubious emotions which could distract a man from the essential matters of human existence and morality, and there was more than a tendency to believe that whatever was enjoyable must in some way be considered to be a sin. From the kirk Fisher received his puritan dislike of alcohol and gambling, even if he did not try to force his attitudes upon those of lesser resistance.

From the Elders, too, Fisher learnt to reject all forms of insignia and awards, mere baubles which sought to lift a man in worth and prestige above his fellows. Yet he did retain a subconscious need to show the world that he was the equal of men who had once been considered his betters. The way this revealed itself was not obtrusive but sometimes surprising. As a boy, it was part of his upbringing to revere Bellfield House, home of the rich Buchanan family in Kilmarnock. In 1912, with a wife and young family, he bought Oakleigh Hall in East St Kilda near Melbourne. This residence was so large that W. M. Hughes gave him a compass so that he could find his way to bed after locking up for the night.[10] The mansion had appealed to Fisher because it was an almost exact replica of 'the big house' of his youth.

Fisher had no need to hide such feelings, because Presbyterianism did not encompass the concept of self-abasing humility. A man of success was entitled to be a man of prestige, provided that he indulged in no vain boasting or tedious self-praise. He needed to have no shame in showing certain egotism with regard to personal accomplishment, a characteristic so necessary for the ambitious politician. This was the lowland Scots attitude of 'walking tall', shared by the Covenanters of the seventeenth century, and it could easily be interpreted as conceit or even as arrogance by outsiders. Fisher did not lack it, despite his basic modesty and inborn tact. He was seldom deliberately overbearing, but it sometimes came as a surprise to observers who admired him that he could show feelings of pride in his achievements, or sometimes talked down to people of greater talents. Associated with this, as his career developed, he also learnt the dramatics of using contrast in his political behaviour. One opponent in Parliament wrote that he 'used occasionally a surprisingly offensive phrase — the more effective because he was usually timidly courteous and conciliatory.'[11]

With this parental and religious background, Andrew

Fisher attended first Rab Porter's school at Draghorn and then the Crosshouse public school under James Wilson.[12] The experience was all too short, and enabled him to do little more than learn to read and write. The first he learnt to love, the second to accomplish well, although he was not, and never claimed to be, a great stylist.[13] His schooldays were brought to an abrupt end in 1872, for his father developed the dreaded 'black lung', the coughing disease pneumoconiosis, as a result of breathing in coal dust for so long. With such a large family, someone had to earn the money and prevent eviction. Despite Forster's Education Act of 1870 which provided for compulsory schooling until the age of twelve, Andrew and his elder brother John were compelled to go into the mine. Andrew's first job was the incredibly boring one of fanning air into the shafts to provide enough oxygen to keep the working miners from fainting. At the age of eleven, family circumstances permitted a few months extra schooling, but soon he had to return to the filthy monotony. With age, he came to be in charge of the horses which carted coal to be lifted to the surface. When he had reached his full strength, he became a miner, and tasted the excruciatingly hard and unpleasant toil of hacking, scraping, and shovelling.

Andrew Fisher's adolescent years were thus spent in being responsible for both older and younger dependants. The feelings of having to look after others never left him, and all his life he was always prepared to act with great conscientiousness on behalf of men and women who had given him their trust. Before long such emotions developed into those of ambition, causing him to believe that it was necessary for him to take the lead. Whether in the close world of a trade union, the wider one of a political party, or in the business of running his Government, as long as he had the support of his colleagues, he never had the slightest doubt that he was the best qualified person to look after their interests.

In doing this, he was also well able to take positive criticism from those who were on his side, while attacks from opponents mostly bounced off him like peas fired at a fortification. But he could never be described as a solid buffer or a sounding block. He was always open to pleasant remarks and to deserved praise from friends and supporters. His later secretary called him 'a man whose nerves thrilled to the touch of popular approval, a man sensitive to defeat, and happiest when he was the bright particular star of his horizon.'[14] This characteristic ensured that when he was in positions of power the way to his favour was through harmonious and appreciative co-operation.

The reverse side was that he could be easily hurt and lastingly upset by men who had treated him shabbily. In such cases, his feelings of resentment could be strong. His religion had place for a tooth for a tooth, and on occasions he was well pleased with what he saw as an appropriate requital. When with a group, he reacted on behalf of them all, and this protected him from unhappy consequences. But when he had a personal grudge, he tended to respond in an introverted manner which only damaged his own interests. He could turn his back on men in a stronger position, or do things which put them ever more against him. Towards the end of his life, such introversion came to dominate him. His final years were far from happy ones, for he had given up on many things which had earlier been the substance of his existence.

As a young and hopeful man with his life before him, this form of negativity was furthest from his thoughts. When he was a miner, he was proud of growing up with a strong physique. He was muscular and well-built, 5' 10" tall, but slender rather than stocky. He was good-looking with exceptionally regular features. His eyes were most striking, beautiful and deeply-set. He knew well how to fix them upon those who were talking to him, and give them a pervading sense of his deep and genuine honesty. He had sandy hair which turned white in his late forties, and he had a broad moustache as soon as it grew. His tastes were always simple, from food and clothes to entertainment. Later in life, he took a great interest in photography and then in golf, but when he was young a favourite pastime was walking in the open air with his father and brothers, where he breathed in the feeling of freedom from coal. He also enjoyed the relaxation that came with fishing. But his time for doing this was so short, and his life was so serious when he was young, that it would have been no wonder if he had been captured for life by the shut-in horror-world of the pit.

His salvation was the Co-operative and parental pressure. His father suffered pangs of conscience that his elder sons were having to work to secure the existence of them all. The Co-operative had developed from being merely a store into a place for self-study where those who wished could educate themselves. A reading room and a small library were opened at nearby Thornyhill. Robert and Jane Fisher encouraged their sons with every argument at their disposal to take the fullest possible advantage of this opportunity. They responded as their

Part One

parents had hoped, ready to do anything not to cough their own lives away. Andrew Fisher completely accepted that education was the way to escape from the clutches of dragging poverty. He invested much of his precious spare time in attending evening classes in Kilmarnock, where he learnt about mine management, in which he hoped to make his career. He developed an ability to read deeply on subjects of interest to him. For his general education, he ploughed through Thomas Carlyle and R. W. Emerson, and made their ideas his own that self-help was the way to be successful. He also loved the poet of Ayrshire, Robert Burns, idealising his hearty and open attitude to life as contrast to the imprisoning blackness of the coalmine.

Through these activities, Fisher became literate far above the average coalminer, but nevertheless he felt his lack of schooling all his life. He sometimes said that he wished he had more knowledge, or that he could give more time to study, yet he never expressed resentment against those of more fortunate birth, nor did he at any time pretend to be something he was not. He knew that he had no capacity to have original thoughts, but he was well able to compensate by using the strengths he did have. He trusted in people who could express ideas of social justice far more potently than he could himself. He accepted and adopted the wisdom of those he admired, and once he had made an idea his own he was tenacious indeed in holding it. He understood the mental processes of what he was doing, and he was always modest enough to listen to expert opinion and act upon it if he was convinced of its probity. Later in life, in the highest positions in politics, without envy or jealousy, which were foreign to his nature, he sought out expert and educated bankers and economists, while remaining determined that the final word of decision should be his. He was never too proud to delegate responsibility, and he was always willing to rely on men whom he recognised as having talents different from his own. His opposite side was his inability to accept new arguments which went against his established convictions. He only liked to read books which agreed with his point of view, and he was apt to get irritated or angry when things did not go the way he had planned. Once his mind had been made up, he could not accept that his opponents might have something useful to say. He would listen to them, but he would automatically reject everything. In the polarised politics which dominated most of his life, this was a great asset to him. He was sympathetic to the suggestions which harmonised with his own outlook, while refusing to have anything to do with those from the other side. Only after August 1914, when his world suddenly became far more complicated than it had ever been before, did his own character become his nemesis, and his career was fated to run upon the rocks.

But as a young man determined to fight for a better world, he suffered from no doubts as to what was right. He was never shy about expressing his opinions in public. From his earliest years he took part in debate and discussion of all kinds. As a teenager he relished the soapbox polemics at the local bridge over the Carmel or at the Bakehouse Corner.[15] Here he got to know the slogans of socialism, and they made a lasting impression on him. All his life 'he loved to coin a phrase and build his speech around it' in the manner he had first learnt at the parish pump while hammering out his arguments on behalf of equal rights for all.[16] Because everyone at the village meetings tended to express themselves in the same direction, early on he saw the positive function of the exchange of views, while well able to distinguish the constructive forms from the destructive, negative, and dead-end sort. In Australia he learnt to modify the quick Ayrshire dialect, which is almost unintelligible to outsiders, so that people could understand him. But he never lost his burr, and few people ever classified him as a good orator. Yet all his life in his speeches he radiated the sincerity and honesty which were such marked features of his personality.

The habits he learnt so young were to stay with him throughout his political career. As the leader in cabinet he was to be renowned for listening carefully to the arguments of his colleagues. He was cautious with new proposals, wishing to consider them from every point of view. Once he had accepted them he was skilful in arranging a compromise when the different opinions admitted of one. He was utterly dependable in backing up his ministers. But he was not strong in setting an independent lead of forceful initiative; far too much did he require a consensus of opinion in the planning of policies. His weakness was in finding a method of resolute control when totally divergent opinions clashed bitterly. Fisher was not a man who liked to give set orders, he had little desire to dominate or to insist on forcing through his will against the fierce resistance of his colleagues, overriding their feelings and principles. Hence at the end of his political career in 1915 he was hopelessly overburdened when his Labor Party began to declare civil war on itself over the matter of priorities.

The Co-operative not only introduced Andrew Fisher to the pleasures of politics, it also became his receiver to developments outside Crosshouse and Kilmarnock. Men like James Keir Hardie were the leaders of the movement to improve the living conditions of the miners and other workers, and also the safety in the pits. Nothing could have been more natural than for Fisher to find his ideals embodied in the work and speeches of such men. There was to be no revolution which caused bloodshed and bitterness with an unforeseeable outcome. Wars were a ridiculous extension of capitalism, which the workers would abolish through international arbitration once they had come to power. Similarly, reason insisted that strikes and direct action were to be avoided if at all possible, and were only to be used as a last resort since if they failed, they brought poverty, anger, frustration, and despair. Far better was to work within the system and try to change it gradually by means of political pressure. That was the lesson Fisher had received as a teenager and retained when he was in a position to transform it into practice. And the important word was 'to work'. To debate and discuss, that might be enjoyable, but Fisher learnt that only organisation and action could bring about the changes which he desired.

Hence he early put his practical abilities at the service of his fellow miners. The work of the trade union was the means to improvement, as all could see, and at the age of seventeen he became secretary of the local branch of the Ayrshire Miners' Union.[17] This work strengthened his attitude that only working together for the common cause could bring about improvements in conditions and pay.

Part One

No body of men was as close as the miners, and none was so united in their fixed idea that it was 'us' against 'them'. Fisher's loyalty to his colleagues, to their organisation, and later to his political party, was unshakeable from the first, and it remained so. But in conformity with his entire character, it was a loyalty of moderation, one which sought the solutions of compromise, not that of aggressive, confrontational leadership. Fisher was never happy, and often helpless, when he had to try to mediate between two seemingly irreconcilable points of view.

Fisher's early work for the miners thus reflected everything in his temperament, always acting on behalf of what he saw to be the general good and always in as friendly a way as possible. This characteristic was a most striking one in him. Almost every account, his whole life long, reports him as being the most engaging of men, pleasant alike to his colleagues, friends and subordinates, easy to get on with, never putting on airs, always trying to find some harmonious solution. But there was iron in his soul. When supported by his own people, his determination was strong, his resolution unbreakable, and his firmness of will intense and lasting. Yet when support was lacking or doubtful, when the middle way could not be found, he showed weakness. He was unable to rise to control the situation, he became morose, withdrawn, subject to sudden anger, and unable to provide a sense of leadership or purpose.

As a very young man, he had his first bitter taste of the grave psychological conflicts he was unable to deal with. In 1881 he was involved against his will in a miners' strike for better conditions and higher pay. Fisher stood loyally with his colleagues while he attempted to mediate with the owners, who were not interested in compromise. After ten weeks the strike was defeated without gains for the miners, and the union was crushed. Fisher himself was blacklisted for his obvious solidarity.[18] He managed to get a job in another pit, but he was lastingly unhappy that he had not found any kind of positive solution. He did not give up after this first setback. He engaged himself in political activity for equality, as when he chaired a meeting at Crosshouse in 1884 against the House of Lords for opposing Gladstone's extension to the franchise,[19] and he worked hard to regenerate the union when it was revived in the same year. Early in 1885, after a new strike, he was blacklisted again. This time he did not only lose his job, there seemed to be no hope of getting a new one. He saw himself as a failure, and he lost heart as well.

And indeed, the situation in Ayrshire was pitiable. Already sunk in depression, and now with a class struggle which the miners had lost, Fisher's methods had achieved nothing a second time. What future could there be in Scotland for a man of his feelings and abilities? His way out was that his dependants were growing up, and no longer had to rely upon his support. Jean had died at the age of twelve, and the rest of the family was beginning to disperse. Of his brothers, John had already gone to become a policeman in Liverpool, and Robert was learning mine management. Andrew's dilemma was solved by his family telling him bluntly that the others could now do their share in looking after their mother and their incapacitated father. Therefore he was able to escape by seeking his fortune in a distant country. He and his brother, James, first thought of New Zealand, then they read the brochures with which the Government of Queensland was promoting immigration to the Colony. They managed to save enough money to add to the subsidy for their fares, and in June 1885 they boarded the train for London. They left England on the SS New Guinea, and landed in Brisbane on 17th August, 1885.

Notes

The background on coalmining in Scotland may be found in R. P. Arnot *A History of the Scottish Miners from the Earliest Times*, London, 1955. J. Malkin, *Andrew Fisher 1862-1928*, Kilmarnock, 1979, is an uncritical essay on Fisher, but the facts have been soundly researched. It is well illustrated. C. Dougan: Andrew Fisher − Scots Collier and Australian Reformer, in *Scottish Local History*, July 1988, copies much from Malkin, with some additional information. G. E. Marginson (See Chapter Two) has other facts, mostly drawn from Fisher's letters which are in the *Fisher Papers* in the ANL. M. L. Shepherd, *Memoirs*, MS A1632 in the ML has many interesting stories about Fisher, written in retirement by his private secretary.

Chapter II

'Parliament was a great deal worse than I had anticipated it would be.'

When Andrew Fisher reached Australia his character was formed but his life was not. He had come in order to find 'freedom' and get out of the mines, but as a fresh immigrant he could find nothing else to do than to go back into them.[20] In September 1885, he and his brother tried unsuccessfully to get work on the Ipswich coalfield, but they were first taken on as ordinary miners later by the Queensland Colliery Company in one of their Burrum pits eighteen miles north-west of Maryborough.[21] Andrew took the first chance he could to get away from the coalface. A new shaft was to be sunk, and he was put in charge of doing it. He did his work well, for he was afterwards appointed manager of one of the company's Torbanlea mines on the Burrum field, where he was also successful. Twelve years later he proudly remembered the 'record efficiency' while he had the job,[22] but this did not help his career. In March 1888 he applied for another managership, this time with the Isis Investment Company, but the position was given to a man of lesser qualifications. Fisher was angry and frustrated, and he saw no future for himself among men who had spurned his abilities.

As in Scotland three years before, he solved his problems by leaving them behind. He took a look at the Gympie reef-mining goldfields eighty miles to the south of the Burrum, and found that there was work for him there.

He accepted a career setback as compensation for starting anew, and went back to hacking and blasting holes in the ground at the No.1 North Phoenix.[23] He transferred his hopes of bettering himself through mine management onto engine driving. He studied for his certificate whenever he could, using well the free time offered to him during the strike at the end of 1890 when he was sacked and blacklisted. In 1891 he passed the necessary tests. He started to drive the trains, mostly in the open air, for the South Great Eastern Extended, and soon became the president of the engine drivers' union.

During these hard and unsettled years, Fisher never lost contact with his family and friends in Scotland through letters. The detailed correspondence shows how much he retained his mental stability by means of the exchange, even if there was much disconcerting news.[24] He was informed of everything that went on, of his father's worsening condition, death and funeral in 1888, and of the problems and hopes of the rest of the family. For years he went through phases of depression because he was too far away to be of help in times of crisis. His subconscious feelings of somehow having failed them made it difficult for him to start any close relationship in Queensland, or even to settle down. It was only the continued dispersal of his brothers which subdued his uneasy conscience. Robert went on to be a mine manager, first in Lanarkshire, afterwards near Carlisle, and he finally accepted an offer in Labuan, North Borneo. James left Queensland in February 1892 to join him, but found no work until months later he reached the Kolar goldfield in South India. Andrew showed no desire to drift around with him. It had taken a long time, but at Gympie he was beginning to settle in fully to the new life and the new conditions in Australia. His experiences on the Burrum had taught him once and for all that individual talent and striving were not enough, and that a man alone was helpless against the arbitrariness of authority.

In Gympie, he did not repeat his mistakes, but at once started to take part in community activities.[25] In May 1888 he joined the Wide Bay branch of the Manchester United Independent Order of Oddfellows. He became active in the Presbyterian Church as superintendent of the Sunday School and in debating. He helped with his great experience to found the Gympie Industrial Co-operative Society in January 1891. He was for a time in the local Defence Force until the heavy drinking drove him away. He joined the Chess Club as an active player and briefly as secretary. He learnt shorthand to do such work better, and also compound arithmetic which later helped him to be appointed Municipal Auditor. But, of greatest importance for his future, he became an activist in the trade union work of the Gympie miners. Thus he was part of the beginning of the working class mobilisation in Queensland which led first to parliamentary representation, and then to an extraordinary political future for himself.

W. G. Spence wrote later that the Queensland Labor movement was 'Socialistic from the jump.'[26] Modern historians have asserted that it was far more pragmatic in its aims.[27] Whichever interpretation may have more truth, it was undoubtedly full of furious indignation against the power of capitalism and the seemingly arbitrary way the law was used on behalf of the interests of property and wealth. Spence's book *Australia's Awakening* may well be subjective and selective, but he shows, with all the brilliance of the highly successful union organiser, the disgust and contempt felt by the activists for their mean and sadistic opponents who were so full of selfishness and arrogance. Spence also shows the conviction of total commitment in his political demands, and in his vision of erecting a proud and enduring system of democratic justice in Australia in place of the revolting machinations of moneyed politics.

In the years when Andrew Fisher was a miner, the activities of his opponents gave such men as he and Spence good reason for their sense of hot injustice. They lived through strikes which were battered into submission by the unrelenting establishment forces of law and order. They saw the blackbirding of cheap kanaka labour for the sugar plantations, with the implicit threat against the jobs of every working man in the Colony. They mocked and derided the rich man's philosophy of liberal equality, whereby the master was free to offer work on whatever terms he wanted, and the man was free to reject them and not get the job. A fertile ground had been prepared for such animated and enterprising newspapers as William Lane's the *Boomerang* and then the *Worker*. Their readers would never again accept the governments of capitalist exploitation with grumbling submission. Two forms of protest were at hand: either there could be the strikes they all knew so well to try to force change, or, for all the boodlers' recourse to gerrymandering and pluralism, the working man now had the vote himself. His elected representatives would even be paid, £200 a year from 1886, raised to £300 in 1889, but reduced by half in 1892 to discourage Labor candidates.

Andrew Fisher was heart and soul a part of the movement of social protest, whereby the working classes should join together to fight for gains for all, and use the power of the State to do it. At first, there was much heated argument with those who said that each group should win concessions for itself. Fisher avoided factious, bitter controversy since it was not in his nature to throw himself into one-sided polemics. But he put all his immensely strong instincts to help the whole community at the service of the Amalgamated Miners' Association whose Gympie branch had led the way in Queensland in 1886 in joining the common cause. In 1890 he became the secretary of this branch, and in 1891 its president.[28] He had no success, for it collapsed after the disastrous strikes of those years. Fisher's view that capitalism could never be tamed by threats and confrontation was confirmed. The alternative method had its first triumph at the exact time of the bitter defeat in Queensland. In the elections of June 1891 in New South Wales, the Labor Party won thirty-five seats at its first attempt. Fisher understood the message. In July 1891 he was an active leader in founding the Gympie branch of the Workers' Political Organisation, the forerunner in Queensland of the Labor Party. He was rewarded by getting himself elected its first president.[29] He identified himself completely with the new movement, speaking as often as he could on workers' rights and the need for the appropriate legislation.

During the first years of the working class political movement in the Colony, one great difficulty was to decide on a programme which would be acceptable to all. Men such as Lane publicised socialist ideas as widely as possible, and found many takers. In August 1890 the first Queensland General Council of the Australian Federation pronounced in Brisbane its aims as being the nationalisation of all sources of wealth and its 'just division among all the citizens of the State.'[30] This went too far for other reform associations, and the extreme demands were dropped. What was left included planks for democratic electoral reform, higher taxation of the rich, and the correct way of dealing with the reactionary Legislative Council. There was to be a state bank, an eight-hour day, pensions for the old and for orphans, and free compulsory education. There were to be Acts for better working conditions in mines, shops, and factories, and protection for trade unionists and others against the conspiracy laws. A general socialistic tinge remained, but the idealism was far more in favour of a step-by-step improvement of society rather than for its revolutionary transformation.

Andrew Fisher was only in his total engagement for the cause different from many others who supported the emerging Labor Party. He had no immediate family responsibilities to distract him from political work, and in Gympie he devoted himself to the organisation of the branch. In 1892 he was its representative at the first Labor Party Convention in Brisbane which finalised the electoral programme for the future.[31] He repeated faithfully all the arguments in favour of political reforms, backing them up with moderately socialistic justifications. His constant activity and utter reliability brought him wide acceptance and his excellent and worthy character made him an obvious favourite to become a Labor Party candidate for the next elections of May 1893.

Fisher saw no reason to restrain in any way the pressure on him to nominate. Far too long had he been on the losing side in industrial warfare for him to want to resist any chance of being able to stand up in Parliament on behalf of the working classes. His gut feelings against the towering injustices committed by greedy capitalists on their fellow human beings had been intensified by his experiences in the recent strikes. His personal ambition to be successful, his needs to help the people he worked with, indeed his entire upbringing, it all had prepared him to make a serious attempt to start a career which a few years before had never entered his thoughts. He nominated to become one of the two Labor candidates for Gympie. At the end of March he topped the pre-selection poll with two hundred and thirty-seven votes, and alone of five men had more than fifty per cent.[32] The second man, his friend George Ryland, was selected in a run-off a week later.

Fisher started his election campaign on 21st April, 1893, later than the other candidates because he had been sick. With great earnestness, no humour, and his accent which caused some problems to his listeners, he demanded the reforms on the party manifesto which he had helped to draw up the previous year. There were no surprises in his speeches, but his utterances and his personality were exactly what his audiences wanted to see and hear. He topped the poll with one thousand and nine votes, nearly two hundred more than the leading candidate of the Ministry, William Smyth. The delighted winner said that his victory showed Gympie to be 'practically democratic in spirit and radical in intention'.[33]

This was true for many voters in Gympie, and also for other mining and working class electorates in the Colony. Sixteen Labor members were returned, an impressive success. But they were only a small minority in a Legislative Assembly of seventy-two members. The representatives of finance and property, helped by efficient boundary manipulation and every other kind of trick, won a handsome majority. They continued their existing alliance with each other, which meant that they went on supporting what was to be called the 'Continuous Ministry'. The general Labor feeling towards this form of worker oppression was expressed by Spence, and was contemptuous in the extreme:

> One Premier after another retired to a good fat billet, his lieutenant took his place, and the Ministry filled vacancies with leading supporters, but it was the same crowd all the time. They were the most capitalistic, commercially governed party ever seen in any State, and none were more glaringly corrupt.[34]

It was true enough, especially from the point of view of the members of the Labor Party, which the Government looked upon at best as an unpleasant nuisance.

The proud sixteen would rather have given their support for legislative concessions than having to remain as complete outsiders. Although initially they signified this by not sitting directly in opposition but on the crossbenches, nobody in power wanted anything from them. Therefore they found that they could do little more than express their points of view angrily, truculently, or rationally, according to their characters. Indeed, they had much to complain about, since 1893 was the year of the collapse of the banks and economic misery, and 1894 of the 'Coercion Act' against striking. They all spoke 'too long and too often', enormous outpourings of words to commend themselves to each other, to their electors, and to the hoped-for reforming tidal wave of the future.[35] For the present, they could do little more than this, and accept the inevitable defeats in important divisions.

Andrew Fisher was walking tall after his election. He was 'quite proud of himself when he first arrived in Parliament. One could see it in his walk, and he had a charming though unobjectionable self-confidence'.[36] He at once started to try to educate his capitalist opponents as to the worthlessness of their opinions. Parliament had barely met when he gave his maiden speech. He first informed the assembly that he had come to learn. Then he praised his party's policy and the good effects which would accompany its realisation.[37] This set the tone for many of his later speeches. With intense seriousness, and never using a short word where a long one would do, he spoke out on whatever course of action would be best for his working-class constituents. He was not the man to engage in vivid, destructive sarcasm against conservative policies. Nor was he strong with lively, partisan criticism in the hope of winning a few debating points or a reputation as a man of thunder. In a painstaking and often tedious manner he attacked whatever the Continuous Ministry was trying to do, and followed this up by trying to be positive in his explanation of the alternative course of action demanded by himself and his colleagues.

In doing this, his technique was still that of the Crosshouse soapbox, modified so as to avoid the cliché of getting all the workers of the world to unite. Now he was full of phrases which demanded 'fair conditions' to give the downtrodden 'the fullest opportunity to rise in life'.[38] This was not so much political thought as his method of thinking politically. He put everything into compartments in the way his religion had taught him. As a man whose perspective was limited by the small towns he had always lived in, he divided the general population into 'the speculating classes' who were 'the systematic swindlers, the commercial men, the squatters and the western landlords', and 'the labouring classes', who were nearly everybody else, and who he hoped were to inherit the better world he was trying to build.

Fisher was always of the opinion that he was a clear and good orator, even if few other people ever agreed with him.[39] In the 1890s, his style of speaking and his simplifications caused no problems of any kind to his opponents, and they seldom paid any attention to him. This dented his beginner's idealism that told him that he could at once do something to help the workers. He found that Parliament 'was a great deal worse than I had anticipated it would be' because of the refusal of the men in power to do anything which was for him so self-evidently necessary.[40] He reacted by concentrating his attention on his own party friends in order to build a reputation for himself as a solid and trustworthy colleague. His plan was to rise in their estimation so that he could have a leading position in the hoped-for time when Labor should have more influence in the decision-making process.

The Labor men in the Assembly reacted positively to his earnest and fully committed explanations of every aspect of their policy. The question as to whether parliamentary or direct action would be more effective was an important one in Labor discussions. From the first, Fisher was wholeheartedly on the side of the political course. With the memories of strike disaster very fresh, such an opinion was in the ascendant.[41] Fisher's utter honesty and sincerity caused him to win the appreciation of his like-minded colleagues. He used this to his own advantage in beginning to satisfy his ambitions. Within a year he was elected vice-chairman of the party in the Assembly. Advance in rank accorded well with his growing opinion of himself, and he used the chance to expand his activities in whatever way he could. He got himself onto several parliamentary committees, including those for standing orders, for the conspiracy and early closing laws, and for party rules and organisation. And he made long stump tours in the outback when the Legislative Assembly was in recess.

Despite such personal commitment, the political situation was and remained unpromising for the Labor men. Their votes had no weight in passing legislation, so there was no need for any leader to bind the party tightly together, as was happening from November 1893 in New South Wales. The Queenslanders tended to engage in theoretical discussions as to what they would do when they could bargain from strength. Should they stay resolutely independent and make no agreement with any other party, or should the method of support for concessions be adopted? From the first, Fisher was for some sort of cooperation as long as Labor remained an independent party and made no compromise on its principles. But he was learning about the devious intricacies of the parliamentary process from the standpoint of a man whose only hopes of real political achievement had to be for the future.

This was the fate of all the Labor men, and their awareness of it and the resultant attitude caused them to neglect what was going on in the present. The next general elections were to be held in March 1896, but they omitted to update the Labor programme. Fisher paid too much attention to what he was saying in Brisbane and too little to constituency organisation in Gympie. His opponents exploited this. One of them, Jacob Stumm, was the editor of the *Gympie Times* and they all did what they could to destroy Fisher's chances of re-election.[42] In particular, they honed in on some of his earlier socialistic statements to show the voters that he could be seen as a dangerous revolutionary, and they all made much blustering propaganda implying that he was allegedly dominated by the Brisbane Trades Hall clique. These smear tactics were successful. The social unrest caused by the strikes of 1890 and 1891 had run out of fighting force. Fisher's majority was turned into a defeat by two hundred and thirty-nine votes, and he again joined the ranks of the unemployed.

He was determined that this setback should not mean the end of the career which had come to appeal to everything within him. He started to do what he could to ensure his re-election in 1899. His chosen method was to start a rival newspaper, the *Gympie Truth*, which would both promote the interests of the workers and support him as their representative. Less than three weeks after his defeat, Fisher chaired a committee to float a company with five thousand shares and two months thereafter, on his initiative, Henry Boote accepted the post of editor.[43] At first Fisher gave him much help – or watched him closely – but Boote did everything he could have desired. After a bout of typhoid in 1897 Fisher let Boote do the job on his own, and confined himself to writing articles for the paper. He also gave money to the venture after he had, with difficulty, found a new job as engine driver at a local mine.

Fisher, therefore, had more time for other political work, and he was given extra motivation when his opponents caused him to be sacked as Municipal Auditor. He did much for party organisation, which was as usual designed to help the Labor movement as a whole, as well as being to his own advantage. On 3rd June, 1898 he was one of the delegates in Brisbane to draw up a modernised programme for the coming elections.[44] The delegates came from all over Queensland in order to counter the nonsense that the party policy was only made by the Trades Hall. In Gympie itself early in 1899, Fisher fought a far more strategic and cunning campaign than three years before. He had learnt not to make unguarded comments in favour of socialism, so he confined himself to the reforms on the party programme. With the help of Boote and his newspaper, he secured a majority of one hundred and sixty-two over his leading opponent in the elections of March.

Fisher was delighted to be back once more in the forum of all his personal ambitions, but his situation in the Labor Party was different from when he had lost his seat three years before. Although there were now twenty-one members of caucus, they were still in a hopeless minority to the Continuous Ministry in the Assembly. It seemed as though this dismal situation would go on forever, so the majority of the Labor men now believed that direct industrial action promised more than pressing for reform laws which might never come. Fisher's three year absence had lost him his high party rank, and there was no chance for him to regain it as a convinced supporter of political action rather than strikes. He was, therefore, less influential in the party than in 1896, even though his upright straightforwardness had not been forgotten, and he still retained much personal prestige.

This was shown late in 1899, when the establishment politicians got themselves into a crisis in November. As a possible solution, on 1st December the Labor leader Andy Dawson was asked to form a Ministry. He included Fisher as its seventh and most junior member, appointing him Secretary for Railways and Public Works because his honesty seemed a good card to play in a Department which had been racked by scandals for years. Fisher had just enough time to copy some documents proving that featherbedding had occurred on the Chillagoe railway, which he later used to embarrass the capitalists in the Assembly.[45] Before he could do more, the opponents of Labor pulled themselves together, and on 7th December Dawson was compelled to leave office as swiftly as he had taken it.

This interesting interlude confirmed Fisher's opinion that Labor had little immediate future as the driving force in Queensland politics. He was longing to do something active for the working classes, yet the forces of property easily destroyed every promising attempt. Across the border in New South Wales the situation was very different. There, the well-organised Labor Party was using its balance of power in the Legislative Assembly to win reforms, first from Reid's Free Traders, and after September 1899, from Lyne's Protectionists. Fisher had attended the Intercolonial Labor Conference in Sydney in January 1894, and had thereafter kept in contact with the party organisers in Sydney. He had been a supporter of the Federation of the Australian Colonies for years, and now he started to realise that his political future might well be bound up with those of his party friends to the South. Queensland had voted in September 1899 to join Federation. There had been a two-thirds majority in Gympie, and this might work to his advantage in the first federal elections. In addition, it seemed to him that wider Australian politics held out a hope which was diminishingly small in Queensland. The main issue was to be the size of the tariff schedule for the whole of the country. It was possible that the Labor Party might become the third party holding the balance between the Free Traders and the Protectionists, as was the case in New South Wales. Fisher decided to take the risk and make an attempt to leave Queensland politics, where his influence within the party had so declined.

The new Commonwealth of Australia came into existence on the first day of the new century. Sir Edmund Barton was sworn in as the head of a protectionist government, to hold office at least until the result of the elections at the end of March. Fisher was nominated as official Labor candidate for the Wide Bay electorate, which had its main centre at Maryborough, but which included Gympie. With his excellent reputation, he won the endorsement of almost all the local working class political organizations.[46] Playing it carefully, he did not resign his Assembly seat until he should have won. At first he had seemed to have little chance of success, for his prospective opponent was Sir James Dickson, Barton's Minister of Defence. But Dickson died on 10th January, and his replacement was the less prestigious J. T. Annear, the Liberal MLA for Maryborough. Fisher spoke to well-attended and enthusiastic audiences.[47] He and the other Labor men praised the party policy of the previous decade in Queensland. Those like Fisher who were protectionists said they would give Barton a chance if they were elected as a third party, and they all promised to send the kanakas home as swiftly as possible. This was enough for the workers of Wide Bay, for they gave Fisher a comfortable majority of nearly one thousand out of nine thousand votes. He was lastingly proud that he had won in six out of the seven voting districts, for he felt that this gave him a mandate to represent the entire electorate.[48]

The change in his political career that this success heralded was paralleled by a change in his private life. His close identification with his birthplace had become blurred after fifteen years of absence. Three of his brothers had died in accidents, James in 1893, Robert in 1895, and John in July 1901.[49] Such blows gradually weakened his subconscious resistance to setting up a new focus for his private emotions in his new country, by showing him how evanescent the old relationships could be, and by giving him a vital reason to establish fresh ones. He allowed himself to fall in love, and economically combined his desire for emotional security with that of having to look after people. Margaret Irvine was the daughter of his landlady, whose husband had been killed in the mine a decade before. She was twelve years younger than Fisher. The marriage took place on 31st December, 1901, after the birth of their first son Robert. Despite being nearly forty, Fisher showed that he was in no way a born bachelor. He became a devoted husband and an excellent, loving father to his daughter and five sons.[50] He unfailingly showed in his family life the same qualities of reliability and loyalty which were of such importance in politics in enabling him to rise above the rank and file, and which, by the time of his marriage, his new colleagues in Melbourne were already beginning to respect.

Part One

Notes

G. E. Marginson, *Andrew Fisher: the Colonial Experience* B. A. (Honours) Thesis 1967, University of Queensland is very detailed and thorough, and goes far beyond the life of Fisher alone. The general background to the rise of the Labor movement is in R. Gollan: *Radical and Working Class Politics: a Study of Eastern Australia 1850-1910*, Melbourne, 1960. The Queensland development is given in detail in D. J. Murphy (ed.), *Labor in Politics*, St Lucia, 1975, Chapter Two, and in D. J. Murphy et al. (eds.), *Prelude to Power*, Milton, 1970. This second book contains an essay by Marginson on 'Andrew Fisher – the Views of a Political Reformer.' Fisher's Papers in the ANL contain letters and other information which reveal something of his early life. W. G. Spence, *Australia's Awakening*, Sydney, 1909, has a splendid and subjective account of the unionist movement in Queensland. A. J. J. St Ledger, *Australian Socialism*, London, 1909 is its reactionary opposite.

Chapter III

'State enterprise through the whole of the Commonwealth has been most successful.'

The results of the first federal elections more than fulfilled Fisher's hopes. Labor won sixteen seats in the House of Representatives and eight in the Senate. As neither Barton's Protectionist Government nor Reid's Free Trade Opposition won an absolute majority, Labor would be in the desired position of being able to offer support for concessions. Barton seemed to have a more hopeful policy than Reid, and caucus agreed to give him his chance. For Fisher, there was a surprise bonus. Queensland, with three Senators and four MHRs, had the greatest numbers in caucus of any State, ahead of New South Wales with six and Western Australia with four. This weight would make the Queenslanders of importance. Fisher at once decided that he would try to become their leading spokesman in party matters, using much the same sort of methods which had been successful in 1893.

At first he went about this with some open intrigue. It was clear that J. C. Watson would be elected leader, since he had been the architect of the pledge in New South Wales, and his experience qualified him best to hold the party together in the tactical manoeuvring which would be necessary. Fisher let it be known that he was a rival candidate, not in the hope or expectation of beating him, but to establish his claims as the leading Queenslander.[51] Once his point was made, he withdrew, so that Watson was elected unopposed. Fisher, victorious in intent, capitalised on his success. He was very active in the first caucus meetings in proposing or seconding matters concerning party policy in Parliament, thus showing himself to be a man of action and initiative.[52] He thereafter assumed every responsibility that he could. He was appointed to the party's committee to consider the draft standing orders. He was later the Queensland member on the important caucus Defence Bill and Tariff Committees. He was the Queenslander who spoke on behalf of his party in Parliament on the death of W. H. Groom, and on the Government's New Guinea policy.[53] From the very first, he worked as closely with his friend Charles McDonald as he had done in colonial politics. This meant that other ambitious men from his State, like Bamford and Page, were unable to make headway against him.

Fisher's more useful contribution to the whole party lay in using his strengths as a man of understanding and compromise. Caucus discipline and loyalty were vital in making Labor into an effective unit. Although all the members agreed on the necessity of the united acceptance of majority decisions, it was not always easy for a defeated minority to surrender gracefully. More than anybody else, Fisher was the man who was able to soothe ruffled feelings, restore harmony, or suggest political compromises. He therefore received much recognition and acceptance as an excellent and trustworthy colleague.

In the House of Representatives, he did not make any similar impact. As in Queensland politics, he was primarily concerned in increasing his reputation within the party, and not trying to impress the rest of the world with a knowledge which he knew he did not have. He later said that, 'I have never risen to speak from a mere desire to be reported',[54] and he made no contribution to debates which needed legal skills or an administrative background. Most of the issues before Parliament required men who had these, so Fisher confined himself to the few matters where he had experience or an electoral commitment. He spoke with much fervour for a White Australia or the need for duty-free tea and kerosene,[55] but nobody outside the party ever thought of him seriously as being anything other than an average backbencher.

The Labor leader, Watson, had a similar opinion. He was well able to use Fisher's abilities, but he did not value him as one of his most intimate advisers. It was Watson's business to decide on tactics as to how to win advantages from Barton's Government. W. M. Hughes was quick-thinking and resourceful, and had shown his cleverness in New South Wales. So had E. L. Batchelor and Senator McGregor in South Australia, and Batchelor had the advantage of a year's ministerial experience. They could react more flexibly than Fisher, who had been an outsider from government in Queensland, and who always tended to see matters with the sort of black and white attitude that had been built into him by his Calvinistic religion.

Fisher's position in the party was thus one of general acceptance without being in the inner circle of greatest influence. Who, therefore, could better be sent to represent Labor at the Coronation of Edward VII? The Boer War was in its final stages, and Fisher and his colleagues considered it necessary to show that they were against military display. Fisher fully shared the general opinion that 'it is our duty as a peaceful community to indicate that we desire peace and to see the representatives of industrial peace at ceremonies of this kind'.[56] His handsome, upright presence would do them all credit, and the choosing of him would honour the strong Queensland section of caucus. Yet his absence for several months would not inconvenience the party leadership. So in 1902 Fisher sailed to the land of his birth, where he did just what was required of him. He maintained proudly the dignity of Labor, even if nobody in high positions in Britain paid any great attention to the workers' representative from the Antipodes. Even when he went back to the Kilmarnock area, he was met with friendliness, but without the huzzas which greeted him nine years later.

On his return to Australia, he continued to be chosen for responsible tasks without being one of the decision makers. As a completely safe party man, he was one of the delegates appointed in June 1903 to try to organise a uniform Labor pledge in Victoria.[57] Three weeks later, he was appointed to the caucus Committee on Finance. And in September, as the most prominent member of the largest State group in the party, Watson asked him to perform an important duty in the House. The Conciliation and Arbitration Bill was not as wide in scope as Labor desired. Fisher was asked to move an amendment that it should include Federal and State civil servants. The amendment failed on 8th September, 1903, but another one moved by McDonald to include railway workers was passed, whereupon the Government dropped the Bill. These events seemed to be of passing importance; eight months later their repetition finally put Fisher's career on its way. But at the time neither he nor anyone else had an inkling that he was shortly to become a man in a high position. When the First Parliament drew to its close, his place in the political scene was symbolised by his being chosen to declare in caucus, 'That we, the members of the first Labor Party ... decide to put on record our appreciation of the great ability, industry and tact', displayed by the leaders in the House and the Senate, Watson and McGregor.[58]

The general elections followed on 16th December, 1903. The main issue was again the tariff. Reid led a drive from New South Wales to lower it, Deakin one from Victoria to retain it. This caused no great excitement elsewhere, and as neither party was well organised in the less populous States, Labor was given an unexpected opportunity to improve its position. Fisher retained Wide Bay with ease against an elderly and politically harmless opponent. The Queensland caucus numbers were increased to seven MHRs and five Senators, far ahead of the next State, Western Australia, with eight. These gains ensured that Labor became the largest party in Parliament with twenty-five MHRs and fourteen Senators. Caucus decided to go on supporting Deakin's Protectionist Government, but as Labor was now stronger in numbers than the party it was keeping in power, many of its members wished to test their strength.

The crisis came soon after Parliament had met. Deakin

let it be known in April 1904 that he was still not willing to let the newly re-introduced Conciliation and Arbitration Bill be as wide in scope as Labor wanted, and that he would resign if anything against his policy was passed. Caucus organised itself to challenge him. There was to be a double attack. Watson again chose Fisher, with McDonald to aid him, as representing the twelve from Queensland, to move the amendment to include civil servants.[59] Despite a caucus resolution that Watson should do it himself, he held firmly to his plan, in the expectation that the amendment would fail but prepare the way for his own hammer of including railway workers. Fisher did as he was asked, and it came as a surprise when he had a majority. Deakin resigned, and Watson was commissioned to form a Ministry. Fisher found himself soaked in the unexpected prestige of being the man whose initiative had brought Labor to power.

In this position, he had the automatic right to become one of Watson's ministers. Many observers outside the Labor Party were surprised at this. They considered it to be a 'fluke' that, seemingly only because of the amendment, he had been put ahead of other Queenslanders who were equally as ambitious and hard-working as he.[60] Watson made him fifth in cabinet rank and gave him the responsibility of Trade and Customs. Fisher had little idea of what he would have to do, but his presence was meant to reassure jittery industrialists that their protectionism was safe with Labor.

The new Minister took his unexpected job as seriously as he did everything in politics. He worked very long hours in order to master its intricacies and so be a credit to the Government as long as it stayed in power.[61] He tried to create an image of electoral closeness by being available twice a week to Victorians and more often to interstate visitors. He was sternly religious in refusing to allow unloading at ports on Sundays. He showed that there would be no favouritism, as in requiring a standard hallmark on jewellery, or in refusing to give a rebate on sugar costs to jam manufacturers. He was anxious to promote Australia, seeking industrialists who were willing to exhibit their goods at an international fair in Italy in 1906. He wanted to have a reputation as a man who made just decisions, as when he considered for days what to do with three customs officials who had been 'careless' with frozen fish from New Zealand. In his four months in office, he had no time to do anything spectacular, but he showed his party, and proved to himself, that he could well be trusted with administration.

Fisher lost office at the end of August 1904 when Watson's ministry was toppled by a coalition of its conservative opponents under Reid, who became Prime Minister with a shaky majority of two in each House. Reid planned to polarise politics into those who were for and against Labor, thereby sinking the fiscal issue and the independent Protectionist Party forever.[62] In March 1905 he started his anti-socialist campaign in the hope of bringing about this situation, and of holding an early election if necessary. Fisher was swift to use the opportunity to consolidate his high party ranking, and to create a personal image for himself not merely as a man who did what Watson wanted. He reacted to Reid's drumming by beginning to inform the public about views he had held in private for years. He praised the workers' ideology, which he had stopped doing in 1893 because it

Part One

gave too much electoral ammunition to his opponents. Now he made a stand against Reid's propaganda by replying appropriately. In April 1905 he was interviewed by the *Worker,* and said that,

> "No Labor party worthy of the name can deny that its objective is Socialism, but no Socialist with any parliamentary experience can hope to get anything for many years to come, other than practical legislation of a socialistic nature ... Take away Socialism and there is nothing left."[63]

The rabid right got hold of this utterance and exaggerated it out of all proportion. This did Fisher no harm in his own party, and he began to be looked upon as the leading member of the more radical faction. This reputation grew in July 1905, when he attended the Interstate Labor Conference and voted for all the more daring proposals, against the express desire of Watson to keep to moderate policies.

In this way Fisher was the man who was needed when there was a party crisis at the beginning of August 1905. Reid's Government had fallen and had been succeeded by Deakin after Watson had promised Labor support. Watson tried to resign because he was fed up with a number of men who were constantly intriguing against his policy of giving Deakin his majority, and insisting that future Labor ministries should by chosen by caucus and not by the party leader.[64] Fisher was the man who had mediated between opposing factions for years. He was completely loyal to Watson even if his attitudes were recognised as being more radical. He seemed to be the man who could best resolve the difficulties and bring peace to the party. He was chosen unanimously on 9th August to become deputy-leader of Labor in the House of Representatives.[65] These tactics were successful. Watson withdrew his resignation. Fisher's main responsibilities were in promoting party harmony, so he continued to make no attempt to upstage Watson by creating a name for himself in the House. The dissidents calmed down, as they saw it would be destructive for their careers to go on fomenting trouble against a leadership which now included a man of similar opinions to their own. Fisher was, in this way, able to help Watson and the caucus majority policy of supporting Deakin's Government. This was thereby enabled to pass much constructive legislation, and Fisher continued to rise in the estimation of his colleagues for the remainder of the Parliament.

The new elections were to be held on 12th December, 1906. Deakin insisted on the need for a higher tariff, and that the so-called New Protection would be linked to it, whereby the workers in the benefited industries would receive higher wages. Fisher followed this line but showed that he was a Labor man by loudly demanding a land tax.[66] It was clear, however, that he was prepared to go on supporting Deakin if nothing better was forthcoming. In Queensland this was of secondary importance, since the Protectionists had but a single candidate in the whole State. In the absence of any other alternative to Labor, Reid's anti-socialist cries were well received. Labor lost two Senators and three MHRs, and with only seven members in caucus, was now third in strength behind Western Australia and New South Wales. Fisher was not hurt politically by this result. He retained his seat by one thousand three hundred votes, and his high ranking in the party was too strong for it to be undermined. The losses in his home State were balanced by gains elsewhere, and Labor won one seat in each House. Deakin's party was reduced to only four Senators and seventeen MHRs. After a sizzling argument in caucus, the Labor majority agreed to continue its support for this remnant, mainly so that the workers could share in the benefits of New Protection.

Fisher tried to continue his dual role of loyalty to Watson while holding more radical opinions. At the very start of the new Parliament, in February 1907, he proposed the motion in caucus 'that we again place on record our appreciation of the splendid services given to the Labor movement' by Watson.[67] But this time he was unable to prevent the wild men from getting out of control. The Interstate Labor Conference of 1905 had limited Labor support of Deakin to the expired Parliament, so they saw no reason peacefully to observe its continuation. By October, Watson had become so irritated with the constant intriguing that he refused to continue as party leader.[68] On 23rd October he announced his irrevocable resignation. His successor was to be chosen by caucus a week later. Fisher was the front runner. Because of his past services as deputy, his election was considered in the press to be 'a foregone conclusion'.[69] However, Hughes, Batchelor and Spence were also nominated at the caucus meeting of 30th October. Batchelor withdrew before the voting began, everyone knew that Spence had no chance, but Hughes had very real support within the party.

He had indeed a lot to commend him. He was a fine

orator, a prolific propagandist, an excellent union organiser with a past history of success, and an accomplished negotiator of industrial disputes. He was bursting with ideas and initiative, and had an Australia-wide reputation. Fisher could match him neither in past achievement nor in brilliance of any kind. But he was solid, loyal, and honest. Many in the Labor Party were uneasy at the thought of giving the leadership to Hughes with his independent ideas. In each Colony or State men had been expelled for twisting or opposing the party line. Recently Daglish in Western Australia and Kidston in Queensland had demonstrated the dangers of self-willed leadership. Even Watson had made his colleagues alert to the danger in federal politics in showing signs of rebellion against the strictures of caucus control.[70]

There was hardly a chance that Fisher would ever do anything against the expressed opinion of the majority. He was outspokenly devoted to the principles of caucus. A year later he showed how attached he was to its discipline in a letter to A. G. Stephens, the former literary editor of the *Bulletin,* in November 1908:

> It has never been a trouble to me. At present it is the finest battleground any political party could wish to have. We are pledged to each other to the same extent as we are pledged to our constituents. No organisation has been successful which has not a guiding principle and a body to which it can appeal for a decision on disputed points in laws and procedure.[71]

And in Parliament he accused his political opponents of

base emotions when they attacked the system:

> Honourable members opposite are envious of our solidarity. They are envious of us because we have a common purpose, and accomplish objects that we have in view, whilst they cannot do so. That being so, they represent that our method of conducting our business is inimical to the welfare of the country.[72]

Such a man would obviously never try to force his own ideas upon his colleagues. There was 'an exhaustive ballot' for the leadership, so on the first attempt there was no decision.[73] Spence was eliminated, and for the second ballot Fisher and Hughes left the meeting and had a cup of tea together. No figures were released, but Fisher won with 'a substantial majority'.[74] The safe man had triumphed, and nothing was left for the one of ideas to do than to move that his rival should be formally elected unanimously. Seldom has a man risen so high in party politics mainly because of what he was, rather than because of his public accomplishments. Fisher's first public statements confirmed his modest view of his new position. The press was told with great firmness that he was in no way the leader, but only the chairman, of his party, although privately he knew well of the great possibilities open to him.[75]

Fisher's style thereafter was completely in accordance with this definition, and indeed reflected his entire character. The main items of policy were there in the party programme. The timing and authority for effecting them was a group decision, where not only the chairman had the right to have the best ideas. In Fisher's opinion, the party, its aims and ideals were important, and the individual only to the extent of his commitment and contribution to working for the common aim. As the top man, it was his business to co-ordinate and support the collective effort, as well as to represent his party with dignity. It was not part of his scheme of things to outshine or to dominate, for he saw himself as a man of integration rather than one of bold, imaginative experiment.

Nevertheless, as soon as he had been elected to the position, Fisher realised that his most urgent need was to create a personal public reputation in his own right. He chose to do this in a speech on the iron industry in Australia, which he delivered on 19th November, 1907.[76] Whereas Deakin's party supported bounties, Fisher spoke for fighting and determined Labor. He used his sledgehammer style of speaking to leave no one in any doubt as to which direction he would take his party. While bounties were all very well, 'My method – the method of the party to which I belong – is nationalisation.' The time was past for any kind of subterfuge:

> It would be cowardly for the man who believes that nationalisation is a proper principle not to express his views in this House. We have too long shrunk from maintaining propositions which we clearly believe in — far too long.

The rest of his speech was devoted to praising the cheapness and efficiency of State-controlled industries in Australia and New Zealand, and to revealing the evils of the 'triumphant plutocracy' of the United States.

This resounding declaration had some desired and expected consequences. Most importantly, Labor fully appreciated this new direction, and that Fisher had made a statement both of policy and of intention. He was approvingly seen to be far more aim-oriented than Watson. He continued to project this forceful image with such comments as, 'I would eat political dirt if thereby I could obtain a Commonwealth old-age pensions scheme'.[77] Temporarily, he might be prepared to support Deakin's compromise measures, but not indefinitely, for 'we must march on'[78] beyond liberal policies. Such utterances provoked knee-jerk horror and amazement from the entire conservative establishment. Its newspapers and politicians rubber-stamped the leftist movement, and especially its leader, as dangerously socialistic. The way was being prepared for Labor to withdraw its support from Deakin's Government, and so polarise politics between those who were for and against working-class aspirations.

During the first year of his leadership, however, Fisher made no attempt to change Watson's policy of keeping the Protectionists in office. New Protection was seen to be of such importance that he did not capitalise on a political crisis in April 1908 which could have been used to eject Deakin to the possible advantage of his party and himself. Rather, he worked to keep Deakin in power even when the tariff had been increased. He wrote to him in June that,

> I will not be a party to your humiliation while you and I understand each other as at present. I

shall go further and say that no carping criticism shall be heard from me even though I may think that you have taken a wrong course.[79]

Yet shortly thereafter, the reaction of his colleagues to events made this impossible for him. The Excise Tariff Act to ensure that good wages were paid by protected industries was declared unconstitutional by the High Court. It began to seem that Labor was supporting Deakin's policy in return for benefits which the Protectionists had no power to deliver. Worse was to come. Deakin promised a referendum to alter the Constitution to make New Protection possible, but he only proposed a change to allow a new Excise Tariff Act. It seemed that his Government was not willing to keep its word.

The feeling grew in caucus that Labor would have to withdraw its support and go it alone. In July the Interstate Party Conference had stated that Labor should make no parliamentary alliances in the future. Fisher played it on two levels. He made a long policy speech in September to show the country that his party was not extremist, for he concentrated on New Protection, defence, and old age pensions.[80] But in friendly circles he became more outspoken in telling everyone that they were all Socialists now, and such statements put him ever more firmly on the side of those who wanted the complete independence of their party from any other.[81] At the beginning of November 1908, the break was made when a caucus majority finally decided to withdraw support from Deakin. In Parliament the opposition groups joined Labor for the purpose of voting him out of office. The Governor-General, Lord Dudley, commissioned Fisher, as the leader of the largest party, to form the next administration. Dudley knew that he was making a decision which would have important consequences. He wrote to the Secretary of State for the Colonies: 'The existence of a Labor Government may probably give an opportunity for the amalgamation of the Opposition forces and render possible the adoption of the two-party system.'[82] But this development did not come at once, and Deakin promised, at least temporarily, to give the new Government his party's conditional support.

Notes

Again, of course, the *Fisher Papers*. In addition, P. Weller (ed.), *Caucus Minutes of the Federal Labor Party, Vol. I 1901-1917*, Melbourne 1975 is useful. There are very many books on early federal politics and on the organisation of the Labor Party. H. G. Turner, *The First Decade of the Australian Commonwealth*, Melbourne 1911 is the conservative and amusing account of a contemporary. G. Sawer, *Australian Federal Politics and Law, Vol. I 1901-1929*, Melbourne, 1956, is dry but objective. J. A. La Nauze, *Alfred Deakin: a Biography*, Melbourne, 1965, L. F. Fitzhardinge, *William Morris Hughes, Vol. I*, Sydney, 1964, and J. Murdoch, *Sir Joe* (Cook), London, 1996 give three accounts from different points of view. Pearce, op.cit., and especially Shepherd, op.cit., have interesting reminiscences.

Chapter IV

'That this proposal will relieve misery, I have not the shadow of a doubt.'

Andrew Fisher had been heaved into the Prime Minister's stool, having hardly made any attempt to get the job until the circumstances presented it to him. The formation of his cabinet was equally unproblematic for him. For the first time, caucus was to recommend the Ministers, so he did not have to face criticism of the choice as Watson had in April 1904. Fisher had the right to allot portfolios to the eight men who were chosen from twenty-one ambitious applicants.[83] Their first duty was clear to them all. They had to survive as a government until the Christmas recess gave them time to plan a forward policy. Hence none of them did anything which could induce Deakin and his followers to become disaffected with Labor attitudes. The new Government completed a few items of Protectionist legislation, and did nothing controversial of any kind.

As soon as Parliament had risen, however, the main aim of cabinet was to justify going it alone by making a declaration of distinctive policy and so prepare the way for the coming elections. This could only propose to effect the legislation which had been demanded by the party for years. At the start of the Christmas recess, the plans were finalised. Fisher travelled to each State to make himself as widely known as possible, a total of over ten thousand miles, and he also attended a Premiers Conference in Tasmania. No word escaped him in advance as to what his speech concerning Labor's future would contain. He delivered this on 30th March at Gympie.[84] It was in no way a reflection of Deakin's in the hope of retaining his support in Parliament for a few months only. Fisher said that Labor wanted to introduce a land tax to break up the great estates and thus promote closer settlement. The Conciliation and Arbitration Act was to be strengthened, and the Government would try to change the Constitution so that monopolies could be nationalised and a full New Protection introduced. Fisher also spoke of the need for a comprehensive Australian defence force. Together with his party, he had been converted from the belief that war was a capitalist conspiracy, so he proposed to introduce a military and naval system according to Labor ideas. Indeed, the first two warships had already been ordered in February.

This speech was poorly delivered, for Fisher was tired after his travels and was not prepared for a fluent delivery. But its message was clear, and it seemed to almost the entire Liberal press to be heralding the introduction of Socialism and worse, even if there was agreement on the need for Defence Acts. The politicians in opposition to Labor acted accordingly. The parties of Deakin, Cook and Forrest united in reaction in the so-called Fusion. At the end of May, they ignominiously voted Labor out of office. The party members were furiously indignant at this sudden reversal of their fortunes. Fisher presided over unforgiving men who were determined to make the life of the succeeding Ministry of Deakin and Cook as difficult as possible.

Fisher was the man whose strength was in conciliation, but politics now demanded Labor retaliation. He was in full agreement, for his personal feelings gave him a great impetus to attack the new government. For years, including twelve months as leader, he had worked hard for Labor to give Deakin his majority. Yet now Deakin, with what seemed indecorous haste, had taken the first opportunity to join and lead his political opponents of nearly a decade. Fisher was personally wounded, saying angrily that Deakin 'knows that I promised him all the aid that I could give him, and I gave it to him'.[85] He was 'very bitter', full of 'sullen wrath', and so he broke off the friendship.[86] He could not see that his Gympie speech had been a sufficient provocation for Deakin's reaction. He felt that Deakin was denying him what he himself had bestowed so generously. Simple justice demanded requital. Therefore Fisher listened readily to the fighters in his party as to the tactics which could embarrass the Liberal Fusion the most.

These men proposed to divide the party into four subcommittees which would each specialise in different aspects of the Government's policies. Fisher agreed, and the party organised itself into an effective system of ferocious opposition.[87] Fisher set an example in his own speeches. He blasted forth in Parliament with a mixture of Presbyterian righteousness and trade-union demagogy, especially against the Fusion policies of borrowing instead of taxing. The effect was not oratory, but it had its own form of impressiveness. One observer described his style thus:

> His voice was harsh, even raucous, a voice capable of penetrating a hurricane or adding considerable volume to the plaudits at a football match on Saturday afternoons. He had none of the graces of speech, the minimum of humour ... and no gift of eloquence of the polished art. He could be vehement in attack, with the directness and clang of a hammer.[88]

This was his method throughout the session of 1909. His colleagues followed his example, and although the Fusion Government passed much legislation, it was done to a continuing clamouring background of Labor protest, obstruction, sarcasm, and bitterness.

This proved to be of great advantage to Fisher in the following election campaign, which started in February 1910. He was able to lead a party united completely in what it was against — everything connected with its opponents — and in what it was for — its own party policy. Fisher's speeches were basically repetitions of that of Gympie of 1909, with their effectiveness increased by his almost missionary zeal to defeat the Liberals. Unusually for him, he even resorted to deliberate misrepresentation, as when he unjustly accused the Defence Minister Cook for thinking that 'River Class' destroyers were of no use in Australia, which had no big rivers.[89] His strenuous efforts took the public with him, for the time had come for Labor. The Fusion Government was routed. Fisher's party made impressive gains nearly everywhere, eleven per cent in Victoria, seventeen per cent in New South Wales, and twenty per cent in Tasmania. Labor won all eighteen Senate seats to have twenty-three against twelve and an independent, and forty-two to thirty with three independents in the House of Representatives. Fisher, the man who stood for the ideals of democratic justice for the workers, had been elected to do what he could as Prime Minister and Treasurer to bring them into being.

It was the triumph of his life that up to the outbreak of the Great War the good qualities which he possessed in such abundance were those which were required by the men who chose him to lead them. Secure in the support of his party, one aspect of his character above all was striking to those who had dealings with him:

> The gentleness and affection which were so charming in his family circle were, in his relations with others, translated into a genial comradeship. He delighted in 'doing a good turn' to anybody, and if he could oblige a friend he did it in a manner which gave grace to the act. He was a very easy man to work with, and obtained the most willing service from secretaries and officials because he treated them as personal friends with whom he was associated for the common good. If his conversational range was limited, it was nevertheless always a pleasant experience to spend an hour with him, because he was so frank, so free, so unspoiled, so quiet and willing to listen to views which did not coincide with his own. A more friendly man there was not in the politics of Australia in his time ...[90]

Part One

But he was not quite the paragon of this description. His secretary wrote of fits of temper against hostile and unfair newspapers or parliamentary setbacks, and he could be difficult to get along with when he was under too much social strain.[91] But these were exceptions, and his normal attitude to his fellow men communicated itself wherever he went. His own electoral base was firm, for the miners of Gympie 'worshipped him' and loyally outvoted his opponents in all six elections from 1901 to 1914. With time and eventual great success he came to have 'a high opinion of his own ability' and he could be 'fearfully patronising sometimes to bigger men but so unconscious of it that it passed'.[92] Yet to the end of his political career, and indeed until his death, he remained the man his upbringing, ideals and nature had made him when he first arrived in Queensland. The Labor Party owed much to his ability to hold its members together and give a sense of honest purpose to the idealistic drive to build a better and more democratic Australia.

It was a tremendous advantage that his Government had no need to scratch around for a policy. It was the business of cabinet to decide when to prepare Bills on the measures which had been proposed up to twenty years before, in what form to introduce them into Parliament, and also the timing of important executive decisions. The general Labor agreement on the programme and the solid majorities in both Houses enabled the years from April 1910 to May 1913 to be extraordinarily productive in both legislative and administrative achievement. There were many reforms for the working classes: the Conciliation and Arbitration Act was strengthened, the land tax was introduced, and preference to unionists was made a principle in Government employment. An attempt was made to change the Constitution by referendum in April 1911 in order to permit a large amount of industrial legislation. This was rejected, so the measures had to be postponed. This left more time for action on behalf of the whole nation. Comprehensive defence schemes were given top priority. The Northern Territory was taken over from South Australia to hasten its development, and work was begun on the railways to the north and west. The foundation stone for Canberra was laid, and the Interstate Commission was finally established. Dozens of other laws were passed in the general interest. It was due to Fisher's personal initiative that the Historical Memorials Committee was established to help Australian art and artists.[93]

Fisher, as Treasurer, was especially concerned with the matters of financial policy. He had the main role in the introduction of what was widely seen to be the risky experiment of introducing Australian paper money. He naturally sponsored the legislation to regulate the finances between the Commonwealth and the States after 1910, to found the Commonwealth Bank, to impose the land tax, and to repeal the Fusion Government's Naval Loan Act. Hostile critics attacked most of his speeches which introduced these Bills, and also his budgets, as being weak and badly delivered.[94] They were often correct, for Fisher 'had the sad habit of always putting things off' when he might have been mastering his facts.[95] Thus he was vulnerable to accusations of not having the complicated statistics under control, and therefore of failing to understand the probable unpleasant consequences of sectional socialist experiments. Fisher

Part One

indeed never claimed to have the detailed knowledge of a specialist. He told one Governor-General frankly 'that he had no knowledge of finance, though he had ideas'.[96] He trusted completely his permanent officials and other advisers to show him how to carry these ideas into effect, and he was good at delegating responsibility on to them. It was justification enough for him that he was doing what his entire life had prepared him for, and which the elections of 1910 had given him the constitutional authority to realise.

It was the same with his work in distributing money. For the first time, the Federal Government had a large surplus, and Labor saw no need to give it generously to the States with their Legislative Councils which blocked every kind of progress. Fisher and his colleagues used this splendid opportunity to help those who needed it. For example, invalid pensions were proclaimed by the Government on 15th December, 1910,[97] and the conditions for the payment of old age pensions were made more generous at the end of 1912. In the same year an Act was passed to give every white mother five pounds on the live birth of her baby. It was a law which Fisher said was the fulfilment of one of the dreams of his life. In introducing the second reading, he made one of his best speeches, for it rang with his profound feelings of sympathy, based on his desire for all people to attain the maximum amount of human dignity:

> I have never dipped my spoon into a soup kitchen, but I have seen others do it under humiliating conditions. I was not many years old when I felt that I would drown myself rather than humiliate myself,

and it is well for the race that, in general, that is the feeling the people have ... That this proposal will relieve misery, I have not the shadow of a doubt. It will also save lives ... Who can say what will be the value to the world of lives saved and lives protected, apart altogether from the misery and the suffering which will be alleviated.[98]

But this had no effect on the Liberals, who were incensed by it all, and fumed that Labor was proving its bottomless irresponsibility in throwing money away and adjusting taxation to pay for wasteful and unnecessary commitments. Fisher was completely unmoved, for he was secure in the support of his party, his majority, and his lifetime commitment to his ideas of social justice.

Nevertheless, some of the mud stuck, and Fisher's lack of expertise has given rise to much criticism as to his abilities or intelligence, notably from supporters of his Minister for Home Affairs, King O'Malley. Who should be considered to be the 'father' of the Commonwealth Bank? Surely not Fisher, who legislated for a bank within the system contrary to O'Malley's progressive American ideas for a central government bank with teeth.[99] For Fisher the controversy, which has lasted until the present, would have been virtually meaningless. He, his government, and his victorious party were effecting a long-standing Labor policy. As Prime Minister and Treasurer it was his duty to sponsor it, but collective responsibility meant that all shared equally in whatever credit might be due. If the bank was not at first as powerful as O'Malley wished, it was better at first to be cautious rather than make the entire establishment go into hysteria against alleged financial revolution. Later governments could strengthen the institution when and if public need and banking opinion found it necessary. Fisher was a man of the Labor movement, not a publicist for himself like O'Malley, who was greedy for personal fame and praise from every side.

In cabinet, in accordance with his principles, Fisher was a leader who worked for a smooth consensus rather than one who sought to impose his will upon his colleagues. For him this was a two-way process. He gave his full backing to his Ministers as long as they showed their loyalty in return. Hughes's biographer described this when he wrote of Fisher as a man who 'had come to lean heavily on his energetic and ingenious lieutenant, who seemed content to do any amount of work without challenging his leadership.'[100] Significantly, it was Hughes who had to smooth matters out when there were temporary difficulties between them.[101] But when things were going well, Fisher allowed his Ministers much latitude in their administration, provided important matters of policy had received cabinet approval. His appreciation of loyalty extended to the grass roots of the movement in whose service he had risen so high. When the unionists of Brisbane struck early in 1912, first he refused to send the military, as the Liberal Premier Denham demanded. He then had the courage to make a speech in Parliament which showed both his support for the workers, and his respect for the way they had behaved under extreme provocation from the State forces of law and order.[102]

Many men in the Labor Party profited from his attitudes. One of them was Charlie Frazer, who had been

The Triumph and the Tragedy

the main annoyance leading to Watson's resignation in October 1907.[103] Frazer knew well how to play on Fisher's need for appreciative feedback, and a genuine friendship developed between the two. It was Fisher who was first able to rein in Frazer's truculent spirit, and both control and profit from his capacity for manipulation. Thereafter, Fisher managed in 1909 to make use of Frazer's talents for tactical organisation and remorseless political in-fighting which were far greater than his own. Then he was able to encourage Frazer's administrative abilities for the benefit of his Government as a whole. Frazer knew well that his personal fortunes were bound up with Fisher's outstanding qualities, and that without his support he would probably never have become more than a disgruntled backbencher. This former problem for the party became completely loyal to his leader, and worked only for the common good. No small achievement of Fisher, and Frazer was not the only man who owed a tremendous amount to the way that he led the party for the benefit of all.

Fisher thus presided over a cabinet which on the whole functioned smoothly, the only exception being his 'hair shirt', the man who had been chosen against his wishes, O'Malley.[104] This ability to get Ministers to work together and to get things done was one of his most important leadership achievements. It was the same with caucus, which he treated with the consideration and respect due to the institution which had raised him so high. He invariably explained government measures in detail before introducing them into Parliament, and always allowed ample time for discussions, even when these were critical of his policy. He caused the rank and file to feel that they were a part of the decision-making process by continuing the system of committees which had been inaugurated to attack the Fusion Government. These were now reorganised to give advice and help to ministers, as well as to defend the Government in Parliament. It was typical of his courteous attitude that it was his habit at the end of each meeting sincerely 'to thank the members for their attendance.'[105] The support he expected and received from the members of his party was based on a mutual trust which he worked hard indeed to create.

His government officials saw a somewhat different side of him. The man whom he promoted to be the permanent secretary of the Prime Minister's Department, Malcolm Shepherd, wrote down in retirement his memories of the early years of the Commonwealth. These are indeed full of comments praising Fisher's character. He is described as being 'a man of singular earnestness and blazing honesty' who, despite his complete lack of humour, was 'essentially and frankly human' and 'the soul of rectitude'.[106] But just as no man can be a hero to his valet, so does Shepherd reveal weaknesses in Fisher. His willingness to devolve responsibility came from the fact that 'a long brain effort tired him very much', so it was easier to let trusted men do the best they could.[107] Fisher indeed relied heavily on Shepherd, letting him open his letters, signing many answers without reading them, and also getting him to prepare his important speeches. The conservative press picked on this lassitude to mock that 'He was a Prime Minister in the rough, and it fell to Mr Shepherd to turn him into the finished article', and that 'although the voice is the voice of Fisher, the brain behind the voice is the brain of Shepherd'.[108]

Fisher knew the press, so he did not take offence at articles which denigrated him in such a way.[109] He accepted the hardest criticism because everything that he did was for the movement he felt highly privileged to represent. The basis of it all was his certainty in the correctness and justice of the whole Labor Party programme. In his personal conduct, he always took great pains to show himself to be worthy of leading what he considered to be a noble cause. He was fiercely determined to uphold in his personal deportment the dignity of his Government and himself. Although he preferred the sober, black clothes of his religious upbringing, and was impatient with fancy clothes, he endured a frock-coat and a top hat because it was expected of him.[110] This had its limits. For the Coronation of George V he reluctantly had to wear court dress, but he tore off its lace with his own hands. [111] Yet he was only content with the best, in order to show that his party should be seen to have become part of the establishment. In June 1910 he was the first Prime Minister to order a government car, a Renault which cost £850. [112] He was not satisfied with the headlights, so he ordered the installation of better ones. All this was part of his insistence that his official appearances should be correct in every particular of protocol.

With his Governors-General he was equally as concerned to do the right thing and to have a good working relationship. This developed into a friendship with Lord Dudley, who with sincerity wrote how delighted he would be if Fisher on a visit to Sydney would stay with him, even if they were not always of one mind on official matters.[113] Fisher was closer to his successor, Lord Denman, who wanted to be godfather to his youngest son.[114] Sir Ronald Munro Ferguson, the Governor-General of his third ministry, soon appreciated his 'attractive personality', his 'native shrewdness and his untiring industry', and was of the opinion that 'no member of the Labor Party is held in higher public regard' than he.[115] Munro Ferguson obviously believed him when he several times 'told me that he did not conceal anything from me'. The worldly Scottish aristocrat found the former Ayrshire miner to be 'a very simple, outspoken person; and therefore it is easy to discover the trend of his mind'.[116] He appreciated that Fisher 'played with all his cards on the table' while 'being absorbed in his own opinions, which are unchangeable'. This inflexibility made Fisher a difficult man to give advice to, but 'nevertheless, such is his honesty and public spirit that it is always a pleasure to confer with him as a friend', and on the occasions when he listened 'it was often useful to do so'.[117]

Fisher's hot desire always to do the right thing sometimes caused problems for himself and his entourage. Late in 1910 he went to South Africa for the ceremonies attending the opening of the Parliament of the Union.[118] His presence was considered necessary in order to show full imperial solidarity, and he also needed a break from the great strains of office. It was his first visit to a country away from those experienced through his working life, and he did his utmost to honour his hosts. He put on 'shiny boots', which he hated, because it was the current fashion. He was so concerned about his own dignity and the need to represent Labor and Australia that he became unbearable through self-importance. Nothing pleased him; neither the reserved places at ceremonies, nor the Victoria Falls or the landscape during a month's train tour of the inland. It took a row with his secretary to bring him down to earth. It was typical of his essential humanity that he could see the faults in himself and restore a harmonious relationship.

Fisher learnt from experience the following year, when he went to London for the Coronation of George V and an attendant Imperial Conference to consider the defence of the Empire. On the way he enjoyed a tour of Europe, and visited all the cathedrals in Italy and France he could. He did not like Lewis Harcourt, the Secretary of State for the Colonies, but he let others mediate for him. He got very tired of the continual festivities, but he put up with them without ill-humour.[119] He was also able to tolerate the tendency of the British to gaff at the only working-class Prime Minister the Empire had to offer. The Conference was for him 'the most important step taken during the present century, from the Government's point of view', since the Dominions were to be consulted as to the common defence of the Empire.[120] He was not overawed by aristocracy, nor by any feelings that a former coalminer might not have the ability to represent his country on an equal level. He and his Defence Minister Pearce put Australian interests forcefully. 'Remarkable was the tenacity' with which they did this, and praiseworthy 'the important precedents for consultation and co-operation which, primarily because of their efforts, emerged from the conference'.[121]

Fisher's successes in Australia and in London did not change his basic personality in the slightest. He managed to decline an honorary Doctorate of Law from Oxford, but with reluctance he had to accept his appointment to the Privy Council so as not to offend the new King.[122] His real feelings were that such medieval trivia unjustly raised some men above their fellows, and in all matters he remained a true democrat. In May 1911 he returned to Ayrshire, 'going back home, back to Crosshouse where I was born'.[123] The reception he received was in accordance with his high position, and on 5th July he was awarded the Freedom of the Burgh of Kilmarnock, which he accepted more not to offend his hosts than because he wanted it. This was followed by the Freedoms of Glasgow and Edinburgh, yet, despite being feted in the social round, at no time did he show any signs of pride or superciliousness. The report about him in the *Kilmarnock Standard* was flowing with compliments:

> Nature formed him ... for the accomplishment of certain specific purposes. She gave him not only gifts but also the wisdom to use them and not throw them away, not so much to make circumstances as to turn circumstances to good and honourable account ... He is not a class leader but a leader of people as a whole ... He is ready to work with kings and emperors, if they are of one mind with him, just as readily as with miners and scavengers.[124]

It was a tribute which did not bear the sound of flattery, but which had the ring of truth and conviction. In describing Fisher, the leader writer had seen the essential man.

Fisher retained his equilibrium and general good

manners despite the continual stress in the jungle of party politics. Everything that he or his Government did was savagely attacked by the Liberal politicians and press. This opposition was ruthlessly determined to destroy the image of Labor for the 1913 elections, and every form of partisan attack was used to try to discredit the Government. The attempt in April 1911 to change the Constitution by referenda and secure the widest powers for the Commonwealth to deal with industrial legislation and monopolies was also rejected by the State Labor politicians. It all focused on Fisher as the Labor leader. He was caricatured as being the poor slave of his party. 'This, O sire, is what I propose doing', the *Melbourne Punch* made him say, while Autocratic Caucus Rex told him `Ah! — But this is what you must do'. Alternatively, he was satirised as totally hard and inflexible, as a miserly Wackford Squeers more or less starving the poor States, or as a mean Scot who was making Australia pay for the tunes he was dancing to.[125] Fisher might protest that to say that Labor was not responsible to the electors was 'a wilful and malicious lie, which has been put forward by liars from one end of the country to the other',[126] but nothing ever helped to reduce the farrago of poisonous abuse.

The way the Liberals wallowed in prejudice against Fisher was most clearly shown shortly before his return to Australia from England in July 1911. The American journalist W. T. Stead reported him as having said, 'If threatened, we should have to decide whether we would defend ourselves, or if we thought the war was unjust, and England's enemy right, we should haul down the Union Jack, hoist our flag, and start on our own.'[127] This was obviously the complete opposite of all Fisher's known opinions, for he was well-known for referring to the Empire as 'a family of nations'. He was on the seas, so he could not defend himself against the distortion of whatever he might have said. But at once his critics started to revel in abuse. The conservative newspapers thought he might have been hypnotised, the Empire League almost went berserk, and dozens of Liberal politicians like Premier Wade of New South Wales demanded his instant resignation. It was all deliberately nasty, for as the Governor-General wrote, public opinion had 'little disposition to credit Mr Fisher with the sentiment attributed to him'.[128] The object of the malignancy managed to hold himself above the vulgarity, only saying mildly that 'Brother Stead' had got everything 'rather upside down'.[129] Since his earliest years he had fought against capitalism and its manifestations of every kind, and he was given the strength to go on doing so by his knowledge that he was fighting for what he and the Labor movement knew and believed to be right.

For the general elections of 31st May, 1913 Fisher continued with his uncompromising course. The main items on the Labor programme had been passed into law, and not too much thought had been given as to their successors. Hence he talked a lot about past achievements in 'a somewhat discursive utterance covering much ground'.[130] The most important positive proposal for the following Parliament was the reintroduction of the referenda which had been defeated in 1911, in the hope that they would be approved and allow the Government to pass a great deal of industrial legislation. This did not happen. The referenda again failed to win a majority, and Labor lost the election by thirty-seven seats to thirty-eight, although the party had a Senate majority of twenty-nine seats to seven. Fisher resigned, and the Liberals under Joseph Cook took office.

The following Parliament was a distasteful one for Fisher, since it was characterised by furious and destructive debates provoked by the strange unbalanced situation in Parliament. The Liberals tried to show how estimable they were by reversing whatever Labor administrative policies they could. Fisher had to react on behalf of his party, and give a lead with the sort of polemical speeches which he disliked having to make.[131] Caucus meetings were dominated by the planning of obstructive tactics. Nothing positive could be done until a new election had brought about a clear position. Fisher had to start a campaign for purely party purposes; that a single dissolution would suffice as showing the will of the electorate.[132] The Liberals naturally wanted to get both Houses dissolved, in order to have a fresh start. At the beginning of June 1914 Cook won through to the double dissolution. The new elections were to be held on 5th September.

Part One

Notes

Sources as for Chapter Three. In addition, N. J. Meaney, *The Search for Security in the Pacific 1901-1914*, Sydney, 1976 shows the development of defence strategy excellently, and also Fisher's contribution from 1908. T. H. Kewley, *Social Security in Australia 1900-1972*, Sydney, 1972, especially Chapters 4, 5, and 6. R. Gollan, *The Commonwealth Bank of Australia*, Canberra, 1968 summarises in Chapter Seven the controversy about Fisher's contribution. Interesting recollections of Fisher are in R. A. Broinowski, *The First Five Prime Ministers of Australia*, in *The Journal of the Royal Australian Historical Society*, 2, 1949. The papers of such men as Watson, Hughes, and Deakin contain material from and about Fisher, which could be used to provide an extensive and maybe unwieldy support to the judgements on Fisher's character and motives. The East Ayrshire Library in Kilmarnock has press cuttings concerning his visits to Britain.

Chapter V

'I have decided to be an applicant for a position in the public service.'

The election campaign of 1914 was started by Fisher at the beginning of July and by Cook a few days later. The unedifying party attacks on each other formed the main excitement of the purely domestic confrontation. The completely unexpected outbreak of war changed everything. Fisher and Cook promised unqualified support for the British Empire and for each other's party over war measures, whoever won. Fisher made the famous promise to support Britain to the last man and the last shilling (which, incidentally, Cook had used in 1899), and he repeated it two months later in Parliament.[133] The phrase was in contrast to his essentially pacifist feelings, which had always expressed themselves as being against conscription and militarism. Additionally, he had often publicly hoped that international arbitration would manage to prevent all wars.[134] He allowed himself to be carried away by the overwhelming surge of Imperialist popular emotion, and he did genuinely believe in the need to help the Empire. His burst of patriotism was accepted by the electorate. Labor won its second clear victory after 1910. The party was returned with forty-two

MHRs and a friendly independent against thirty-two Liberals, and with thirty-one senators to five. Fisher was given the trust of the nation to lead the country in the conduct of the war.

And this was to be his personal tragedy. He was a leader of consensus, whose great strengths were in taking already existing ideas and policies and giving them effect. He was strong and determined when he knew that he could rely on the support of the men with whom he had to work. These conditions were no longer present as during his previous Ministries. A war needs a leader of instant decision, flexible, adaptable, and able to take a forceful lead against all and any resistance, one who can make and create instant policies to react to new events. Fisher was not this man. Furthermore, the war came more and more to divide the members of the Labor Party. Many of them saw the priority of the war effort to be paramount, since of what use would reform legislation be in a country which had been conquered by the enemy? But the need for Labor laws remained the dominating issue for the rest. Cabinet might have given Fisher good support, but only three of his former colleagues were elected to it, and the team spirit was gone. Although the Governor-General wrote that, 'The Government is full of confidence, and its personnel commands much respect',[135] it reflected the divisions in the party, and it was noticeably weaker than its predecessor. Both cabinet and especially caucus, which had formerly worked for the common aim, increasingly became the forums for bitter, divisive quarrels.

Fisher at first tried to satisfy both groups. The War Precautions and other Acts were passed, and the executive decisions were made to give effect to censorship and every kind of regulation. The organisation was perfected to train as many soldiers as possible. All this was a great strain on Fisher, since it went directly against the ideals of his lifetime and he was mentally incapable of swiftly changing his attitudes. Despite his belief that Australia had to fight, he hated having to announce that further quantities of soldiers would be sent to Europe, since in his own eyes this made him into one of the warmongers he had always despised. He did not put his full heart into campaigns to persuade them to enlist, and he never appointed a Director-General of Recruiting after the British model. Instead, he tried to compensate with legislation in the interests of Labor. The land tax was raised and an income tax introduced, so that borrowing alone would not have to finance the war effort. When it became clear that taxation could not cover all the costs, he reluctantly gave notice of a Bill 'to supplement the revenue at any time by loans'.[136] Because 'he much dislikes having to borrow in the open market', he added the sincerely meant, but vain, hope that they would be redeemed before a year had elapsed.[137] Fisher also tried to align himself with Labor opinion by extending the powers of the Commonwealth Bank. This failed to placate the party, and incurred the bitter hostility of the Liberals. Most productive of strife of all his new measures was the attempt to change the Constitution to give more powers to the Federal Government to pass industrial legislation. This was to be decided upon for a third time at a popular referendum.

Fisher increasingly found that a man who dances at two weddings is popular at neither. As early as

September 1914 the first party radicals attacked him for rewarding Belgium with £100,000 for its 'magnificent defence' against Germany. Frank Anstey and four others furiously condemned this gift to a Government which a few years before had shot some striking workers down, and whose King was far richer than the richest three Americans together.[138] Yet others in the party increasingly compared working-class reform to Nero fiddling while Rome was burning. Fisher was not the man to try to force the competing sides to subordinate themselves to his will. He wanted to please both – but only drove himself towards nervous collapse. He was constantly in Parliament, trying to maintain a complete oversight of events which had long since passed out of his control. In the year up to October 1915 the index in Hansard of his speeches and statements is eleven columns long, a record. But he became wary of facing the critics in his own party. He appeared less regularly at caucus meetings, and went increasingly into cover. He delegated many of his powers of office to Hughes to administer the country on his behalf. He devoted himself above all to internal Treasury affairs, where he could be 'absorbed in finance' to try to forget the world outside.[139]

Shortly before Christmas 1914, he tried to flee from the insupportable tensions within himself and within his party. He chose the time carefully so that nobody could say that he was deserting his post. He went to New Zealand, the land of his youthful hopes, ostensibly for war talks, but in reality to have a break to try to recover his sense of purpose and his mental strength.[140] Hughes, who thought he was well in command of the situation at home, begged him to stay as long as he felt the need.[141]

Fisher's sense of duty compelled him to return, but it did him no good. His condition was worsened by a psychosomatic cold which he was unable to shake off, and he spent much of his time in bed.[142] In caucus he had ever less authority and control. He became psychologically incapable of answering bitter attacks on his Government's financial policies. He could only helplessly try to avoid the conflicts by vaguely saying, 'Finance, finance, finance', to the fury of his critics, especially Anstey.[143] An even greater stress for him was the Liberal demand to introduce conscription. He opposed this as being unnecessary and potentially capable of dividing the country. But the demand grew in intensity from April 1915. His refusals to consider it were made harder for him in the knowledge that some of his own party's members believed that it would have to come. He continually had to give ground. By September 1915 he was saying that, 'the Government will not do anything without consulting the people' by means of a conscription referendum, and this was a long way from his earlier promises that under no circumstances would he ever consider it.[144]

The idea of being Reid's successor as High Commissioner came early in 1915. Fisher's opinion was that Reid was 'lazy and getting old', and that he could do the job much better himself, although he denied for many months that he had any 'aspiration' for it.[145] He hung on to the Prime Ministership in case some miracle should end the war and leave him in the best position to plan the reconstruction. He tried to lighten his burden by pleading with his Liberal enemies in Parliament to give him the fair play he claimed to have given them in August 1914.[146] His increasing loss of a sense of political reality was revealed when he said that 'only an earthquake' could prevent the industrial powers referendum,[147] although nothing enraged the Liberals more, and the chances of a successful outcome were almost nil. By the beginning of October 1915, he had finally been driven harder than he could bear. At the end of the month, he left the House of Representatives for the last time, telling Pearce in a fury that its members could all go to hell.[148] He had finally regressed to his old solution of running away from insupportable conflicts. Still correct in procedure, he informed caucus that he wanted to be Reid's successor. Humane as always, he left Oakleigh Hall in his absence to be a convalescent home for returned soldiers. At the end of October, in caucus, he abdicated the problems of the party, the government, and the war.[149] His successor by unanimous vote was Hughes, who showed that he was a very different man. Whereas the party had destroyed Fisher's career, Hughes destroyed the party, and scrambled over its wreckage to further personal success.

Fisher as High Commissioner was not in a position where he could fulfil his own needs. He represented no political party, and his main responsibilities were to do what his Government required of him, in particular the administrative work to establish Australia House at Aldwych in the Strand. Such paper work had never been his strength, and he rapidly found that he had not retired into a job which would be a form of relaxation for him after the soul-destroying first year of war. He did his best on formal occasions, but he was not made to be a polished diplomat. Far worse for him, Hughes was in England for months in 1916 and again in 1918-1919, and treated Fisher with insulting indifference.[150] He consulted his former chief on nothing of importance, and left him only routine work. When they went on tour together in 1916, Hughes got all the cheers and attention, and also the freedom of most of the great cities of England, while Fisher got nothing. It was galling for him to think that had he held on to office, the positions would have been reversed. He reacted later in the year with a form of introverted revenge. Hughes needed every kind of support he could get for his conscription referendum. Fisher refused to make any public statement in its favour, but his commitment to his lifelong principles rebounded against him. Any chance of trust between the two men disappeared forever. Hughes thereafter relied on the journalist, Keith Murdoch, for information from London and for help in persuading the soldiers to give a positive vote.

Fisher's resentment showed itself when he indulged in a copious exchange of letters with friends and former colleagues who found Hughes to be unsympathetic, dictatorial, and worse. 'Hughes has out-Heroded Herod in his treachery ... He has resorted to every sort of trickery and used the powers at his disposal in the most unscrupulous manner to gain his ends ...' wrote one close friend of many years.[151] This helped Fisher in knowing that he was not alone in his feelings, but it did not improve his position in London. He continued to do what he was supposed to do, and was offered the Legion of Honour by the French Government for his work on the Dardanelles Commission which investigated the mess of the Gallipoli Campaign. His principles about such awards had not changed, and he declined. But more and more he withdrew into himself. According to Pearce, by 1918 he had become 'capable of little concentrated effort' and a year later was 'beginning to fail'.[152] His work suffered greatly, and the conditions in Australia House became 'in sad need of overhaul'.[153] Fisher ended his term reclusive and saddened by the experience.

When his appointment as High Commissioner was over, on 21st January, 1921, only disappointment awaited him. He had had thoughts of going back to Kilmarnock and entering British politics as a Labor member, but at Paisley he was rebuffed. He returned to Australia, where the rejection was even more bitter. The West Sydney electorate became vacant on 1st August, 1921 because of the death of T. J. Ryan. It had been Hughes's seat as a Labor man, and Fisher nominated for pre-selection for the by-election. Victory might have sponged out the memories of his humiliation by Hughes in London. He was not chosen.[154] In his usual manner when faced with overwhelming emotional problems, he decided to leave Australia and the Labor party, to which he had given so much, but from which he was receiving so little. Even the thought of his beautiful home could not keep him. His time was past. He preferred to live in obscurity in a country that owed him nothing than in one which only showed ingratitude. He went again to the anonymity of London, although this had the consequence of splitting up his family into those who chose to live there and those who preferred Australia. Fisher's final escape from the insupportable difficulties was in his steadily weakening health until his death on 22nd October, 1928. His wife outlived him by nearly thirty years.

At least he was honoured by a memorial in

Hampstead Cemetery, paid for by Australians living in London and unveiled by Ramsay MacDonald on 7th February, 1930. In Gympie, the house of his early married years in Maori Lane was restored and erected in the grounds of the local museum. In Crosshouse in 1978 a garden was laid out with a cairn with four plaques, from the Community Council, the District Council, the Government of Australia, and the Ayrshire miners. It is not much to honour a man who had been so successful as Prime Minister between 1910 and 1913, but, after all, Fisher was never one for meretricious show.

Notes

The most useful additional sources are E. Scott, *Australia During the War*, Sydney, 1936, and L. F. Fitzhardinge, *William Morris Hughes, Vol. II*, Sydney 1979. J. R. Thomson, *The Australian High Commission in London, its Origins and Early History*, Ph.D. Thesis A.N.U. recounts the background up to Reid's retirement, with some references to Fisher. There are many books about the conscription issue.

PART TWO

The Leader Whom They Chose:

Frank Tudor and the Labor Party after Hughes

As I have said to many others, I know that the position [of leader of the Labor Party] is one of the most difficult to fill in Australia at any time, and it will be particularly difficult for some time to come, but I will do my best, and no one can do more than that.

Frank Tudor to Andrew Fisher
27th November, 1916
Fisher Papers, ANL

While I hold that Frank Tudor is one of the cleanest and whitest men in the Labor movement, we must realise it, and even Frank Tudor realises it – that one man stands head and shoulders above everybody else, and that is Thomas Ryan.

Tom Butterfield
at the Labor Party Conference
2nd October, 1919

Chapter I

'In a shop in which I worked in England, they turned out a thousand dozen hats a week.'[155]

John Tudor was born in 1829 in Milford in Pembrokeshire, Wales, and Ellen Burt in the same county eight years later.[156] They migrated at the end of the 1850s to Victoria, not in the hope of getting rich from gold, but to find a better life than that offered by the docks of Swansea or Cardiff. John was a ballastman, and earned enough to afford to get married in Melbourne on 10th October, 1861. The couple went to live at Williamstown. Their first children were Frederick and Charles, but they both died before they were four years old. Their third son was born on 27th January, 1866. He was named Francis Gwynne, but he was always called Frank. Ten years later the family moved to Richmond, about four kilometres south-east of the centre of Melbourne.[157]

This working-class 'Struggletown' had enjoyed its own local government since 1855, and was created a city in 1882. It was not salubrious. The Yarra constituted half its boundary, and 'the wide river flat proved irresistible to noxious trades seeking both a river frontage and a captive pool of labour living on their doorstep'. Richmond became 'dingy and crowded', full of stinks

Part Two

from such places as the tannery, the wool-washing plant and also the open drains. Although there were 'pockets of gentility', especially during the boom of the 1880s, there was an enormous amount of human unhappiness of every kind in the many tiny dwellings and hovels. But there was a good side, because 'poverty and prejudice welded its people into a richly human community'.[158]

The young Frank Tudor absorbed both aspects of Richmond as vital parts of his nature. He had a deep and ever-enduring sympathy for the exploited and the poor, and he never grew away from his origins. The support of the people of his city enabled him to become a successful politician, and he returned their faith by not moving to a better district, and by always identifying himself with their problems and their aspirations. His life long he did what he could to improve the human condition of those he knew so well. In return he won his strength from the multitude of close relationships which were the essence of life for the working people who had very little else.

Frank was brought up in this strange bipartite world of fundamental human values and of atmospheric stench to be a practising Christian in the Congregational Church. He learnt early that the need to help and to love were not just pious texts. His formal education was not so easy. He went to the Central State School at Richmond. The experience was less than uplifting. The classes were overcrowded and the buildings insanitary. The pupils 'were given levels of literacy and numeracy fit only for the factory'.[159] The boys were taught a little wood and metalwork, but nothing to help them become skilled tradesmen. Frank was industrious and somehow managed to acquire more than the absolute basics. He early showed the precise accuracy which was to be a great strength to him. He was competent at arithmetic, good at English, and his handwriting was readable even if not handsome. At sports, despite his small size, he did well. He particularly enjoyed everything to do with water, and he won a bronze medal for lifesaving.[160]

Despite their son's obvious intelligence and ability in school, there was no thought in his parents' minds that he should stay there longer than necessary. He had no particular idea as to what he wanted to be, and at first he worked in a sawmill and then in a boot factory. He found that he preferred supple materials to the strength of wood or hard leather, a predilection which was later reflected in his character in politics. He found his place in the felt hat industry, a booming trade since it was an epoch when a man in public thought he was half-naked without one. He became an apprentice in 1882 at the Denton Hat Mills in Abbotsford,[161] and went through all the stages to become a master hatter.

He was too ambitious to spend his life at the workbench. His hopes were to become the manager of a hat factory and make it into one of the most progressive in the world in the quality of its goods and in pay and conditions. He realised early that all this could only come about when management and men co-operated in using more efficient methods to make a better product. Hence, while he remained a man who always wanted to do what he could for the workers, he never recommended the hard policies of industrial unrest and strikes, and he was always for compromise when it seemed possible.

Part Two

As a young hatter, anxious to get on in the world, he saw that he would have to study the industry in other places than his home city in order to learn about the improvements that could be made. He decided to travel to increase his knowledge of the hatters' world. He left home, first to go around Victoria to find out about the raw materials and also the hat opinions and needs of future customers. Then in 1890 he travelled steerage to England, an experience which gave him a lifelong dislike of third-class conditions on ships.[162] His intention was to investigate the most modern methods in the centre of his hat world, in order later to help introduce them to the Victorian industry.

And he was a good learner, because he had grown up to be a young man of many positive qualities. He was friendly, open and easy-going, with no signs of malice of any sort. He was both understanding and kind to his large circle of acquaintances and friends. He was tolerant of the social vices, while showing no inclination himself to relax with cigars, alcohol, gambling, or any sort of doubtful company. He was always ready to give lavishly of his time to people who were a part of his world and to make their concerns his own if he could see his way to helping them. Thereby he was a good mediator who was proud of doing a good job himself and encouraging it in others. Ambitious as he was to rise in his trade, he had the necessary qualities of reliability, honesty and tenacity of purpose. He was responsible with figures and funds, painstaking and utterly correct with all matters of administration which came within his province. He had an unbreakable sense of loyalty to his friends and any group of which he was a part, and he was exceptionally dutiful in carrying out whatever tasks he had been entrusted with.

But his personality, so bountifully equipped for success and popularity in working-class Richmond, was less endowed for leadership in more demanding circles. He never had the burning, egocentric drive of the man who uses a cause to help himself to power. He could not dominate, and never did he try to force his ideas upon anyone. He needed an amiable consensus of opinion to be able to function properly, but although he was amenable to persuasive argument, he was not particularly good at it himself. He completely lacked the killer instinct with intransigent opponents, for he showed 'no indication of cantankerous fighting blood'.[163] With his friendly openness he was not the man to engage in intrigue or hard political bargaining. He was an excellent representative of any organisation with which he had identified himself, purposeful in putting forward ideas which everybody could share, but he had no imagination or initiative to propound new ones when boldness of action was required. He was persistent when the direction had been set by the general situation or by other more decisive men, under whom he was always ready to do what he could, but he never won deep personal loyalty from those who required a forceful command, however much they liked him for his admirable and genuine human qualities.

But as the young man eager to make a career in the hat trade, his lack of hard leadership abilities was obvious to no one, and of neither interest nor importance in any case. He arrived in England with letters of introduction, and went the rounds of the hat factories between London and Lancashire to gather information and experience. He was particularly impressed by the headquarters of Tress in Denton near Manchester, where many thousands of hats a week were turned out, of such high quality that people boasted about them being snapped up by presidents and kings.[164] Here he learnt about English management and organisation, and also that the methods in the United States were more modern than those in Europe. So he crossed the Atlantic with fifty dollars in his pocket, and worked in the felt hat trade in Connecticut and New Jersey.[165] He became a member of the United Hatters' Society of North America, and found out about the 'union label', whereby a stamp of quality was given to products made entirely by trade unionists. He was very enthusiastic about this device, since it encouraged both unionism and high standards, in that the Society 'only places the label in perfect hats'.[166] Later, in Australian politics, he was seen by his colleagues to be the expert on the subject in general.[167]

Despite his positive experiences, his stay in America was not prolonged. He wanted his future to be in England, since Alice Smale of Denton was awaiting the return of her young and respectable career man. He came back to her in 1892, and they married on 2nd January, 1894, at her local Congregational Chapel. She became pregnant, and Frank had little thought of returning to Victoria, particularly as the colony was suffering from a grave economic depression and his career in England was starting to flourish. Shortly after his marriage he became assistant to the general secretary of the English Hatters' Union and vice-president of its

London branch.[168] As a zealous reformer he used his growing influence to help promote the union label. He later said proudly that, 'I was so satisfied of its beneficial effects in America that I moved a motion to introduce its use into Great Britain. Our union was the first trade union to endorse the label there.'[169]

Despite this attempt to integrate himself into the English hat world, Tudor's life was not to be spent there. Alice and baby Alfred both died at the birth. The subsequent emptiness of his life induced the unhappy widower to return home to the emotional security of his family and friends in Richmond. When he was there he looked for a job for twelve weeks until finally Denton of Abbotsford took him on again.[170] Thereafter he never looked back. His world experience was at once found useful by his employers. He automatically helped to effect his ideas for improving production efficiency and working conditions. He settled down completely and finally, and sealed this by his second marriage, to Fanny Mead, on 6th January, 1897. He became a husband and father with all the good qualities of his kind and generous nature to his wife and brood which came to number three daughters and three sons.[171]

His career blossomed with the pressure of a growing family behind him. He became admired for his achievements to the extent that he rose to be President of the Felt Hatters' Union, and this gave him a seat on the Victorian Trades Hall Council. Here he progressed swiftly in the estimation of his colleagues, and in 1900 was elected by them to be their president. The position was one for which he was entirely suited. His need to help the men and women he had been brought up with and knew so well found its appropriate outlet. His duties were clear in trying to co-ordinate the interests of the working population and pressing for the necessary legislation.[172] The lines of general policy were established by the situation, so there could be no great differences of opinion among his co-workers. He was thus able to maintain his friendly profile while being active for the common good. He was seen to be approachable, hard-working and efficient, and at no time did he let his distinguished position go to his head.

Hence at the start of 1901 many people in Richmond saw in Tudor the fitting Labor Party candidate for the working-class seat of Yarra for the first federal elections which were to be held at the end of March. He was very attracted by the idea. His work on the Trades Hall Council had introduced him to the parliamentary scene from the point of view of the lobbyist. The thought of being a legislator himself and thus in a position to help pass beneficent laws appealed greatly to his social instincts. He was given every encouragement by the men in the Denton factory.[173] He showed how much he wanted the party nomination by saying that, 'The Trades Hall mark should be put upon the most suitable candidate', meaning it of course the other way around.[174]

He had to control his impatience for some time, for his party only got around to forming a Labor League in Richmond in the middle of February.[175] It was not until 6th March that he won the pre-selection on the first ballot against three rivals. This was ratified on 10th March by the Political Labor Council, and he made his first speech four days later.[176] The main issue was the tariff, and as a Victorian from the hat industry he was naturally for the highest duties. He also showed that he was a solid Labor man by demanding such reforms as conciliation and arbitration, old age pensions and the Commonwealth Bank, and he was very outspoken for a White Australia. His speeches appealed to the working-class electors of Richmond, but he won mainly because the vote against him was split between three protectionists. In this fortunate way he was returned as one of the original twenty-four members of the federal Labor Party, only three of whom came from Victoria.

Part Two

Chapter II

'I should go back to my trade if I left political life.'[177]

From the start of his new career as politician, Tudor's character made it easy for him to be an excellent constituency representative. Because Parliament met in Melbourne he was one of the few members who could live permanently at home. The whole year round he made it into his office for the people of the district with their problems. He was conscientious in doing whatever he could to help and he showed his closeness to local opinion by preferring to hold evening street meetings rather than official ceremonies. He was never proud or conceited, and his style was well appreciated, as the following recollection manifests well.

> I cut my teeth hanging on to my father's hand listening to [Tudor] speak from the back of a wood carter's truck with a hurricane lamp, expounding his policies. And to get [the people] there they used to borrow the auctioneer's bell and go round the streets. And they'd come out in their hundreds... The peasants liked to listen to their parliamentary representatives, and they'd stay there until 10 or 11 at night.[178]

It was good entertainment from a man who was seen by his audiences to be one of themselves. Tudor enjoyed the continual contact, later saying proudly that 'most of the people [in my electorate] are personally acquainted with me'.[179]

He consolidated this good reputation by taking part in the widest variety of district activities. He supported numerous sport groups, and he was a long-serving President of the Victorian Amateur Swimming Association.[180] Another particular interest was the Richmond Australian Rules Football Club, of which he was also president for many years, and which was almost a religion in the area. He went to as many games as he could, and not only of the first team. He was a member of the local militia and also a highly respected member and deacon of the Congregational Church. He had a great sense of fun, and he took part in all kinds of outings, whether organised by the liquor trade or by anybody else. He was a good mixer, and did not talk over people's heads. He was far happier to chat about developments in the hat business, which he followed with enthusiasm his whole life long, or to gossip about who was getting married to whom, than bore anybody with reports of what was going on in federal politics. For his first career always remained in some inner way more real to him than his second ever became.

This closeness and friendliness to everyone earned him criticism from sour extremists who wanted him to support their own particular crusades. One acerbic polemicist for social revolution wrote that,

Part Two

his electorate comprised Protestants and Catholics, Sinn Feiners and Orangemen, Loyalists and Pacifists, Socialists and Conservatives. How to represent this jumble of interests would present a problem to the ordinary man, but Mr Tudor tactfully solved it by doing nothing.[181]

Not quite true, because he was not always so bland, for instance supporting Home Rule in 1905. But impartiality was his considered personal policy on his home patch.[182] His sound tactics of non-partisan lack of involvement won and kept him the support of the majority, whose general opinion was expressed by his parliamentary colleague, Richard Crouch. He noted in his memoirs that Tudor 'was a good friend and an indefatigable member for his constituents'.[183]

Tudor was also able swiftly to rise in the estimation of his Labor colleagues in Parliament, although the opportunity was due less to his intrinsic personal merits than to the needs of the party. The first leader, J. C. Watson, and his closest adviser, W. M. Hughes, were both from Sydney electorates. Senator McGregor from South Australia was the party spokesman in the Upper House. The strong Queensland bloc of seven ensured that their Senator Stewart became caucus secretary. To have left Victoria out of the party executive altogether would have been a gratuitous insult. Tudor was generally seen to be the most able man of the three from his State. J. G. Barrett was an undistinguished junior senator who seldom went to caucus meetings. J. B. Ronald was a clergyman who never dispelled the rumours of alcohol which persecuted him like a hangover. Therefore Tudor had general support in being elected assistant secretary of caucus, its treasurer and its whip for the sixteen members in the House of Representatives.[184]

His careful and responsible nature enabled him from the first to be competent with his new duties. To be treasurer involved only the modest finances of the party in Parliament. His work as whip was made easy by the party rules which ensured discipline, and as well the numbers to be organised were not great. He was busier as secretary, since Stewart increasingly left him to do everything. It was typical of Tudor that he made no grumbling attempt to be installed in his place. He continued his efficient work, always acting in the interests of the party leaders and the general Labor movement.

His idea of loyalty was to be unfailingly on the side of Watson, who was tactful and friendly but firm of purpose, and had a similar attitude to Tudor's as to how to serve their electors. Watson knew well how to make use of this undeviating support. He got Tudor, as the representative of Victoria, on to such important all-State committees as that to recommend a uniform electoral law, or that to update party policy for the 1903 elections.[185] Tudor was his leader's sidekick at the second Commonwealth Labor Conference in Sydney in December 1902. And he was appointed to be the standing party delegate to the Political Labor Council, where he invariably represented Watson's opinions.[186]

In the House of Representatives he made a similar impression as a man to be relied on. He followed the party line faithfully on matters like the minimum wage and conciliation and arbitration, and he saw the need for bonuses in order to establish the iron industry in Australia.[187] He went to any amount of trouble to get his facts and statistics right, and when he was well prepared his explanations could be clear and precise. He was effective in the long tariff debates in which he invariably supported the highest proposals. He had his best moments when the matter under consideration was hats. He passionately employed such arguments as that the import of them into Australia had almost tripled since 1895 as the consequence of lower duties which therefore had to be raised, and later he dissolved into paroxysms of indignation over the well-publicised case of six immigrant hatters whom he thought to be superfluous.[188]

Despite such obvious enthusiasm, he was not a 'good or deep' speaker when he was making purely political speeches.[189] He had no compelling qualities in his voice, and his delivery was dull. He was often repetitive and monotonous with lists and details which bored his audiences. He tried to bring colour into his orations by using the same sort of biting metaphor which Deakin or Hughes could employ so well. But his efforts tended to be limp or absurd, as when he supported the Immigration Restriction Bill. He told an inattentive House that in his election campaign he had gone,

> further than most honourable members, when I stated that I was prepared to stop the influx of coloured aliens immediately. I preferred to cut off the tail of the dog at once, instead of taking off a joint at a time – as much for the sake of the dog as for the sake of the person performing the

operation.[190] Additionally, he could not react sensitively to the mood of his audiences either in Parliament or on the platform. He sometimes became heated or even sarcastic, but as he had no gift of repartee it was easy to side-track him with interjections, and his arguments often became confused.[191] This led him on many important occasions to be 'very ineffective'.[192] In consequence he had at best the qualities of a backup, for he could never set a vigorous or inspiring oratorical lead himself.

Tudor, therefore, was on all sides seen to be a splendid colleague and an excellent party hack, but not to be full leadership material. This was shown four months after the second general election of 16th December, 1903. The voters of Richmond had recognised Tudor's splendid constituency work, and started the tradition of making Yarra into one of the safest Labor seats in Australia. The overall results were even more pleasing for the party, because it was returned with twenty-five MHRs and fourteen senators. At first they continued to support the minority Protectionist Government, but this fell in April when Deakin refused to consider Labor demands for a wide Conciliation and Arbitration Act. Watson was commissioned to form a Labor administration. He and his closest associates chose the other ministers.[193] Balanced State representation was an important matter for them. Their Victorian choice was not Tudor, but the radical Protectionist, H. B. Higgins, who became attorney-general with the agreement of his leader, Deakin. A main reason was that Higgins was a very experienced lawyer, and Hughes – only recently qualified – did not yet want the portfolio. But Watson did not consider Tudor for a minor post. He showed no signs of being upset. He went on with his usual party functions and soon became promoted. Stewart gave up all pretence of doing any secretarial work and on 27th June, 1905, caucus gave Tudor his job.[194]

He continued to use his increased influence on behalf of Watson's interests. In July 1905 Charlie Frazer and others initiated a strong movement against Labor giving backing to a new minority Deakin Government, and Watson tried to resign the irksome leadership. Tudor was one of those who persuaded him to remain. Thereafter he went on giving his fullest encouragement to Watson's and to Labor's support for Deakin, mainly because he saw New Protection as a splendid way to integrate worker interests with a higher tariff and the general welfare of the country. When Fisher replaced Watson as party leader on 30th October, 1907, Tudor transferred his loyalties. He saw in Fisher a kindred spirit, friendly, honest, reliable, and devoted to the Labor movement in the same way as he was. The trust was returned, because when Fisher was on other business he relied on Tudor to chair caucus meetings in the manner he wanted.[195]

This undeviating co-operation worked to Tudor's personal advantage. On 5th November, 1908, a caucus majority decided to withdraw party support from Deakin. After the government fell, Fisher was invited to form the next administration. In contrast to 1904, there was no thought of including a man like Higgins from another party. Caucus had to select the eight ministers from twenty-one of its own ambitious aspirants. It was important to have at least one Victorian, and Tudor was widely seen to have by far the best record of the six from his State. Fisher made him minister for trade and customs, in the correct assumption that a man with an unimpeachable high tariff record would show nervous industrialists that they would be safely protected under the new Labor Government.

The position fitted Tudor admirably. He had been very active in supporting the first tariff schedule of Kingston in 1901-1902 and then the higher one of Lyne in 1907-1908, but of course in neither case had he borne any responsibility for them. That heavy burden was now in the past, together with the need to control the tedious and intricate debates and endure the constant pressure of group interests and lobbyists. Tudor's task was to administer the accomplishments of other men, wearisome indeed, but requiring neither a heavy hand, nor great initiative, nor the fighting qualities he knew he did not have. He listened attentively to his permanent officials and was prudent in acting on their advice. He treated his ministry more or less like a chain of hat shops, where the head office gave the branches directives and attended to complaints. In the geographical conditions of Australia the method was effective. He won a reputation of being a conscientious administrator who was not likely to start anything in the nature of risky socialistic experimentation.

His first experience of office was a short one. During the parliamentary recess of 1909 Labor's opponents united in what was called the Fusion, and Fisher's ministry was discarded into opposition on 27th May. The tactics of the defeated Labor Party consisted of organised obstruction. This was not the best environment for Tudor's meagre debating skills, but he fought along with the others, notably making the longest, most tedious and most irrelevant speech of his life on a no-confidence motion.[196] He retained his stature in the party, and benefited accordingly. Labor won the general elections of 13th April, 1910, with a convincing majority, sweeping back into power on a great wave of public confidence that the party would start to build a finer country. Caucus elected Fisher's ministry on 29th April. Tudor showed how he had retained his prestige as the leading Victorian by being chosen on the first ballot.[197] Fisher without hesitation appointed him again to trade and customs.

As in his previous cabinet experience, Tudor was a good and undemanding colleague. He was content for Fisher and Hughes to work out the direction of government policy and parliamentary tactics. He never caused problems of any kind for them, even if he sometimes needed help in making even the smallest decisions, as in trivial matters like the wording of a job advertisement for a lighthouse director.[198] He concentrated fully on his ministry, and he always liked the personal touch in his relationships. For example, he wrote to the Australian piano-maker, Hugo Wertheim on the excellence of his product, congratulating his firm 'on turning out such a magnificent instrument'.[199] Of far more general importance, his legislative record was beneficial and sound. Much of it concerned useful amendments to existing acts. Some were new, and he was ready to extend the bonus system of giving government help to develop fledgling industries. Two reform measures in particular were of great value to the Commonwealth. The Lighthouses Act 1911 improved coastal safety. The comprehensive Navigation Act 1912 introduced a sensible plan in the interests of both ship owners and seamen. Tudor showed much competence in piloting the bills through Parliament. He prepared himself thoroughly for his speeches, and was clear and informative in their presentation. He was particularly happy with the sections of the Navigation Bill 'to improve the lot of the seaman, and to secure fair treatment for him' in stopping such abuses as crimping and shanghai-ing.[200]

The consequence for Tudor was widespread recognition for his diligent and careful work. Even the Liberal opposition 'admitted a promise of administration which ... was scarcely to be looked for from a felt-hatter'.[201] This opinion was shared by a governor-general, who wrote that 'on the whole he has given ... considerable satisfaction to both sides of the House', and, even better, that 'his common sense and scrupulous fairness won golden opinions from the merchants who did business with him'.[202] Tudor was naturally delighted at the general approval. His personal fulfilment was in the feeling of being a useful member of a dynamic reforming government which was doing everything it could both in the interests of the nation and of his constituents.

This excellent record of Fisher's Government was not a recipe for continued success. In the elections of 31st May, 1913, the Liberals under Joseph Cook scraped into office with a majority of one in the House of Representatives, although they had only seven seats to Labor's twenty-nine in the Senate. The political situation resolved itself into an undignified brawl. The Liberals demanded a double dissolution so that Parliament could start again with a clean sheet, and Labor reacted that a dissolution only of the House would suffice as showing the opinion of the electorate. The political tumult which ensued was elevating for neither party, and Tudor contributed by holding his fair share of long and boring speeches. The position was resolved at the start of June 1914 when the Governor-General granted Cook his double dissolution. The following election campaign began as a purely party struggle, but it came to an end with the events of late July. Both party leaders unhesitatingly committed Australia to the Empire effort. Andrew Fisher for Labor promised support for the war 'to the last man and to the last shilling'.

This was the promise which received the greatest resonance in the country. On 5th September, Labor won forty-two seats to thirty-two, and could count on the support of the independent. In the Senate there were thirty-one party members to five Liberals. Caucus met on 17th September to elect Fisher's ministers. Tudor had lost some political weight as the result of the new experience of having a Victorian colleague of first-class abilities. J. A. Arthur was a lawyer who had been elected in 1913, and who had quickly made an excellent impression. But Tudor still had just support enough, and he tied for last place.[203] Fisher for a third time put him at trade and customs.

And in this congenial atmosphere he was very glad to be. He was an imperial patriot like all his cabinet colleagues, but he had no desire to do anything other than share collective responsibility for the politics of war. He did not query what Fisher, Hughes and the Minister of Defence Pearce decided, since he had no alternative ideas to offer as to how to control the price rises, unemployment and consequent labour unrest which were besetting the whole country. He devoted all his energies to reorganising his ministry to cope with the new conditions and to adjust the administration to the falling revenues. He only left his burrow when he was required to support recruiting drives, or when his presence was needed at conferences which concerned his department.

Nevertheless, his close relationship to his working-class constituents was beginning to make him uneasy with some of the policies of the government of which he was a part. At the end of 1915 he was having private doubts about Hughes's performance as Labor leader, for he had abandoned the referenda concerning the transfer of many powers to the Commonwealth to control wages and prices. The increasing tensions in the Labor movement were indeed creating a situation, 'already far advanced, of a party which was disintegrating because of the irreconcilable attitudes prevailing among its members towards the war.'[204] But although he was giving 'long and careful consideration' as to what he should do,[205] Tudor made not the smallest sign in public of his doubts, and he remained a fully loyal member of the cabinet. He had no wish to cause any problems, and even less ambition to make any kind of challenge for a more important position in the party. The idea that he would become its leader one day simply did not exist.

Part Two

Chapter III

'I candidly admit that I cannot bring myself to send men out of Australia to fight.'[206]

During the first months of the war the Labor Government efficiently equipped and trained large numbers of volunteer soldiers. Tudor was an advocate of the policy. The first serious demands for the conscription of young men came after the losses at Gallipoli at the end of April 1915. The loudest cries were from the Liberals, but a few Labor politicians also supported the call. Tudor was at first influenced by them. He made a speech in Richmond in favour of universal service, but he soon began to have doubts. He was the only MHR in the ministry who lived in his constituency all year round. As he had never stopped being in closest contact with his voters, he was subjected to a continuous and growing barrage of working-class opinion. As always, he had an open ear for what he was hearing. He soon gave his full attention to those whose sons might be forced to go to war and then be killed. He also agreed with them about the moral turpitude of the Liberals, who were unwilling to countenance the conscription of wealth in any form.[207]

Elsewhere the demand for the conscription of men grew in intensity, and reached an organisational high point in September 1915 with the formation of the Universal Service League. A month later Hughes became Labor Party leader and prime minister by a unanimous vote of caucus after Fisher's retirement. He was away from Australia from January to July 1916 on a visit to England, where he received a great number of ovations and honours. He accepted that the conscription of soldiers was the only way for Australia to honour its war commitments to the Empire. In this he set himself alongside the entire Liberal Party. It is unusual in parliamentary politics for a prime minister to adopt the official policy of his rivals, which it had been since Cook had held a long-awaited speech in the House of Representatives on 10th May, 1916, but this is what Hughes did. The Liberals wanted conscription to be introduced directly, although Cook had said that, 'I, for one, would welcome a referendum' because he was sure it would be successful.[208] Hughes followed this line. His popularity in England seemed to have gone to his head, for he convinced himself that he could carry his own party with him and make them acquiesce in what the rich and the comfortable told them was their duty.[209] There was much evidence that very many Labor people would never agree with the policy, but he discounted their negative reaction as if his own incandescent leadership would be strong enough to keep his party together under all circumstances.[210]

Hughes thus decided to hold the referendum in the belief that a positive result would bring almost his entire party to a grumbling but peaceful submission to his will. Tudor was one of those whom he placed in a great dilemma. The organisations in the Yarra electorate were increasingly coming out against conscription, the Labor one as a matter of course, then the local branch of the Australian Natives' Association in May, followed by the Richmond Council early in August.[211] Tudor was in full sympathy with them, and had made up his mind by the middle of August not to follow Hughes if he continued with his policy.[212] He delayed making a statement as long as he could, hoping that a majority in cabinet, including himself, could somehow compel or persuade Hughes to back down. He was to be disappointed. In a series of angry party meetings at the end of the month Hughes first won cabinet support and then a caucus majority of twenty-three to twenty-one to hold the referendum.[213] The necessary bill was quickly prepared, and it was to be introduced into Parliament on 13th September.

This meant that Tudor was no longer able to avoid making his position public that he was on the side of his local organisations and of the great majority of his constituents, over seventy-two per cent of whom were to vote 'No'. He was consequential in what he did, for he not only declared himself to be against conscription, but he also resigned from the cabinet which was supporting it. He made his official announcement recalling the time when he and Hughes had worked on the Lighthouses Bill together. For now, Hughes 'has stated that he has "seen the light" and that he intends to follow it. Apparently he and I are looking at different lighthouses. I have not seen the light in the lighthouse he has seen'.[214] Tudor had no feeling of being disloyal to his colleagues, since he knew that it was Hughes who was distancing himself from the Labor movement.

Tudor was the only member of the government to

stand early and consequentially to his principles. It made him automatically one of the most prominent federal politicians who were against the referendum. He made no attempt to exploit the situation, partly because he remained an Imperial patriot and never ceased to advocate voluntary recruiting. More importantly, as a former member of the government he had no desire to cause it additional trouble, so he took no leading part in the 'no' campaign. He was at none of the important anti-meetings in Melbourne or elsewhere. He was indeed appointed to be the Victorian anti-conscriptionist to act with the federal executive, but his most notable public performance was to make a list of his party colleagues who had similar opinions to himself, as an answer to their rivals who had only half as many in the party.[215]

Hughes was not similarly reticent. He scythed into the campaign for which he was responsible with fiery and ferocious arguments, some of which now appear absurd, such as that Germany intended to 'prussianise' Australia.[216] His mainly Liberal audiences gave him tumultuous receptions, but he had erred grievously in his assessment of the general situation. He was swiftly expelled from the New South Wales Labor Party, then by the two trade unions he had led, followed by his own electoral council.[217] His opponents throughout Australia used their chance to roar out their opinions as loudly and as often as they could. Hughes reacted to it all with storms of abuse and undemocratic power tricks which lost him much of what was left of his working-class following. He lost still more because the Liberals enthusiastically copied his demagogic tactics. When the referendum was rejected narrowly on 28th October he had but little Labor prestige left. Only a few of his own party members still believed in him. Many of the rest craved to expel him from the federal party and from all his remaining offices.

Caucus met on 14th November with the militants in purposeful anticipation of doing exactly this. Hughes took the initiative away from his enemies. Before they could vote to throw him out, he abandoned the meeting to do whatever it might wish. Thus, instead of the planned lonely exit in disgrace, he was able to take with him two dozen followers. They left behind them twenty senators, a majority in their chamber, and twenty-four angry and astonished MHRs, some of whom were reduced to tears by the shock.[218] They were all faced with the business not only of indulging themselves in righteous self-justification, but also of reconstructing their devastated party. After a night of unhappy indignation, they met again to elect the new party leader.

There were two serious candidates for the position, Tudor, and the Speaker, Charles McDonald. Tudor had not sought the job and he had made no attempt to win any support. His name was put forward because he had resigned early from Hughes' ministry in what were seen to be virtuous circumstances, as opposed to others who had clung to office until the last moment. He was, in character, the opposite of Hughes, whom he now regarded as being a discredited dictator. His record of party service was long and honourable, and he had done well as Cabinet Minister. His friendly manner was redolent of that of Fisher, whose leadership of integration had brought the party so many successes before the war. This characteristic of 'he having no spite in him' was decisive in giving him a very narrow victory over McDonald.[219] The sociable master hatter thus became leader of his political party which had been preparing to destroy itself for months and which, after having successfully done so, was in a state of extreme despair.

And the psychological consequences of the Hughes disaster were grave indeed, both deep and lasting. From the early 1890s the party had grown in electoral strength and political achievement. There had been few serious setbacks, and the Labor Party members had developed a kind of collective vision of a new and better Australia which they were being privileged to initiate. And now such leaders as Hughes and Pearce, Thomas and Spence, who had all helped in the struggle for two decades and more, men who had required and received party trust and support, men who had seemed to bear worthily the responsibility and cares of progressive government, these men had adopted the policy of their despised political rivals, and in their apparently malignant attempt to effect it, had risked and then forced the split. What value could now be put on their past services for democratic rights? What trust could ever be placed in political leadership again, now that the idealism of Hughes and his gang was seen to be a sham, their promises dust, their loyalty a betrayal? Stupefied were they all, those who were left, by what had been done to them by those whom they now saw to be the perfidious Prime Minister and his morally despicable followers.

In this dismal situation Tudor accepted the leadership. He did not do so from personal ambition, and he realised that he would have a very problematical time. He unburdened himself to Fisher, writing candidly about the difficulties he would have to try to overcome.[220] Yet he did think that he had a number of qualities which would help in restoring his party to health. His life experience and his character caused the notion to well up from his subconscious that just as he could aid his individual constituents, so could he save his party in distress. He thought that by being sympathetic to everyone he could be an antidote to Hughes, relieve the general tension and bring about again the common purpose he remembered so well from the pre-war years. With his kind personality he was always prepared to see the goodness in others, and he persuaded himself that by presiding over the meetings of caucus and by speaking on its behalf in Parliament, he would be able to set a positive and inspiring example to his colleagues.

In addition, he felt that he was the right man to re-establish the relationship that had existed before the war between the Labor voters and their legislators. For him, the parliamentarians and their leader could indeed propose matters of policy, but the power of decision as to their acceptance lay elsewhere. He trusted in the wisdom and righteousness of the workers' movement, and believed that if he were open to its wishes as expressed in party conference resolutions he could continue the Labor rhythm of electoral success. He also saw himself as the agent of caucus decisions and not as their initiator. This concept of leadership was the opposite of that of Hughes's in 1916, and he approached the party ideal of the representative who uncritically and faithfully carried out the wishes of those who had elected him. Tudor hoped that by working diligently he would lead like a kindly light away from the gloom caused by Hughes into the democratic future of his wishes.

Despite such convenient self-suggestion, and despite the fact that his colleagues had no real alternative, their choice of Tudor as leader was of doubtful value. His entire political life had been one of worthy service, but the initiatives and direction had always come from other men whom he had been content to follow. Now he had taken on the responsibility of starting the return of his party to stability from the psychological shambles in which Hughes had left it, and of remaking it as a redoubtable political fighting force. Pleasant-natured he was, a figure of reliability and of honest purpose. But now he took over the leading position in an atmosphere of ferocious and bitter party politics, at a time of a ruthless fight for power, all against the backdrop of a terrible and devastating war.

From the first he had no appropriate concept of what he had to do. His opinion of himself had slight relevance to Labor's real and immediate needs, which were those of a political party requiring hard decisions on how to deal with a crisis. Loyal he was to group interests, obedient to the outside authority of party conferences, courteous to men of different opinions, and considerate in finding the way of compromise. But while he was always ready to listen, he was seldom prepared to lead. He reacted to situations rather than trying to create them. The men who chose him wanted the soothing reassurance that he would never jerk their party into another self-willed catastrophe. But this guaranteed also that he could not inaugurate a new course of action, regardless of how necessary it might be.

The opposite was the case with Hughes, whose hold on office was more than precarious, but who acted at once with determined resolution. Almost everyone of political importance helped him to stay in power. The Governor-General admired him, and commissioned him to form a new ministry from his handful of followers, thus giving him temporary security while the politicians of all three parties worked out their own destinies. The Liberal leader, Cook, was indecisive, calling plaintively to Hughes to take the first step.[221] The Liberals reacted to his irresolution by failing to agree to any course of action. Some of them wanted a new election, anticipating a Liberal victory over a split Labor vote. A majority, including Cook, thought that a split conscriptionist vote would bring Labor back to power, so the last thing they wanted was a new election. This incapacity to unite on what to do about the situation thereby countenanced its prolongation.

The Labor Party under Tudor made no intelligent attempt to profit from the confusion. Its members were so certain of their own righteousness that they rejected any kind of political understanding with their rivals. Yet they accepted the new minority Hughes Government unconditionally, to the extent that they at once started sending delegations to Minister of Defence Pearce to resolve injustices caused by Hughes during the referendum campaign.[222] At the same time they hoisted the traditional banner of Labor Party purity and independence from everybody else. They fired at all their opponents a constant barrage of verbal small-shot and derision, although such a strategy was neither helpful nor constructive. Their main idea was to hold new elections as soon as possible in the conviction that they would win. But as this result was also anticipated by Hughes and his entire party together with Cook and a majority of the Liberals, the repetitive Labor demands to go to the country had the effect of the beating of spoons on a toy drum.

Even more counter-productive were their tactics in Parliament, for they did the exact opposite of stirring up the violently disagreeing Liberals into a state of complete chaos. All they could think of was to introduce a no-confidence motion against Hughes into the House on 29th November. Tudor indeed made an indignant opening speech, but he miscalculated the mood of his traditional opponents.[223] The Liberals were united only in their determination to do anything rather than have Labor return to power. None of them supported Tudor's motion, since if it had been successful the Governor-General might well have commissioned him to form a new ministry. The only result of Tudor's initiative was to isolate Labor completely from the other parties, and to give Hughes more time to strengthen his bargaining position with the Liberals.

In any case, the Labor Party was far too preoccupied with itself to make Hughes's life miserable, and its decisions closed off all his options of political survival except that of coming to an understanding with the Liberals. A special interstate Labor conference was held at the beginning of December. Tudor was in attendance, but typically not as an official delegate. There was no discussion of a forward policy, for they had met to expel Hughes and his apostates formally and forever from the party.[224] Tudor afterwards presided over a series of caucus meetings whose agendas were notable only for their trivial content. Nothing more serious could be decided upon than to use the Labor Senate majority to limit supply to two months instead of passing it for the usual three. The intention was to give Hughes the opportunity to secure a double dissolution,[225] although he had no more intention of doing so than Labor had of welcoming him back. He indeed hoped with most of the Liberals to extend Parliament and so avoid an election altogether. All Tudor did was to surrender the initiative to the man who was supremely capable of using it.

And Hughes indeed exploited with purposeful skill the time which had been given him after Parliament jolted its way into the Christmas recess. He set about organising his own party – from the top, since matters were far too urgent to bother about grassroots support.[226] About two hundred rich and influential men met in Melbourne on 9th January, 1917, to bestow upon him their praise and offers of help. Strengthened in this way, he became ceaselessly active in trying to form a national government with himself as its leader. Tudor and his party were hopelessly outclassed in the wheeling-dealing. They not only failed to hinder or annoy Hughes in any way, they actively assisted all his bargainings with the Liberals, of course without the slightest intention of doing so.

As an example, early in January Hughes' efforts to form his own organisation began to offend many Liberals. They feared that their sudden rival might cut into their own following. Tudor did nothing to stir up the situation. He said only that Labor would 'make no move until the caucus had discussed the position, and that there would be no party meeting until the eve of the reassembly of Parliament'.[227] Even more significant was the Labor answer to the Liberal proposal of 19th January that a national government should be formed from members of all three parties. Tudor and his colleagues might have caused difficulties by playing around with the suggestion. They only taunted Hughes and Cook that they would never consider anything so grotesque, but that their official decision would have to await the rubber stamp of caucus.[228] This ideologically correct but utterly impolitic reaction was fully in line with past Labor Conference decisions, but it only brought upon the party a general odium for the automatic refusal to sink personal differences in favour of patriotic purpose. The Governor-General wrote that Tudor was 'always digging up old speeches and old issues' instead of doing something positive and constructive.[229] Even more disadvantageous, Hughes knew exactly what to expect from the tramline attitude of Labor, so he was given two full weeks to work out the conditions with Cook for a coalition of their two parties.

He made the best use of the time, and understandably ignored Labor altogether. He concentrated his powers on Cook and outmanoeuvred him on every important matter. So when caucus on 7th February made the, by now, empty rejection of the proposal for an all-party government, Hughes had the Liberals where he wanted them, and controlled completely the final bargaining rounds. In this way, when the Governor-General commissioned the coalition ministry on 17th February, Tudor and Labor had put up a wretched showing. They had been neither flexible nor clever, but had held fast to old habits and patterns of thinking. They had been neither successfully obstructionist nor positive in action. They had only done everything possible to further the interests of all their opponents. It was almost as if Tudor had subconsciously continued his lifelong habit of doing what the man in authority expected of him.

Even so, the Labor Party was not yet in a hopeless position. The new ministry was so obviously opportunistic that its members feared the voters, and the crushing defeat of the equally opportunistic Fusion Ministry in April 1910 was constantly in their minds. The obvious solution was to put off elections until people had forgotten or become malleable. Labor could prevent this by means of its small majority in the Senate. Hughes tried to manipulate the situation by the subversion of some Tasmanian and other senators, but failed when two Liberals refused to go along with his double-dealings which appeared to include bribery. The charges of corruption enlivened the political scene in Parliament and in all six States. It was seen that only a general election could resolve the crisis, so one of the first acts of the new coalition ministry was to get the Governor-General to dissolve the Parliament whose proposed extension had been one of the main factors in bringing them all together.

The Labor members received this news with rejoicing, because it represented the fulfilment of their own policy which they had been unable to bring about themselves. Tudor was confident that he and his party had a number of very considerable electoral advantages. But the combined anti-Labor forces were in no way without resources. Hughes, with poisonous attacks against his former party, and Cook, with feverishly exaggerated propaganda, led their drive for the electoral confirmation of the patriotic motives of the coalition. They sought to remove one obvious weakness by promising not to introduce conscription unless the war situation required it and a second referendum were to approve it. Most of the press gave them rabid support, using highly emotional anti-socialist and anti-I.W.W. polemics to try to destroy voter faith in the Labor Party which less than three years before had been given overwhelming support to lead Australia's war effort. And also on the side of the coalition, although they could not be aware of it, was the general Australian refusal to give a majority to the party which was believed to have a less active policy on defence – only on a single occasion, in 1929, has this not been done.

Against all this, and to make full use of his advantages, Tudor would have had to be a different man with a different policy. He would have had to be more crafty than Hughes, more ferocious than Cook, and also able to show the press that Labor would really wave the flag of Empire to the last man. He was personally in the wrong weight-class and politically in the wrong league. He did his best in his policy speech on 29th March which followed faithfully his party's manifesto. But he was not convincing in his assertions that his party would use voluntary recruitment to conduct the war 'with vigour and determination', and so be a viable alternative to Hughes.[230] His pride that his first son, Gwynne, had recently volunteered on his eighteenth birthday was not enough to convince many voters that the whole of the Labor Party would follow his example. The press found Tudor to be 'feeble', and in addition held Labor accountable for the fact that the I.W.W. and other left-wing organisations were against the war. The electorate reacted accordingly. Tudor's party won only twenty-two seats out of seventy-five in the House of Representatives and none at all in the Senate.

In triumph, the victors reconstituted themselves on 13th June to form the united Australian National Party. It was a second and even more devastating hammer blow for the Labor men after November 1916. They did not see Hughes as a masterly politician who had 'coped successfully with difficulties that must have overwhelmed a less indomitable spirit', nor as 'that small figure ... [who] evoked my admiration',[231] but only as a heretic of no loyalties whose hunger for acclaim and power had destroyed his judgement, character and moral sense. And now this traitor, whom they saw to be so much in the wrong, had been seen by the great majority of the country to be in the right.

Chapter IV

'I sometimes long for the old times when we were fighting together.'[232]

The calamity of the 1917 elections finished Labor off as an effective political force and demolished Tudor's prestige as leader. He feared that 'the movement will be put back at least ten years', and he was full of nostalgia for how it had been before the war.[233] He still felt very close to 'the old brigade' who had stayed within the party. But he was too hurt by the bitter opposition of those who had left with Hughes to make any constructive plans to start improving the situation.[234] Moreover, the sad few who had been elected were dominated by left-wingers to whom he had no real contact. In any case, as a small minority they were all helpless to do anything worthwhile in Parliament and undecided in any case about what to do. The party outside was ridden with faction and highly distrustful of politicians as men to whom honour was an unknown concept. Labor conferences were full of the idea that strict conformity would early have put Hughes under party control, and their delegates set themselves to restrict the freedom of their own representatives. In the years after the split, any independent political action was punished by the expulsion of its perpetrator. Thus Labor lost all the vision and breadth which had made it so successful before the war, and developed into a pale imitation of what the Bolsheviks were doing in Russia.

The party needed either a narrow doctrinaire leader to work with this feeling outside Parliament, or one who could creatively start to rebuild Labor along the pre-war model. Tudor fulfilled neither role. He disliked the witch-hunts but could do nothing to prevent them. His passive attitude made him acceptable to those of inquisitorial mentality, since they could do what they wanted without any obstruction from him. Yet he never satisfied them, or those who worked for the party to regain a wide electoral appeal. He had neither the personality nor the initiative to start the reconstruction of the old party form, whose successes had been based on the need to pass a number of long-standing reform proposals into law.[235] Tudor had no inspiration as to what a new policy should contain. He was so depressed by the result of the elections that he made no positive attempt to develop one out of the many proposals worked out by some of his colleagues. He only waited until a party conference should tell him what to do. Additionally, neither he nor any of his party friends had a real idea of what attitude to take towards parliamentary bills directed against extreme left-wing groups, and their feeble compromises damaged their image even further.

All this meant that Tudor in effect did little more than go through the motions of leadership. He chaired the caucus meetings and made a large number of speeches in Parliament. These were often long, sometimes informative, and they invariably expressed the party line, but they were never inspiring. Tudor's successes were confined to small strategic victories in the House, which may have embarrassed Hughes for an hour or two, but which had no more lasting consequences than the landing of a paper dart.[236] And even the one great Labor triumph of the Parliament, the rejection of the second conscription referendum on 20th December, 1917, owed little to him. He inaugurated the 'no' campaign in a speech on 13th November.[237] But although he was, as always, well prepared, he failed to grip his audience. He was full of details where something more polemical was required. Thus he went on being little more than a mediocre figurehead, and the organisation, power and drive for the 'no' cause came from elsewhere.

An example of his inability to take the offensive occurred after this second referendum had been defeated. Hughes had promised that in such circumstances his ministry would make no attempt to carry on the business of government. Faced with the unwanted need to keep faith with the electors, there was much confusion within his party on the proper course of action. Finally on 8th January, 1918, Hughes resigned, but gave the Governor-General no advice as to what to do next. Munro Ferguson consulted all the leading politicians and Tudor was among those whom he interviewed.[238] He was certainly in no good position with his small numbers, but he was unable to exploit the situation since he had only waited upon events. He did no more than tell the Governor-General that a minority Labor administration would have as much chance as Hughes fourteen months earlier. He left it to his colleague W. G. Higgs to say that Hughes had to honour his promise. The Governor-General was not impressed by Tudor's uninspiring performance, and disliked his party in any case.[239] He was not prepared to commission a Labor ministry which would at once have to ask for a dissolution. He therefore took no serious notice of Tudor's advice, and invited Hughes to form a new government, which he did using exactly the same men who had resigned with him two days before.

It was no secret that Tudor lacked genuine leadership qualities, although the Labor press was not zealous in revealing his demerits. Others were less discreet. Hughes commented aptly that Archbishop Mannix was his real opponent in the second referendum, and by March 1918 it was being stated in the less friendly papers that 'Mr Tudor has many excellent qualities and his services are highly valued by his colleagues, but he is not sufficiently picturesque to grip the imagination of the general public'.[240]

Tudor was not a vain man. He was the last person to cling to the leadership against the wishes of the Labor movement. But after the dreadful experiences of 1916 he was obsessed by the need for preserving party unity. The example of Hughes had made him apprehensive of men with too obvious ambition. He would only resign when a deputy had shown himself to be a person of integrity and ability, and when he was certain that the change had the support of the overwhelming majority of his colleagues. Until this happened, he felt that it was his duty to stay where he was, a figure of integration even if of average abilities who would act in accordance with the general Labor will, and make no attempt to shape its direction himself. And the fact that he had no characteristics like Hughes was reason enough for his colleagues to make no attempt at undermining his position.

The problem was to find a suitable successor. Within caucus, only Matthew Charlton had the necessary ambition, but he had not yet proved himself. Tudor favoured him as 'one of the very best',[241] but his leadership weight was too small to influence people to his opinion. Besides, Charlton came from a New South Wales electorate, the Victorians stood by their own man, and there were other State jealousies in the party. The more obvious candidate was the highly successful Premier of Queensland, Thomas Ryan, but there was caucus opposition against inviting him to enter federal politics and then seeing him jump into the first place.[242] So although the demand for him was increasing, the matter could be postponed since it was a long time to the next elections. Tudor accepted the situation, and made no serious attempt to lead his colleagues into finding an early solution.

Outside Parliament he was similarly without drive, and he was regularly upstaged. The Governor-General called a conference on recruitment in April 1918.[243] Tudor stated the Labor position that the idea of conscription had to be abandoned, that the rich had to be taxed, and that the War Precautions Act must not be misused. But W. A. Holman ran rings round him in the discussions, and Tudor had to rely on Ryan to answer him effectively.[244] Then he was invited to attend the seventh Interstate Labor Conference in Perth in June. He tried to defend the rights of Labor Parliamentarians, but he had little influence in the ballots in which he was not allowed to vote.[245] By May 1919 he had no longer any genuine recognition. One of his own colleagues of the past called him patronisingly 'a good little fellow' and hoped that

Andrew Fisher would be asked to resume the leadership which he had given up in great despair in October 1915.[246] This was clearly a negative solution since Fisher's time was over, and it only showed how any replacement for Tudor was being thought acceptable. Yet caucus would still take no firm action as to what should be done.

This enduring procrastination ensured that a decision was finally made elsewhere. The situation became critical after Hughes returned in August 1919 from the Versailles Peace Conference to vast public rejoicings at his having achieved a great diplomatic success for Australia. A general election was called for December so that the Nationalists could profit from his popularity. Leading Labor men outside Parliament understood that Tudor alone would never inspire a majority vote against him. A party conference was hurriedly called for 2nd October.[247] The general feeling was in favour of asking Ryan to enter federal politics. Bailey of New South Wales said that 'his leadership would have a great effect on the Labor movement', and the South Australian Butterfield that 'he stood head and shoulders above everybody else'. By nineteen votes to ten the invitation was made official.

Tudor's reaction showed his apprehension that so bold a plan might have adverse consequences for party unity. He reassured Labor that he would go on being party leader during the election campaign, by means of a public denial that he had ever promised to stand down for Ryan.[248] Privately, he was perfectly willing to do so as soon as the new man had shown his worth and had a united caucus behind him. Ryan had far more confidence in himself. He believed that he would become prime minister in the event of an electoral victory.[249] Therefore, as soon as a safe seat had been found for him at West Sydney, he accepted what he saw to be a summons to action.

It was symptomatic of Tudor's loss of prestige that he had neither been in the Victorian delegation at this conference, nor did he attend as a visitor. The Governor-General correctly saw him as being no more than 'nominally leader' of his party, while Ryan was the 'actual champion'[250]. Ryan was also appointed campaign director over his head, and he was the inspiration behind the election manifesto, which Tudor did little more than approve and sign.[251] Ryan tried to set a new direction for his party. He prepared a policy redolent in the scope and number of its proposals to that of before the war. Profiteers were to be dealt with ferociously, ex-soldiers, pensioners, widows, orphans and invalids were to receive generous gratuities or pension increases, all to be paid for from a wealth tax. There was to be a national medical service, workers' compensation, and everything possible was to be done to assist primary producers. On the other hand, Labor remained narrow in some of its views, and opposed Hughes's proposal to transfer by referendum industrial powers to the Commonwealth for three years, on the grounds that this should be permanent. The idea of progress through compromise which had been so successful before the war with Deakin had been forgotten.

Inspiring leadership from Tudor was necessary to bring Labor's programme to the voters, and counter Hughes's popularity. He could not give it. His experiences of the previous three years were not a motivation, and in addition he was still depressed by the death in late June of his younger brother. He had no real hopes of winning the election, he knew he had aged, and it showed in all his public appearances.[252] He had even lost prestige in his own electorate, for he had to beat two rivals for pre-selection. Additionally, he was suffering from a heart condition and its associated illnesses. His policy speech on 4th November followed closely the manifesto, but it was burdened by all the old faults of dullness, so that there was no good reason for the press to transfer its main coverage and support from the excellent entertainment provided by Hughes.[253] In the middle of the campaign Tudor had two haemorrhages and was thereafter incapacitated. Everything was against Ryan's revival, and Labor suffered a second shattering defeat, winning only twenty-six seats in the House of Representatives and but a single one in the Senate.

Even after this second catastrophe under his leadership, caucus could not find its way to separate its destinies from Tudor. He was re-elected leader so that Ryan could gain experience before taking over. In the following months Ryan tried to organise sensible parliamentary tactics, based on the success of the Country Party which had profited from the introduction of preferential voting by winning eleven seats. The Nationalists and a couple of half-hearted allies had a shaky thirty-eight, a very insecure overall majority of one. Ryan's, strategy was to pick constantly on the blunders of the Government in the hope of making common cause with the Country Party and the waverers, and so tip the balance in Parliament and force a new election.

Regrettably neither the Labor Party nor Tudor gave him efficient support. A party conference expelled W. G. Higgs in January 1920 for having spoken on behalf of

Hughes's referendum, and he strengthened the Nationalists by joining them in September.[254] Hugh Mahon exploded against the Empire in November, was voided out of Parliament, and his seat was similarly lost to Labor.[255] Tudor introduced a number of censure motions with weak speeches which lost their way through his inability to ignore or parry interjections.[256] This laid him open to counter-attacks from his opponents. Even more fateful, some of his own party members indulged in self-destructive tactics in the subsequent debates by criticising violently the Country Party whose support they hoped to win.[257] Additionally, Tudor was unable to prevent many of his New South Wales colleagues from jealously supporting Charlton instead of Ryan for deputy leader. This led to unfortunate 'knives-drawn' scenes in caucus when he was away sick as to who should get the job.[258] Even when Ryan won out, he diplomatically declared that he had no ambition to replace Tudor during the Parliament,[259] and this kept the increasingly unhappy leader in the seat which he no longer had any wish to occupy.

Tudor was indeed becoming ever more incapable of doing anything of use or value. His chronic heart condition had for many months been weakening his purpose and his resolution. His increasingly listless performance deteriorated until his final appearance in caucus on 28th April, 1921. Even then his party did not let him honourably retire. He was formally advised to take a holiday of two or three months to recuperate, and he left for Rabaul at the end of May.[260] Two months after his departure, and while he was still visiting Papua and the Mandated Territories, Ryan died suddenly on 1st August.

Part Two

Instead of using the unhappy opportunity to replace Tudor, caucus in September expressed its 'desire that he should continue' in office, together with 'the hope that he will be sufficiently recovered in health to soon take up his political duties'.[261]

There was no chance at all that he would ever be able to do this again. His heart condition was worsening, and he hardly ever went outside. Yet his sense of service stayed with him to the end. He remained as an absent figurehead while Charlton gained the necessary experience of managing his unattractive party. When Tudor died in his home at 263 Stawell Street on 10th January, 1922, there was no obstruction to Charlton taking over officially. Yet he proved himself to be as unsuccessful in leading a Labor revival as Tudor had ever been. The true rebirth did not occur until an entire new generation of Labor politicians won their way to office nearly twenty years later at the start of a second and even more disastrous war.

PART THREE

And Who Awakened When?

The Political Philosophy
of W. G. Spence

For in times when new nations and new principles of government are being formed, men are moved by appeals to the imagination – a fact far too often forgotten in our modern analysis of the history of such periods. Imagination is the force that propels, though statecraft may guide.

> G. M. Trevelyan
> *The Rise of the Roman Republic*
> Chapter Nine

The greatest difference of all between Labor and other parties lies in the fact that Labor has an ideal.

> W. G. Spence
> *Australia's Awakening* 1909
> p.277

Chapter I

Three Score Years and Eight

The tiny island of Eday lies a couple of miles north-east of Kirkwall in the Scottish Orkneys. James Spence was a stonemason, a respected profession in a treeless windswept place where houses could only be made out of the local granite. He married Jane Guthrie, and their son William was born on 7th August, 1846.[262] The excitement at the Victorian gold rush was the motive for the family to leave a place where it is cold most of the time and the sun hardly appears in winter. They arrived in Melbourne early in 1852, and the following year settled near Creswick. William experienced both 'the firing and the digger-hunting' which led up to the events of the Eureka Stockade in 1854 and the cruel injustice of the police and the authorities thereafter.[263] It all made a great impression on him, and helped push him in the direction of the political attitudes he had for the next sixty years.

James Spence had no success at getting rich, and his son accordingly never had any kind of pampered upbringing. His was at first an untrained mind, for he never went to school, even if he did get 'at odd moments' teaching from a graduate of Trinity College, Dublin.[264] Physical work had been the life of his father, and it was the most important thing in his own early life as well. He was a shepherd at thirteen, a butcher's boy two years later, and a miner in between and afterwards.[265] In the alluvial mines at Creswick, he learnt indelibly what unrestricted capitalism could do with unorganised manual labourers.

> We are told that a man will not live where a candle will not burn, but [I have] worked many an eight hours' shift where no candle would burn, and where light was dimly secured by placing two candles one on the other horizontally in the mouth of the air pipe. The two candle flames would unite, and what air came through the pipe kept them supplied with oxygen, but left little for the miner working six feet away.[266]

The consequences were an accident rate of over fifty per cent, ghastly lung diseases and wage exploitation. Spence very soon had a sense of burning injustice against the system. He developed into a remorseless foe of capitalism, a friend of socialism, and ready to fight for anything which might help the workers. He read such writers as Bellamy, Blatchford, Ruskin and Morris 'in a curiously miscellaneous way',[267] and he became infused with the idea that he was a man who could help to bring about the vitally necessary changes to the system he so despised.

This realisation matured suddenly as the result of a riot in Creswick in July 1878 caused by wage reduction.[268] In the excitement of the sudden strike of three hundred men, Spence was spontaneously elected secretary of the upsurge, and made his first stump speech, appropriately on what was left of a cut-down tree. His natural talents welled up, and he organised pickets with such vehemence that within a week he tasted the exhilaration of victory. The miners won everything they were striking for, and under Spence's leadership managed to resist later revenge attempts to get them all sacked. In the flush of success, Spence and his friends got them to join the Amalgamated Miners Association. His activism made him a marked man, and the bosses took the first chance they could to blacklist him.

> This turned out a good thing for me, however, as I have not done any mining work since; and it really gave me greater freedom to become a bigger thorn in the side of capitalism by my being able to devote my whole efforts to organising work and extending Unionism.[269]

And he remained the Creswick branch secretary for sixteen years.

In this position he learnt to improve his extraordinary talents for organising the men in the union and negotiating on their behalf. He wrote the essence of his methods down in detail, and not without vanity, since he described his opinion of himself in the requirement of each union to choose 'the best man and the most intelligent among themselves' to be the secretary.[270] Moreover, the paragon 'needs to have energy, enthusiasm, calmness, good judgement, and tact. He must have a knowledge of men – of human nature'.[271] What stopped this from being conceit was that Spence really

Part Three

did have all these qualities to the full, and he used them to great effect in the cause of trade unionism and winning benefits for its members. He travelled at least fifteen thousand miles a year to make his personal influence as great as possible.[272] For all his activities he received just recognition, and in 1882 he became the general secretary of the A.M.A., and retained the job for a decade.

In his positions of importance, Spence was totally on the side of the underprivileged, identifying himself with them since he had been one from his birth. His strengths were pre-eminently practical. He won respect by never being only a man who kept his hands soft for office work. He was excellent at handling people of all kinds, and he loved the rough and tumble of it all. He was a man among men, and was particularly happy to do the dirty on non-unionists whom he rejoiced in calling scabs. Naturally he did not tell the public about anything he had perpetrated himself, but he recounted with relish such stories as a good way of converting a scab on a frosty morning to more positive ways of thinking.

> He tried moral suasion without avail, and finally he dropped the scab from the bridge into the cold water. The poor fellow came out still loyal to his desire to oblige the employer, so he was again pushed in. He came out the second time still a hardened sinner, and after some further parley was again dipped under the cold water. He repented this time, and came out a convert to Unionism and a monument to the efficacy of cold water in judicious quantities properly applied.[273]

Elsewhere Spence was more honest, although still full of cynical understatement, when he said that scabs became civil 'when threatened with drowning'.[274] His full antagonism came out in another story of 'a very fine young woman' who give some scabs 'such a dose of jalap in their tucker that they were unable to work for a week after. Her name was Martha Davis, and may good fortune attend her. Scabs deserve no better treatment'.[275]

Spence was equally rampant against those who were unfortunate enough to have skins of a different tincture to those of himself and the people he trusted. There were good economic reasons for this racism. The Chinese and the Kanakas were willing to work for dribbles of money which would undercut everything tending to preserve the lifestyle of the whites. The coloured servility therefore seemed to menace the jobs of each and every one of the upright beneficiaries of pinker skins. Spence wrote of many incidents of 'The anti-Chinese movement [which] was one of the early developments of democratic feeling in Australia',[276] and he was fully on the side of hostile and violent mobs to repel the oriental invasion. He took for Labor the credit that if the workers had not made a stand, 'Australia would not have been a white man's country today'.[277] Had the alternative come to pass, the dreadful consequences would have been that the Anti-Socialists would have got used to being in command with the automatic disappearance of every kind of manly virtue and a concomitant perversion of moral values.[278]

Spence, despite his red rage against such creatures as scabs and Asiatics, was, in industrial matters, never a man of small thoughts. He rejected the viewpoint that it was every trade union for itself. He set out in 1882 to unite the miners throughout Australia and New Zealand, and later turned his attention to the shearers. In 1886 he was appointed the first president of their union. He saw well that he was the spear point of a genuine people's movement, 'a conscious awakening among the workers'.[279] He was proud of himself and his fellow activists for increasing union membership with great speed and efficiency, and for the many successes of their negotiations with the bosses. He did not lose prestige after the union defeats in the strikes of the early 1890s, but he grew ever more convinced 'that union principles must be applied politically, and reform and better conditions sought through political machinery'.[280] He became secretary of the Australian Workers' Union in 1894 and its president in 1898. He considered it to be the industrial wing of the Labor Party, and thought as a matter of course that no one was in a better position than himself to represent it in Parliament.

Accordingly, he tried to enter a Legislative Assembly. His first attempt was in Victoria in 1892, but he had to wait until 1898 until he was successful, for Cobar in the northwest of New South Wales. He received much recognition for his past achievements, but in the solemn halls of political intrigue he was unable to add to them. He was hardly more than an addition to a formal party organisation which was already working well. The leaders, McGowen, Watson and Hughes, knew what they wanted, and had become clever at exploiting parliamentary procedures and the Labor Party's numbers to get it. Spence found that his bush methods were out of place, and that he was only a single vote pledged to do what the caucus majority decided. It was possible that in the Commonwealth Parliament, with everything starting anew, he would have more chance to make a name for himself. He was elected in March 1901 as the first member for the Darling electorate which included Cobar. At fifty-four he would still be young enough to make a great impression on his colleagues from the other five States, all of whom admired him for what he had done for unionism.

He failed to make use of the opportunity. His attendance at caucus meetings in the first three years was sporadic, and he was chosen to be on none of the important party committees.[281] He was not a political tactician, so he could be of little help in winning advantages in the House. He had no particular causes which he could get others to identify him with, apart from those like unionism and the need for a White Australia, which all the Labor men shared as articles of faith. He had too much fame to be a water carrier for his more important colleagues, and he was never at home with the formalities and procedures of Parliament. Accordingly, he devoted himself more to the world where he had been successful for years, and where he still had an enormous amount of prestige. He continued with his organising work in the trade union movement, and in negotiating settlements with highly intransigent employers.[282]

This meant that other New South Wales men from outside Sydney became more useful to the movement within Parliament. They used their chances of advancement to sweep past Spence in caucus estimation. David Watkins of Newcastle was to become whip and party secretary. Josiah Thomas of Broken Hill was made postmaster-general in 1908, again in 1910, and minister of external affairs in 1911. Up and coming enthusiasts like J. H. Catts and William Webster were clearly men with a future. With such competition, Spence seemed condemned to stay as a backbencher who was renowned only for his past achievements.

He was not content to remain a man of reputation but no great political success. With increasing age, the once 'bête noire of the squatters and their advocates had become ... a genial, pleasant-spoken, mild-mannered man,'[283] but he still retained his ambition to be a politician of substance. When Watson retired in irritation as party leader in October 1907, Spence made an attempt to become his successor. He hoped that the top candidates, Fisher and Hughes, would cancel each other out so that he as the compromise figure would get the nod. He was disappointed, but he did not give up. His second method to win regard was to write a book on the achievements of Australian trade unionism and the Labor Party, of which he was so proud of being a member. He had the help of his son-in-law, Hector Lamond, the editor of the *Worker*, in its composition, but the form and the ideas were his own. It was published in 1909 as *Australia's Awakening*, in good time for the 1910 elections. He followed up his literary success two years later with *The History of the A. W. U.* also written with the help of Lamond.

These two books are as entertaining as they are subjective, and show Spence's apparently undying commitment to all the ideas of his younger years. Their success was excellent for his reputation in his party. He was not voted into Fisher's ministry, but he was offered the speakership, which he declined. Thereafter he was given important responsibilities in the caucus treasury committee. After Labor's narrow electoral defeat of 31st May, 1913, he was elected to his party's executive on 8th July. He attended almost all its meetings, but as he was sixty-eight in 1914, there was apparently no hope for him to have any further political successes. He seemed to be ending his career and his life as a party man of great stature because of his prestigious past. He was revered as a man who had written down his experiences and his ideals in a form which would ensure his lasting reputation as a fighter for the rights of the workers long after he had passed from the scene.

Part Three

Chapter II

Exploiters, Angels and 'Scum'[284]

Spence wrote his book *Australia's Awakening* to show how the main cause of the social evils in Australia was the unpleasant characteristic of capitalists never to be satisfied with having almost everything. In their insatiable grasping after riches and power, they lacked even the most elementary form of normal and natural ethics. They were responsible for making a society which confirmed the sombre writings of Malthus, in that,

> the weakest are crushed out; the strong, the heartless, the least scrupulous, survive ... The few required to attend to the machines are but a part of the machinery of the factory, and are counted, not as human beings, but as 'hands'.[285]

Each of those who were on top, later calling himself an anti-socialist, was 'a born tyrant', and these men,

> care not for the masses, except insofar as they are useful to maintain the rich in unearned luxury. Economically ignorant, they cannot conceive it possible that the present social system can be improved.[286]

That it could was his life's work as he saw it in 1909.

His further descriptions of his soulless opponents show his contempt for their abysmal characters. These 'wily schemers' used every kind of oppression to keep the great mass of humanity not only in economic bondage, but also 'in mental slavery and ignorance'.[287] The dreadful suffering of their fellow-creatures was a matter of total indifference to them. The foul reality was of 'Millionaires' wives spending fortunes on dog and pig parties, freak dinners, and the like, whilst those who provide the wealth are in dire want within a few yards of them'.[288] Thereby they were incredibly idle and in their worship of money had not the slightest understanding that good moral character could be of any value at all.

Such generalities show well the cast of Spence's mind, but he made them as a result of long experience. In his career as union activist, he had needed to contend with all the scurrilous manoeuvrings of his opponents who had wealth, influence and power on their side. He knew the squatters who felt sick at the thought of unionism, of those who paid nothing for a pen of shorn sheep because only a single one of them was not clipped cleanly enough.[289] He had seen them blacklisting and boycotting his friends, and trampling over any sense of fair play. Why should he have any trust in the Pastoralists' Union which broke solemn agreements, for the employers were men who had 'absolutely no sense of honour when acting together'?[290] These deceitful rogues were full of every kind of mean and petty trick for their own advantage, as well as being only corrupt when it came to money matters. They were for class warfare when the unionists wanted co-operation, friendliness and peace.

Part Three

A dreadful lot, yet at least they were representing their own interests. Worse were their paid lackeys, the hirelings who, for money, were ready to betray themselves and their class. The press was submissively dependent, and the Mounted Rifles were prepared to fire on peaceful demonstrators – indeed, a medal was given by the President of the Pastoralists' Union to a scoundrel who had shot a unionist.[291] The magistrates bent to the side of power, giving penal sentences for unproved and mostly uncommitted offences allegedly caused by innocent unionists.[292] The worst of all were men like the paid secretary of the Employers' Union, who said in 1902 that,

> marriage is a luxury for the workers, as are also long sleeves, attending theatres, and the like; and it is not fair to compel employers to pay for such things.[293]

Such toadying was hardly worth a contemptuous comment. Spence's reply showed his essentially humane attitude, in his observation of shop assistants who had been given their evenings free by the Early Closing Act of 1900:

> I remember one scene with pleasure ... On the night of the first half-holiday under the Act, I chanced to visit the Theatre Royal, and found on getting inside, that the family circle had been almost entirely filled by an early-door crowd. That in itself was nothing, but I soon observed that they all seemed to know one another, and

were remarkably jolly and happy. Upon enquiry I found that they were all employees of one of the big firms which had always fought against early closing, and which previously used to work its shop-hands up till nine o'clock at night. This was the first opportunity they had ever enjoyed of attending a theatre, hence their excitement and pleasure.[294]

Subjective this may be, but who of us is not on the side of Spence?

With such an opinion of his opponents who were so full of indifference for the well-being and happiness of their exploited employees, it is no wonder that Spence rejected totally their liberalism which expressed itself in the economic principle of freedom of contract. This was a dismal doctrine which purported a semantic equality but which was only to the advantage of the privileged. It stated that the employers had the freedom to offer work according to whatever conditions they wished, and the job hunters had the freedom to accept or go somewhere else. Spence printed in full such a contract, which was in fact a recipe for serfdom.[295] Even worse in his eyes were the combinations of rich men who met in secret to hammer out schemes on how to destroy unionism, and then render it illegal in order to treat with neither pity nor humanity the wretches who had been left without protection of any kind. Whether or not such meetings and agreements took place, Spence believed that they had, and he used it all to stiffen the resolution of the workers who read his books.[296]

Such propaganda, in his opinion, was vitally necessary,

because so many of the workers were regrettably slow and sometimes stupid in catching on to what had to be done to defeat the machinations of rabid capitalism. 'The worker,' he wrote, 'has ever been foolish, and he is only slowly awakening.'[297] Far too many a wage slave was 'so mentally lazy that either he takes his cue from the boss or the Press'.[298] There were thousands of such men, and only unemployment could get it 'into their thick skulls that the existing order of things is not exactly going right'.[299] Fortunately, those of progressive ideas had already seen the light, and were leading their more tardy brothers and sisters towards a worthier future for them all. These intelligent people were the trade unionists, and Spence was as full of praise for them as he was of contempt for their disgusting oppressors.

They were, in the first place, men of splendid moral character. They were full of independence of spirit, and knew of no distinctions of class or sex.[300] They had an unbreakable sense of loyalty to each other and the movement. Nothing could make them 'crawl and cringe', but they were monuments of 'long-suffering patience' against unnecessary tribulations.[301] They were men of great honour towards the fair sex. Spence wrote of one Nat Lewis, who 'thrashed that big buck nigger until he was anybody's dog' because he had insulted 'a decent young woman'.[302] It was automatic that trade unionists were smart, swift to learn, and well able to become 'clever strategists' to get what they wanted from the bosses.[303] Resolute and firm of purpose were these men, some of whom 'have starved, rather than accept work' under dishonourable conditions.[304] As a matter of course they were 'braver men' than anybody else, of 'a high average intelligence', and invariably the best workmen'.³⁰⁵ Many were prepared to go to prison rather than work against their fellows. To sum it all up, 'The trades unionist workers – men and women – are the true heroes and heroines of the world.'³⁰⁶

In the honour of being in the position to record the truth, Spence was full of stories as to the nobility of this splendid army of righteousness. A union shearer, 'who looked a quiet, simple chap', unexpectedly flattened in the first round of a fair fight one of five pugs who had been hired to protect some scabs.³⁰⁷ During the Broken Hill strike of 1892 'the strike leaders kept splendid order'.³⁰⁸ As a matter of course, many peaceful unionists were cheerfully ready to walk thirty miles, or ride up to two hundred, to vote for their own representatives.³⁰⁹ Spence sometimes had a little difficulty in rationalising scenes of violence, as when union men burned the *Rodney* at Swan Hill on the River Murray. But then the boat was carrying forty scabs, and whoever had actually perpetrated the offence was never brought to book, since P. M. Glynn secured the acquittal of the accused.³¹⁰ Therefore, Spence was able to excuse the incident, since the men had obviously been provoked beyond endurance by the mere existence of the snivelling creatures of the capitalists.

And it was these sub-humans who most of all provoked Spence's contempt. At least the employers were being true to their class, and the occasional one was not beyond all reason and fair play. Some, indeed, were 'unconscious of evil motive'.³¹¹ But scabs, and, even worse, anti-unionists, were traitors to their own side, persons therefore of 'a very low class' who ought to be treated like smallpox, because,

> they belong to the criminal type – the person who cares for nothing but the gratification of his present wishes, regardless of what effect his actions may have on anyone else ... in my thirty years' experience and association with many thousands of men, I have never known [one] who was any good.[312]

They had no pleasant characteristic of any kind to redeem their abysmal perfidy. Every single one was

> by nature narrowly selfish ... whilst he will cringe and crawl after the boss, he will act just as unfairly to him behind his back as he does to his fellow-workers when it suits him.[313]

It completed Spence's attitudes towards the men he knew and worked with; a simplistic view, dividing his world into devils, angels and trash, but sincere, and based upon his experiences in the world of industrial action.

Chapter III

The Vision ...

From the very start as trade union organiser, Spence's experiences with capitalism and his deep sense of democratic social justice made him determined to do what he could to change the system radically. Although he had nothing against rubbishing a scab or two, he was against organised violence as provoking retaliation and hate. Negotiation might work more slowly, but in the end it would be far more effective in sharing fairly the wealth of the world and thus bringing about a just apportionment of the means of production, distribution and exchange. The successes of his first ten years of activism seemed to show that he was right in his insistence that the real future lay in collective action. The weight of numbers gave him the bargaining strength to make the employers give in to unionist demands. The result was that Spence and his colleagues improved everything, simply because the bosses were frightened of the potential massed against them.

> Man generally has a respect for power, and anything big is treated with much more consideration than anything weak and unable to hit back. Man crushes an ant under his heel, but gets out of the way of a bull.[314]

Part Three

It would have been better if the capitalists had given way having understood the workers' point of view, but then Spence never expected too much from the enemy.

His emphasis was therefore on the need to organise white workers everywhere, so that the trade union bull would become unbeatable. His openness for socialism was fully understandable. Here was the justification for working-class collective action which directly confronted the liberal apologia for the economic and political freedom of the individual. Spence never formulated a doctrine for Australian unionism, but he was highly receptive to the ideas of others which supported his gut feelings. The interests of all white workers throughout the world were identical, and his own methods of organisation would be equally effective everywhere.[315] Hence he saw worker idealism as the driving force of the whole unionist movement. The purpose was not merely to secure better conditions and wages, but to change society completely and irreversibly.

This was done first by the normal everyday contact of workers being on the job together: the A.W.U. men 'are united by a common ideal over the whole continent, and thus tend to leaven the minds of those amongst whom they work with advanced industrial and political thought'.[316] More important and effective was deliberate missionary activity, undertaken by the friendly press, the *Worker*, and by the peripatetic A.W.U. organisers. These were excellent people, and in their selfless proselytising of the cause, they

> are the educators of our members. They give extension lectures. They tell of progress made.

They set forth the ideals of the great Labor Movement. In that sense they do University work and the cost is more than repaid in the enlightenment of our members, who are notoriously the best informed of Australian Unionists.³¹⁷

His portrayal is like the spreading of the gospel, and he did in fact make the comparison himself.³¹⁸

However subjective such observations may have been, he was not exaggerating the emotions of himself and his fellow activists. The capitalists could not ignore this growing enthusiasm for creating a better world at the cost of everything they possessed. They were not simply going to melt away in the increasing heat of unionist inspiration, and they were not lethargic in defending their own interests. They learnt much from Spence, but not that they were selfish and immoral and ought to change their ways. They saw that his methods of organisation were an excellent way of fighting back at their originators, and they too formed themselves into unions. The contest was joined in earnest in August 1890 with what has become known as the Maritime Strike, and continued by the shearers the following year. The anti-trade unionists had the powers of government and the law behind them. Spence might write that the workers had never wanted the conflict, and that only their heroic self-control had prevented a civil war,³¹⁹ but the result was a victory all along the line for the men of money, and the innocence of the workers that through organisation and negotiation they could build a better world received a beating that none who lived through it would ever forget.

Part Three

The noble fighters were not going to give up merely because they had been knocked about in the opening rounds. If the capitalists could learn from the trade unionists, so could the unionists learn from the capitalists. The aim of creating a better world would not change, but the means to do it would. The rich men had won in 1890 and 1891 because they had made and controlled the law. Therefore it was the duty of the workers to use their enemies' methods to win control of the law themselves. Spence saw clearly that the strike defeats had brought about the realisation that, through the ballot box, they could win a majority to make the legislation they wanted and needed. Capitalism would be crushed with the weapons it had itself created, and the laws which performed this essential task would also create the better world. Of eighty outstanding issues, no fewer than seventy-three could only be solved in this manner so Parliament had to become the battleground.[320]

Thus trade unionism assumed an additional responsibility; that of organising for votes as well as for membership. Spence's idealism was well able to accommodate itself to this new dimension. He became as fervent for the unity of the Labor Party as he was for that of the unions. He described the splendid political fraternity throughout the country when Labor succeeded in getting into Parliament: 'A Labor member visiting any State or the Federal House walks right into the Labor Party's rooms, and is welcomed as a comrade and brother.'[321] Furthermore, in the years since Labor had entered politics, the results had been entirely beneficial, because 'the character of the several Parliaments has been raised' in its tone and behaviour.[322]

~ 176 ~

Spence's certainty in his beliefs and his moralising led him to indulge in romantic descriptions of the sort of society which would emerge from the ever-extending process of worker co-operation. The capitalists would, of course, lose their monopoly of power and money. Nationalisation was the preferred method to accomplish this virtuous necessity. The impartial, yet beneficent, state would take over the regulation which had previously been brutishly performed by the morally worthless capitalists. The excellent results could be seen in the many state- controlled industries which had been already set up in Australia.[323] With their extension, the transfer of wealth to the workers would bring about a greater efficiency of production and a far more humane system of doing it.

This, in turn, would result in sensible and rational profit-sharing because 'the wage system is itself wrong, and must be abolished'.[324] As the automatic consequence, work for the liberated wage slaves would become safe, well paid and enjoyable. The world, for the white workers who had the good fortune to inherit it, would become a far brighter and better place.

> With all workers organised and acting together ... injustice will disappear, a new and healthier environment be created, and mankind raised to a higher plane of existence ... Those who join become part of the grand army working for better and saner conditions of life.[325]

When this had been achieved, the happy citizens would be able to take advantage of it all for their mental development. Crime would gradually become a forgotten part of the capitalist past, and everyone would have the good sense to use his spare time profitably.

> The increased leisure will give opportunities for the cultivation of all those higher faculties latent in man, but now repressed by the pressure of a social system which makes the satisfaction of mere material wants an all-absorbing struggle.[326]

An entrancing prospect, and it added to the depravity of the bosses that they were too arrogant even to think about it. All they cared about were their own shabby bank accounts, upon which Spence sourly commented that,

> every one of them wants to retain the present awful, wicked system, wasting time and trying to hide glaring evils by putting patches on them to cover them up until after [the] next election.[327]

This picture in the roseate colours painted by Spence has all the aspects of a pious belief, and indeed he wrote that innumerable workers took to unionism as to a new religion, which 'came, bringing salvation from years of tyranny'.[328] The ultimate aim was indeed one directed at the destruction of evil. Spence did not wish to improve capitalism, nor to civilise it, he intended to obliterate it utterly in favour of co-operation and humanity. Organisation, both of the trade unions and of the Labor Party, was the way first to weaken and then to extinguish the system of oppression. To Spence it seemed as self-evident as it was simple. He wrote that 'When man gets time to think, he will realise that all Nature's forces — all material things, such as land and machinery — should be the common property of all', and there would always be enough, for 'Nature has ample stores and is ever ready to supply all human needs, leaving man to the development of his wonderful mentality and the enjoyment of all which high intellectuality brings to his ken'.[329] It was necessary only to remove all the obstructions which the wicked capitalists had erected in their vile intention to bar the way to everything that was good.

This desirable process seemed to Spence to be virtually inevitable, since,

> soon in every State and in the Commonwealth the masses will elect their chosen representatives who will make laws for the welfare of all the people; and class misrule and misgovernment, with all its attendant injustice and misery, will have become a thing of the dark ages of the past.[330]

He stressed that the renewal of true humanitarian values had to be accomplished slowly, for,

> Revolutionary Socialism is an impossibility. No practical man can conceive it possible. It is not a healthy form of doing things ... There is ample work for a succession of Labor Parliaments.[331]

So it would all take many years for the malevolent castle

of capitalism to fall and be reduced to rubble.

Therefore Spence was content with parliamentary gradualism. The early Labor Party members had acted as watchdogs, and they had done good work in bringing to light and in preventing examples of capitalist corruption. The future struggles would include abolishing the reactionary Legislative Councils which were hindering, for a time, every kind of humane reform.[332] Many years would go past, but the steady and peaceful revolution would automatically bring about a change in favour of all the good qualities of the human spirit. For the destruction of privilege, of capitalism, of conservative liberalism, indeed of all the enemies of human happiness and fulfilment, it all was only a question of organisation, of unity, of perseverance, and of time. And it would have no limits, for 'The extension of Unionism over the world will do more to bring peace than all that can be accomplished by Hague Conferences'.[333] So Spence, who had been so successful in confrontational action, foresaw a future where only the virtues of co-operation would be required.

And this was the vision of a man who was happy to have been a part of what he believed to have been the opening stages of change. His pride was to have helped at the start of the realisation of a glorious concept. It was indeed a splendid belief, one which transcended the means which had to be used to achieve it. Spence wrote with deep emotion and sincerity of his profound conviction that,

> Labor undertakes to change the whole tenor of the world's ideas. It undertakes to change a social system which has been the growth of

century upon century ... Give Labor a chance – give it reasonable time – and it will start such an era of growing prosperity in Australia as will make it the envy of the world.[334]

No small claim. No wonder that it provoked reaction from the men of wealth who felt everything about them to be undercut and threatened.

This reaction was expressed in their ideals of liberalism, which they took from the century which had passed. Their almost hysterical defence of it showed how serious they considered the Labor ideals to be. With every form of propaganda at their disposal they pleaded for the freedom and the rights of the individual from the tyranny of government control. They saw this as mind-deadening compulsion which would reduce Australia to a grey and initiativeless pudding society. They could not know before the war broke out that what they held to be sacrosanct was to be as evanescent as the colour of the last red clouds of evening. Nor could they know that the Labor Party, and not their own, was directly within the trend of the twentieth century towards machine majority politics and the democracy of strict party organisation. Yet Labor too was enjoying a vision which was soon to be no more. Distance became smaller when masses of men could be shipped across the world. And the naivety, the splendour and the parochialism of the beliefs of people like Spence were exposed to brutal facts when so many of these men did not return again.

Part Three

Chapter IV

... and the Void

The ideals and hopes of both of the Australian federal political parties had seemed so vivid and strong before August 1914. The catastrophe of prolonged war destroyed the island perspective. In the contest between pastoralists and shearers, one pointed gun had been a most serious matter, a unionist who bared his breast and said with scorn, 'Shoot away, you bloody bastards', a hero to his mates.[335] Yet what was all this beside the hell of what was happening in Europe? What mattered the little disputes in Australia beside the ghastly events of bloodshed? In the cataclysm of ever-fresh horrors, the old fight between property and have-nots seemed, to many people, to have become irrelevant, and the world of before the war was smashed and lost forever.

From the first, the Liberals were dominated by the overwhelming need to save civilisation from the evils of Prussian militarism. On behalf of this greater cause to preserve the freedom of the world, they compromised on their peacetime principles. Regulation, censorship, government control of every kind, and then the drive for conscription, caused the freedom of the individual, for which they had formerly fought so hard, to lose itself in the shadows thrown by the overwhelming need. In 1917 the Liberals even snuffed out their own party in order to unite with former rivals and thus be better able to indulge in war.[336]

It was harder for the Labor Party. At first, the great majority was as eager to help the Empire as the Liberals. But as time went on, a division appeared in the ranks. There were those like W. M. Hughes who agreed that nothing mattered except victory, for of what use would reform legislation be in a land which had been taken by the Hun? Yet the others feverishly demanded that the working-class experiment had to be continued. For two years the conflict grew. It destroyed the career of Andrew Fisher in October 1915, and became ever hotter in the months thereafter. The crucial issue was that of conscription, on which both the Liberals and Hughes' men became fixated, even though it was essentially irrelevant: how could the Germans be beaten by a few thousand extra men from the Antipodes? Yet in the cause of Empire unity, Hughes risked and then brought about the destruction of his party.

Spence was close to the centre of this development. The war and Labor's electoral victory of September 1914 had surprisingly caused a surge in his political fortunes. Many people had become completely insecure. At sixty-eight, Spence seemed, in his person, to offer a kind of old-world wisdom and stability. He was elected by caucus to Fisher's third ministry, mainly through the votes of the more radical members who were the most apprehensive about the future. He was made postmaster-general, but the appointment was disastrous for him. He was too old to learn the intricate business of bureaucratic administration, which had never been his strength in any case. He did everything on the initiative of his permanent officials. He thereby lost his personal touch with the trade unionists in his department, and accordingly 'failed to give satisfaction to them.[337] He became a disappointed failure, and when Hughes and caucus reconstructed the ministry after Fisher's resignation, he was dropped.

But his close working relationship with the proponents of conscription had left their mark on him, and he listened far more to their propaganda than to that of his former friends who were against it. He had been for compulsory military service since the foundation of the Commonwealth, so he followed Hughes faithfully in the campaign, and was praised by Creswick Liberals early in October for doing so.[338] He then made the mistake of his life in following Hughes out of the caucus meeting of 14th November, 1916, which split the Labor Party asunder. It was later said that his son-in-law, Lamond, had pushed him into doing it,[339] yet Spence made no attempt to show contrition and return to the fold. Indeed, he did the opposite. Hughes made everybody who had ranking of any kind into a minister in his minority interim government which lasted until 17th February, 1917. Spence became Vice-President of the Executive Council, but the position was only formally of importance because he had nothing essential to do. He paid for this fleeting triumph by being thrown out of the Labor Party to which he had given his life, even though, because of his services of decades previously, he was graciously permitted to resign.

His next personal tragedy was in losing his seat in the general election of May 1917, but he did not thereby retire into obscurity. As a member of the National Party, he won a Tasmanian by-election against Labor on 30th June, 1917. His new colleagues were a mixture of conservatives and discarded radicals, and included representatives of the establishment he had spent his life fighting against. Ambition and desire for recognition are curious emotions, and they allowed Spence to sit beside such men as whom years before he had only met across the negotiating table.

Yet he had no real contact to his new colleagues and electorate, and neither trade unions nor Labor Party wanted anything more to do with him. He made a number of long and rambling speeches in the House, but he was given nothing of importance to do. He lamented that, 'All my life I have found the greatest pleasure in work, and it is an awful punishment for me to be idle'.[340] He made one last effort to be accepted by those he knew so well. He was the Nationalist candidate for a working-class Melbourne electorate in the general election of December 1919, but he was not successful. His career flickered out in a dismal ending for a man who had hoped to make a second and political attack on privilege in the service of the cause, but whose talents had always been, and so remained, only those which had given so much inspiration to the first. In December 1926, he died.

Spence's idealism and vision were thus one of the casualties of the Great War, and in this he was not alone. The others who followed Hughes out of the party derailed themselves as well. Yet those who stayed within it were by no means happier. The eager proponents of workers' rights could no longer believe that the organisation of their forces could build a better world. Their demands for reforming laws became little more than the cries of a self-centred pressure group. The electorate reacted by taking away their majority. Labor endeavoured to recapture the earlier spirit by declaring socialism in 1921 to be the official party policy. The manoeuvre had no effect, for nothing could bring to life again the burning hopes which had inspired them before the war. The vision of them all, both of those who stayed within the party and of those like Spence who had left it, was not to be revived. It had been destroyed, like so many of the men who had shared it, on the murdering fields of France.

PART FOUR

The Leader Who Never Was:

The Short Life of Charlie Frazer

Charlie is an amusing cuss. His faith in his own powers should be quite capable of shifting continents.

The Kalgoorlie Sunday Sun September 1903

There is an exhilaration about federal politics akin to that of canvassing for photo enlargements - you never know what a streak of luck the day has in store.

Charlie Frazer, 1910
The Melbourne Punch
15th March, 1917

# Chapter I

'In this country 'tis "Youth must be served".'

James Frazer was born in Glasgow in 1831, but left that damp and chilly city for ever when he heard of the gold strikes in Victoria. He landed in Australia in 1852 and followed the rush to Forest Creek, later named Castlemaine. He had some success, for he was able to buy 280 acres of land at Keilor Plains, although he did not stay there.[341] In 1862 he married Susannah Atkinson of Melbourne, and the birthplaces of their nine children shows something of their peripatetic life. Robert and Florence were born at Ballarat in 1863 and 1866, and Adeliza, who died, in 1864 at Daylesford. A second Adeliza was born in 1870, at Maidstone, John and William in Geelong in 1872 and 1875.[342] The responsibility of so large a family finally made stability necessary, and they all moved north to find it. Mary was born at Lake Rowan in 1877, the year in which Susannah's sister, Ellen, selected 195 acres in the nearby parish allotments a mile south-west of Pelluebla.[343] James selected a property of 248 acres next to hers a year later, and at first they all lived close together in huts of wattle and daub.

Pelluebla, later called Wilby, was a tiny cluster of buildings about twenty miles south of the main district

Part Four

centre of Yarrawonga. This town is on the Victorian side of the River Murray westwards from Albury. The name is taken to mean 'water running over rock' in the local aboriginal language.[344] The first white men to report on the area were on Hume and Hovell's expedition of 1824. The first pastoral lease of 85,000 acres was as a matter of course made out to Elizabeth Hume in March 1842. In summer it is hot, there is an average rainfall of about twenty inches, and the land is flat enough to have surprised the early settlers with unexpected floods.

Yarrawonga was first opened to closer settlement[345] in 1869, followed by Pelluebla four years later. The farmers spent the first years learning to live with the elements and trying to bring under control diseases in wheat and livestock. The Frazers arrived when Yarrawonga had become 'a flourishing township' in an area where 'some of the best wheat in Australia is being produced'.[346] There were 1,204 ratepayers in 1878. Four years later there were two banks and several insurance agencies to look after the finances of the provident. There was a local paper, three churches and six hotels for entertainment of various kinds. Employment was to be found in a saw mill, brick works, several stores, and a soda-water factory.

James Frazer, from the time of his arrival, showed much interest in taking a lead in local political affairs. In July 1879 an overfilled public meeting was held in Pelluebla on the building of the railway line to Yarrawonga.[347] Frazer proposed the motion, which was carried unanimously, that the meeting support the government's scheme to lay the tracks from Benalla rather than Shepparton, and therefore through their own district. He was appointed to the committee to co-operate with other leagues of the same opinion, and to dish their opponents. They were successful. The railway was built to pass near Lake Rowan and Pelluebla, and it reached Yarrawonga in 1886, although the river still had to be crossed on large flat ferries locally known as punts.

On the new Frazer property, Susannah gave birth to her last two children, Elizabeth in 1878 and Charles Edward on 2nd January, 1880. He was named after the Stuart succession, even though his father had been brought up as a Presbyterian and remained vaguely within the influence of the sect. At first the baby was his mother's bonnie prince, but to everyone else he was always known as Charlie. As a boy he went to the next door Pelluebla South School which had been opened in September 1877. It almost immediately suffered from overcrowding, partly because of the Frazer brood, although families of eight and more children were common in the area. Charlie and his older brothers and sisters were clever but not brilliant, for they appear from time to time in the local press as winning minor Sunday School prizes.[348] In Pelluebla South, Charlie learnt the three R's thoroughly and well. Figures and finances were to cause him no serious problems later. His handwriting was confident, clear and attractive, and his spelling good. He could write adequate essays without having any claims to being a stylist. He later said that he was a great reader, but he made no literary references in any of his political speeches. The qualities of friendliness and approachableness, which were so much a part of his character, were doubtless obvious to all who had dealings with him as a boy.

Charlie Frazer was brought up more to work on the

farm than at school. His father's priorities were clear, for he was fined in the 1880s for keeping his children at home to help him.[349] Charlie grew up to believe that long hours were part of life, and he never had any problems with working from dawn until dusk. He also learnt for politics that whoever sows well now will reap a fine harvest when the time comes. But he never got used to working alone in old clothes in hot and sweaty conditions, and he was far too gregarious to enjoy being in the paddocks. Consequently, he had not the slightest inclination to follow his father, although he learnt early to keep his opinions to himself. One of his strongest characteristics was to present to the world the front which he wanted people to see and to keep his own counsel about his innermost thoughts. Only to his mother, and later to his wife, was he able to break this reserve.

Another reason for him not wanting to stay on the land was that the farm never prospered as his parents had hoped. In the first years there had indeed been much optimism in the area, and between 1885 and 1890 more land was granted there than anywhere else in Victoria. But at the end of the decade the crops were failing due to drought and locusts. Susannah's sister gave up in 1887, and made a present of her property to James.[350] Then came the years of depression in Victoria, with the abyss of the bank crash in 1893. The good mood in the area vanished completely. By 1895 the Frazer family was making preparations to move once again, this time to Mulwala, just across the river from Yarrawonga in New South Wales, where the financial position was less catastrophic than in Victoria.[351] Their property in Pelluebla was sold to Leonard Inchbold in 1896.[352]

Charlie became ever more unwilling to go with them. The threat of being engulfed by the drudgery of a farmer's life caused him very early to feel the urge to escape from it. He was so young that he could hardly identify the restlessness which was driving him, nor what his real interests and abilities were, but he knew instinctively that they had to be realised somewhere else, as far away from closer settlement as possible. He had listened avidly to his father's stories of the Victorian gold rush, and he had inherited his readiness to move around. He made up his mind to do what his father had done thirty-four years before. Accordingly he left home, but not on the spur of the moment, for although he liked taking risks he never did anything without calculation. He had no intention of being an aimless wanderer who accumulated experiences before settling down. Streams of Victorians were leaving the Depression for the newly discovered goldfields of Western Australia. Charlie felt that in the euphoric atmosphere of the west, so different from that of his home, he would be able to find personal fulfilment. He travelled through New South Wales to Sydney.[353] Then he took ship to Fremantle, arriving some months after his fifteenth birthday as one of the 29,523 immigrants of 1895.

When he first reached the west, he found that the time of picking up nuggets was past. He had no inclination to engage in prospecting of any kind, and even less to work in the mines. He became an apprentice in the locomotive shops of the government railways at Fremantle.[354] The work was far from being without sweat, but it was congenial to him in that he was working as a man among men. He at once showed characteristics which were to be

Part Four

prominent throughout his life. He was never shy of anyone or anything, and he quickly adapted to the manners and habits of the railwaymen. He learnt to drink, to swear, to smoke cigars, and with time, that he was liked by girls. He became an excellent poker player, a game which suited perfectly his temperament of hiding his real feelings and taking calculated risks, and he had enough sense not to play at the same time as having a beer. He hated cheating of any kind, and held grudges against men who deceived him in any way. He had a razor-keen willingness to learn from experience. He watched the most respected and influential men, and followed their instructions and advice. He seldom made the same mistake twice, and not surprisingly soon became fully accepted.

Working in the engine sheds was only a first stage for him, and after a few months, far below the usual age, he became a fireman on the trains during the construction of the track between Southern Cross and Kalgoorlie.[355] At first this was undertaken by a private company. There was a newspaper story about when he came for his first pay.[356] He was told to go away because the only Frazer on the list was a fireman and he was too small to be that. His mates convinced the paymaster that he was the man, and he was so astonished that he paid him half a shift too much. The windfall was celebrated by a party for all, which was paid for by the delighted beneficiary.

The work on the railways introduced Frazer to trade unionism, which was to have a great influence on his development. In Fremantle he joined the Locomotive Drivers', Firemen's and Cleaners' Union. His great self-confidence was based on having made his own way in life away from his parents' farm. But the union and the men who organised it were the bedrock of his stability. The feeling of being part of the union formed his character, not in terms of what he did not want to do – the breakaway from Yarrawonga – but in terms of what he did. The loyalty which the unionist sentiments induced in him was strong. The union was making it possible for him to grow up and become what he wanted to be, so he would stand by the unionists. In this way he soon began to understand the emotions which constituted the essential part of his nature.

Foremost among these was his desire to be a manager of men, which he first sensed in the shop meetings when he was an apprentice. He had inherited all of his father's political instincts, and far more besides. His needs were to make the group interests his own and to speak out on behalf of them. His talents, as he quickly discovered, were to manipulate and to lead, and his fulfilment was to represent his colleagues in assemblies of every form and kind. If ever there was a natural-born politician it was Frazer, and his aptitudes and instincts were coupled with a far-sighted ability to plan ahead. His deep feelings for unionism channelled the personal ambition which was early a prominent feature of his character. Long before he came of age, he knew that he wanted to go into politics and rise to the highest possible levels in order to affect the policies of the unions and the Labor Party.

As these feelings developed, he automatically accepted the attitudes, ideals, and prejudices of his colleagues, whose existence and whose organisation were giving purpose to his adolescent strivings and hopes. The government took over the construction of the railway to

Part Four

the goldfields. Frazer followed the unionist opinion concerning the self-evident superiority of employment by the state. The locomotives and also the mining machinery were fuelled by wood cut in the bush by gangs of southern Europeans who seldom spoke any English, and then brought to Kalgoorlie and Coolgardie on hurriedly laid railway tracks which were anything up to one hundred miles long. Frazer shared the union's hostility to all such immigrants, and he expressed himself bombastically against their undesirability. He also repeated uncritically all the old saws against Asians, such as their desire to corrupt pure Australian womanhood whenever they could.[357] He early developed a rough, outspoken and fearless goldfields' style of speaking which appealed well to his first often unwashed hearers. He had a particular talent for expressing himself coarsely about the alleged bad qualities of his capitalist opponents.

As soon as the railway was completed, Frazer went to live at Boulder. Here in 1899 he qualified as an engine driver with a first-class certificate.[358] He joined a new union, that of the Certificated Engine Drivers. He started work as a driver first in the Hannan's Star and then in the Boulder Perseverance Mines. He sometimes drove the trains on the electric railway between Kalgoorlie and Boulder with its highly efficient service of up to sixty-one trains a day. Settled as he now was in one place, he invested in a part-ownership of a Boulder hotel.

Yet it is possible that early in 1900 he allowed himself to be sucked into adventure. There is a cutting in his scrapbook from the *Perth Daily Standard*. This states that he volunteered for the Boer War, and that his service was short but distinguished. In February 1900 he was selected by General Buller from seventeen volunteers to take a message to Field Marshal Roberts. For nineteen nights Frazer went through Boer country between Colenso and Paardeburg, and returned with Roberts' orders for Buller. He was wounded in five places, recovered in hospital and returned to the goldfields.

There is no confirmation in the official records that he was in South Africa. Yet, from a psychological viewpoint, the account may well be true. Frazer was an avid poker player who loved to bluff and conceal, but who abominated lies and falseness of any kind. It would have gone against his character to win credit by boasting about something he had never done. Also, he cut out and kept the article, which he would hardly have done if it had had no substance. Whatever had happened, by 1901 he was against the war on humane grounds. He made a speech in Kalgoorlie against it, but his audience, full of Imperialist loyalty, rushed the platform, and he had to escape.[359]

It was a brave enough action of so young a man to risk facing a hostile crowd. But he had plunged into union and municipal work, and he used any occasion to increase his public image and thus establish his name among other men in the Kalgoorlie area who had strong political ambitions. There were many of these. Frazer already knew well John (Honest Jack) Scaddan, who had often been his driver during the construction of the railway from Southern Cross, and who was to become Labor Premier of the State in 1911. In Boulder he got to know Hugh de Largie, a rabble-rousing union organiser who presided at the first Western Australian Trades and Labor Congress at Coolgardie in April 1899, and who became a federal senator in 1901. He was on friendly terms with Tom Bath, who edited the *Westralian Worker* at the turn of the century, and also with union organisers like Jabez Dodd, Robert Hastie, John Reside and William Johnson. All of these men made it into the Legislative Assembly. He knew Paddy Lynch, who was elected first to the State Parliament in 1904 and then to the Senate in 1906. The T&LC brought him into contact with the coastal organisation's George Pearce and John Croft, both of whom also became senators for the State.

These men in private and in public spurred each other on in ambition and achievement. The goldfields became a breeding ground for Labor political development. In such company Frazer's political feelings matured quickly, and they were not modest. From the first he concentrated his hopes on federal politics. This was partly because there would be less competition from his older colleagues who were more committed to local affairs, and some of whom had families which made the distance to Melbourne insupportable. But it was more because his own ambition could not be confined to the parish pump. His interests were clear in January 1901 when he cut out a long report on Barton's formation of the first federal ministry, and also accounts of speeches of such leading Labor men as J. C. Watson.[360] He followed the election campaign of March 1901 closely. In Kalgoorlie the Labor candidate withdrew after an internal quarrel on who should support whom, and this left the radical free trader and editor of the *Kalgoorlie Miner*, John Kirwan, without competition from the left, and he beat the Protectionist mayor of Boulder, J. M. Hopkins, easily.[361] The election of Labor's, Hugh Mahon, in neighbouring Coolgardie caused the first grumblings that the whole of the goldfields should be represented by the party. There was place for a tribune of the people to come forth to stake his unassailable claim in Kalgoorlie for the next elections. When none other appeared, Frazer, young as he was, made up his mind to be that man if he possibly could.

His ambitions had been sharpened by the political situation in the first Federal Parliament. The Protectionists had won thirty-two seats out of seventy-five in the House of Representatives and could only count on a majority in vital divisions because the sixteen Labor members offered conditional support. Frazer understood the benefits of the party giving its votes for specific items of legislation, but from the distant goldfields he felt passionately that there were not enough of these, and that the Labor leader, Watson, was too accommodating and did not press enough for reforms. His irritation was one of his motives to try to win the Kalgoorlie seat, and then do his best to ensure that Labor should show more fight and not give in to the blandishments and promises of opportunistic middle-class politicians.

In making his long-term plans, he realised that it was necessary to create a reputation both as a hard worker for party and union interests, and to overcome prejudices against his age. He knew well that he had to fill positions of responsibility in order to start building an electoral base for himself. His first attempt was a failure, for he aimed too high too soon. In August 1901 he stood for election as secretary of the goldfields T&LC, but Tom Bath beat him by 389 votes to 123.[362] He continued to be tireless in his efforts to win older men on to his side, and he soon had his first success. On his twenty-second birthday, celebrating to the full, he was elected President of the Boulder Engine Drivers' Union.[363] This was only a step to higher things. He showed that he could take responsibility, and resigned the position when he was appointed secretary of the Eastern Goldfields District Council.[364] He had already made a name for himself in the Boulder and Trafalgar branch of the Western Australian Natives' Association, never losing an opportunity of loudly proclaiming his racist opinions in speeches against non-British immigrants who worked for low wages. In 1902, after only two years' membership, he was triumphantly elected president, and in April 1903 he was the Kalgoorlie delegate at the eighth annual ANA conference.[365] As a bonus, to show his heart for basic human needs, he was active in the work of local friendly societies.

Together with such work on behalf of people and politics, Frazer won the essential reputation of being a good mate and a loyal friend. He had grown up to be extremely good-looking, well built with dark hair, a small moustache, warm eyes, and regular features. His pleasures were those common to the men of the goldfields, and with his sociable nature he enjoyed constant company. Although he was always willing to listen to jokes and to laugh, his humour was more a learned grace than a vital part of his personality. In his free time he became something of a dandy, enjoying wearing good clothes. His particular hobby was horseracing. He went to every meeting he could, and his ambition was to have a stable of his own. With his habit of taking risks he was always good for a bet, both on the horses and on taking shares in a new mine. But one popular form of Kalgoorlie entertainment was not for him. On the goldfields there were many more men than women. A considerable percentage of the young women worked in the brothels, where tokens were given to the customers and whoever collected five had 'one on the house'. Frazer had little need for such distraction, for he was one of the young men with a steady girlfriend. She was Mary Kinnane, a cashier in the Hannan Street branch of Brennan's stores. Mary was no great beauty, but she was always well dressed. She had a lively and determined personality, later being known as 'deservedly – the most popular of goldfields politiciennes'.[366] From 'the first she gave her full support to all Frazer's schemes, defying her Catholic parents who objected to him as having the wrong faith, and not very much of it in any case.

With this background, Frazer felt self-assured enough at the age of twenty-two to attempt to go into town politics. He was one of six men who stood for four places in the elections of 19th November, 1902, for the Kalgoorlie Municipal Council. The unionist newspapers, whose editors he all knew well, were on his side despite his youth, and their readers stood by him. He polled three hundred and thirty votes to take fourth place, thirty votes ahead of the fifth man.[367] He was by far the youngest councillor in Kalgoorlie's brief history, and was sworn in on 3rd December.[368] The *Kalgoorlie Sun* wrote that he had been elected 'in order to make things hum when he gets among the old fogies in the Council'.[369]

This description of his fellow councillors was hardly appropriate. Kalgoorlie had been a few years earlier 'a collection of canvas tents and hessian humpies' with no roads but enormous amounts of dust and millions of flies.[370] The rates from the income from the gold had been well used to build in the shortest time an exceptionally modern town. An Irish member of the British Parliament visited the goldfields in 1903 and recorded his opinions of what he thought the councillors had done.[371] Kalgoorlie produced nearly £9 million worth of gold a year, half of the Australian production, and the town had become 'the real wonder' of Western Australia, in fact 'one of the wonders of the world'. He described it as being 'a perfectly up-to-date city, with wide streets, electric lighting, fine shops and hotels, and a race course, and one of the best tramway services in the world'. He also praised the water supply line, just being finished when Frazer became councillor, and commented that Kalgoorlie was a magnificent example of what Home Rule could do. He wrote that it was 'a marvellous place for ten years' growth; and presents the most wonderful evidence of startlingly sudden development which the whole world can show today'.

In this atmosphere of swift development there was little sparkling initiative which the youngest councillor could take. After his election, he was appointed to the works committee, which was responsible for buildings, water supply, parks and reserves, roads and footpaths, and baths. In this necessary, but less than exciting position, his most important contribution was to propose a successful motion to give 'priority of employment to local householders'.[372] On 22nd June, 1903, he was transferred to the electrical supply committee, which supervised precisely that, including street lighting, and in addition the administration of the by-laws. His most noteworthy action was to second a motion which reduced work on Saturdays by an hour.³⁷³ On 3rd December, the committee's duties were enlarged to include the supervision of rates, markets and office staff. Frazer's success in larger politics prevented him from enjoying the increased responsibilities, and he resigned on 4th January, 1904.

The year of his being a councillor was thus not studded with extravagant successes. But Frazer had not wasted his time in dusty offices. As always, he was loudly vocal in telling everybody his views, and he began to establish a reputation among his friends as being 'an energetic and uncompromising advocate of municipal as opposed to private enterprise'.³⁷⁴ He was full of schemes to help the Kalgoorlie unemployed.³⁷⁵ He was always ready, with extraordinary precocity, to take the side of the workers in any industrial dispute. He helped organise a pay rise for the employees in a Kalgoorlie hotel. When the owners sacked them two days later, this fitted in with his dislike and disgust of unrestricted capitalism.³⁷⁶ He repeated his opinions on every possible occasion, and swiftly won a fine reputation, being 'looked upon as a powerful and fearless advocate of workers' rights' so that 'he enjoys the entire confidence of the goldfields workers'.³⁷⁷ He was not slow to use such popularity as a stepping stone to his own advantage. He resigned from the District Council on being elected at the second attempt on 23rd March, 1903, as secretary of the goldfields T&LC. In this position he fired off urgent letters to high circles to take instant action against the 'influx of aliens' to the State.³⁷⁸ He won enough popularity to get himself elected as a vice-president of the Western Australian division of the Australian Labor Federation.

Part Four

In these positions of responsibility, Frazer knew well how to pull strings to get union acceptance as the leading Labor runner in Kalgoorlie for the second federal elections. He was already getting tips from insiders in January 1903, almost a year before they were to be held. Richard Crouch, thirty-one years old and the youngest member of the first House of Representatives, came to the town for the opening of the water pipeline. He and J. M. Chanter, both radical protectionists, 'urged Frazer to go on' with his efforts to win the seat.[379] It was widely thought that he had little chance. Kirwan was also radical in his opinions, and highly influential with his connections to the *Kalgoorlie Miner* and its Sunday edition, the *Western Argus*. He was widely popular among all sections of the electorate, and because he was a free trader, it was hardly noticed that the voters were ready to vote for a protectionist like Frazer. The general opinion among the cognoscenti was that his re-election was as good as certain, so that Frazer's candidature was seen as being for a hopeless cause. Why should the free and independent miners be ready to vote for a man shackled by the Labor pledge and machine, and moreover for one who was so young and who had just scraped into the local council?

Frazer's instinct, however, told him that the time was right, and his willingness to take risks was far stronger than any advice to wait that he might have received. In addition, according to Crouch, he had won a thousand pounds in one night at poker, so he had more than enough money to contest an election.[380] He easily became the selected Labor candidate. His main opponent, T. J. Boyle, was a miner who was injured at work and could make no attempt to present himself. The other, C. J. Ricks, withdrew because he wanted to leave the area and become a farmer.[381] Frazer resigned his vice-presidency of the ALF to show his laudable intention to concentrate on the one task. On 22nd September he polled 920 votes to Boyle's 398 and Ricks' 29. He showed his pleasure by keeping the ballot paper with the official result on it.[382] Kirwan later wrote, snuffily but correctly, that he had won the Labor nomination only 'because no one wanted it' on account of the seeming hopelessness of anybody's chances against himself.[383]

The electorate, which the apparently long-shot Frazer hoped to win, occupied the whole of the arid southeastern part of Western Australia. It extended from Broad Arrow and the Phillips River to the South Australian border. By far the greatest industry was gold mining. The bulk of the population lived in Kalgoorlie and Boulder, although there were several other mining centres such as Leonora, Laverton and Menzies to the north-east, and Norseman to the south. There were three tiny landing places on the Great Australian Bight, one at Eucla for the telegraph station, the others at Esperance and Hopetoun, which catered mainly for scattered pastoralists. The electorate had the perennial grudges of being underrepresented in State politics, and of having difficulties in getting the less than sedentary miners onto the rolls.

Kirwan's over-confidence that he would be re-elected worked to Frazer's advantage. Kirwan omitted to organise his supporters in any way, assuming that his return 'was considered certain no matter who stood against me'.[384] The Labor Party made no such error. There was a systematic effort to win the unions and the miners

Part Four

onto Frazer's side. This was led by the unionist press which supported Frazer with great praise and coverage in everything he did or said. He did not enter the campaign brashly. Made wary by the attitude of the Kirwan party, he began at Hopetoun to test his way of speaking and improve it before going on to the more important centres. From here he took ship to Esperance, where he spoke on 26th October.[385] He then took five days to ride a bicycle to Norseman, both to show that he was not a man of airs and graces, and to be able to chat to anyone he met on the road. It was not until 7th November that he trundled into Kalgoorlie and, having found his style, made his official policy speech.

This was tailor-made for the workers, who came in great numbers to hear him. Election campaigns were entertainment in a place where it was possible to get bored from spending too much time in hotels. Frazer played up to the crowd. He roared and jumped around like a pop star, and got his audience to participate by baiting them to answer all together as to whether they wanted or did not want particular items of policy. He appealed to all the prejudices of the miners, especially by means of a farrago against everybody who was not British. Large parts of his highly partisan speech consisted entirely of clichés, in order to make the most basic kind of appeal.

> The time has come when the workers must make their political battleground against all who are the enemies of progress, and to fight monopoly and individual selfishness in all its stages. We must secure for the workers of the

Commonwealth a fair proportion of the products of their labours. The past has been to the party of reform, as a night of tribulation and sorrow; but the beams of light can now be seen on the horizon, and the Labor Party, with their faces turned towards the East, see the first gleams of the coming day.[386]

But in between it was possible to find a policy. Australia was to stay white, and though he was a protectionist, Imperial tariff preference should only be given if the coloured people of the Empire were not helped by it. He vigorously supported the widest application of compulsory conciliation and arbitration, old age pensions, and direct taxation to hit the rich and to finance the desperately needed railway to the east.

The unsubtle propaganda of Frazer's campaign and its effect among the workers was later described by his opponent Kirwan in dismissive terms.

> The Labor enthusiasts who arose everywhere became fanatical in their zeal. My supporters were not concerned. They thought – and they were right – that at that time the Labor supporters were in a minority.[387]

In fact his own men were in no way unmoved by the success which Frazer was having. The obvious method was to attack him as a juvenile, inexperienced and silly, cartooned as hardly more than a baby with a rubber nipple in his mouth. Frazer's answer, which he helped compose, was printed in the unionist *Kalgoorlie Sun*. The

Part Four

doggerel of the limericks was of such awfulness that it is still fun to read them.

> I'm Frazer! You'll say, Sir, with truth
> I appear little more than a youth,
> But the man who takes me
> For a mud MUG
> Will be left in the consommé, in sooth.
>
> I am young but I'll soon mend o' that
> And I know pretty well what I'm at,
> If I'm hairless of face
> With perhaps e'er less of grace
> There is other than hair 'neath my hat.
>
> 'Age and Wisdom' I've often observed
> Is a coupling not always deserved
> I am wise o' my day
> And make bold here to say
> In this country 'tis 'Youth must be served'.[388]

And in the electorate of many young people, his age was clearly not seen to be a disadvantage.

Recognition of this caused some Kirwanites to indulge in tactics of peculiar nastiness. Perhaps it was normal for Kirwan's papers to ignore his speeches, or to misrepresent him when they did print them. He was quoted as opposing the building of the Kalgoorlie to Esperance railway where he had said it was a State concern. But an attempt to blackmail him was odious.[389] A man named Owens told Frazer that he and his friends would change their votes from Kirwan to himself for five pounds a week. Frazer refused, but Owens went public that his offer had been accepted. He also claimed that Frazer's election as president of the Engine Drivers' Union had not been clean. Frazer at once went to court, and it was proved that he had acted properly throughout.[390] The affair won no prestige for the man whom Labor termed 'Cur-wan' as a result, even though personally he had never been in contact with Owens. However, it was a factor in his poor showing in the election, which Frazer won easily by 5,820 votes to 2,913.

The disgruntled loser, his life long, was convinced that he had lost because a cyclone struck Kalgoorlie on polling day, so that 'No one thought of the election, except Labor Party fanatics, who, notwithstanding the elements, polled every vote ...' while 'Many of my friends didn't vote because they thought I was safe' and devoted their time to rescue work.[391] He thus twisted the fact that less than forty per cent of the electors voted. Yet this was far more than elsewhere in Western Australia. Kirwan also failed to note that Labor was in ascendancy in the entire State, for the party won all three Senate seats and four of the five in the House of Representatives – only the prestige of Sir John Forrest prevented a whitewash. What he could not be expected to understand was that the victory was part of the pre-war Labor surge that led to the great electoral victories of 1910 and 1914. None of his utterances were of the slightest importance to the workers of Kalgoorlie, who paid no attention to him. They wined and dined their new MHR over Christmas and into the New Year. He was given a final rousing send-off party by his old mates of the Engine Drivers' Union on 8th January,

Part Four

1904.[392]

Frazer left for Melbourne to become part of a complex and difficult parliamentary situation. Labor had gained nine seats in the House of Representatives and six in the Senate to number twenty-five out of seventy-five and fourteen out of thirty-six respectively. But Deakin's Protectionists and Reid's Free Traders each had also about a third of the seats. It took many months for the leaders to determine finally who should form a government with the support of whom. For Frazer, personally, the conditions were very favourable. Whereas the Protectionists were dominated by Victorians and the Free Traders by men from New South Wales, Labor had very significant representation from the less populous States. Of the thirty-nine members of caucus, twelve came from Queensland, eight from Western Australia, and six from South Australia. This meant that Labor would not be dominated by their seven representatives from New South Wales or the four from Victoria, and that the interests of all the States would be integrated into party policy. This was early seen by the Labor members to be national politics in addition to the demand for working class reforms. Thus from the start of his career, Frazer's tub-thumping for such local matters as immigration restriction to the goldfields and the construction of the transcontinental railway tended to be accepted by his colleagues as part of a larger perspective.

Frazer, of course, never realised how parochial some of his opinions and attitudes were. He saw himself as a practical idealist who was challenging the conservative establishment on behalf of the new, positive and self-confident forces of democratic equality. He wanted the future to be one where Labor would destroy all the privileges and advantages of birth and money, where he personally would have a leading role and if possible, with time, the leadership itself. This outlook showed a great development from that of Labor of the early 1890s, when the workers' representatives had thought of themselves mainly as a pressure group to win a little more 'of the world's leisure, pleasure, and treasure' from the stony-hearted employers.[393] Frazer's hopes were based upon such opinions but went far beyond them. His gut feeling was to help to build a new Australia – white, equal and proud in its knowledge of being further ahead in social justice than anything known in Europe, the United States, or anywhere else. As a very young man, crammed full of idealism, ambition and determination, he was one of the first elected Labor men to have to the full this vision and sense of national purpose, together with all its attendant characteristics of pride, naivety, righteousness, self-assurance, arrogance and drive. The vision came to be shared to a greater or lesser extent by all his colleagues.[394] It was an intrinsic part of the strength and dynamism which led to the successes of Labor in State and federal politics before the Great War, and before the split of 1916 turned the remnant of the party in upon itself and caused it to revert to much of the narrowness of its earlier ideals.

Frazer, fierce as he was to impress his personality and ideas upon his party, found caucus to be a splendid forum to start making a name for himself. The parties of Reid and Deakin met irregularly and rarely, and never to allow backbenchers to have a significant say in the making of policy.[395] Labor, by contrast, met weekly when Parliament was in session. Each member was entitled to

Part Four

make proposals. Both the party policy and its tactics were formed by majority vote, in accordance with the decisions of the Interstate Party Conferences which met every three years. Certainly the leaders of the party had more influence, but they had no more rights than even the youngest of their followers. It was a system which Frazer was to manipulate well to his own advantage as soon as he had arrived in Melbourne to start his new career.

Chapter II

'He has improved out of sight since he bounded into Parliament.'

Shortly after Frazer had become by far the youngest MHR, he had a splendid piece of luck. True to his betting nature, he and his friend George Mayman were in on the ground floor of a seemingly hopeless claim called 'The Hidden Secret'. It struck good, but Frazer was not the man to rush around and start telling everybody, especially as the syndicate had been organised by southern Italians.[396] He kept his winnings as much of a secret as possible, and only after many months did journalists find out that he was 'probably the wealthiest of the Labor men', and 'a standing example of the proverb that it is better to be born lucky than rich'.[397] He began to invest in such luxuries as a motor car and a part-share in a couple of racehorses. And Mary Kinnane was not a girl to let such a splendid prospect slip out of her hands.

The wedding took place at the end of August 1904 at St Peter's Church in the Melbourne suburb of Eastern Hill.[398] To the displeasure of her Catholic parents the Reverend Frank Anderson of the Christian Science Church officiated, and they stayed away. The bride was to be given away by her brother, but an hour beforehand he backed out because of family pressure, and Frazer's friend, Crouch, agreed to take over. Many Labor Members of Parliament came, with a gift of a set of silver-backed toilet brushes, a dozen silver fruit knives and forks, and a silver cake basket. After the wedding breakfast at Parer's Café, the couple went on their honeymoon to the family property and the Yarrawonga area. Frazer had never lost touch with his relations and birthplace, and later visited nearby Tungamah on occasion to 'address political gatherings, and his undoubted ability as a speaker and politician was fully recognised and appreciated'.[399]

Frazer's financial windfall did not cause him to distribute his wealth among the poor and needy, but neither did it make him modify his working-class principles in the slightest. Once in Melbourne, he wanted to create an immediate sensation as a fighter for social justice. Even before Parliament had met he was seconding motions in the Labor caucus, and he got himself elected as one of a seven-member Labor deputation to urge Prime Minister Deakin to administer more strictly such matters as immigration to the Western Australian goldfields.[400] There was no stopping him from holding his maiden speech in Parliament almost before he could find his way around the building.[401] It was a catastrophe. He was full of self-important phrases like: 'I hope to see the measure placed on the statute book at an early date ...' or 'I was very pleased with ...' His cumbersome attacks on the opposition Free Trade Party as suffering from 'hopeless dry rot' might have gone down well at Boulder, but appeared tasteless from such a young and new backblocks politician in the big city. No one was interested in the unpleasant details of the election campaign in Kalgoorlie, and his blunt racism and absurd generalisations against southern Europeans in the west and Chinese in Melbourne were received as being coarse and prejudiced. He succeeded only in getting a reputation as a parliamentary larrikin which the conservative press remembered whenever it seemed appropriate. The *Melbourne Punch* recalled him five years later as having been in 1904, 'a violent, loud-mouthed Labour man – a typical demagogue. He had rough angles and callosities all over him.'[402]

In addition to this miserable beginning, Frazer at first miscalculated his position as a Labor member of caucus. He agreed to vote for an amendment proposed by his protectionist friend, Crouch, against the agreed policy of his own party. In Kalgoorlie, such brashness might have been applauded as good mateship. Not so in Melbourne, where he was given 'a fearful wigging' by the party leader, J. C. Watson. Frazer was angry and upset at the summary treatment, telling Crouch that, 'I am their slave, but I am not here for that'.[403] He was intelligent enough to understand his mistake, and thereafter worked only within the rules of caucus discipline, learning swiftly how to exploit them for his own purposes.

For, despite these early setbacks, he never for an instant relapsed into passivity. The main issue of the 1904 session of Parliament was the Conciliation and Arbitration Bill, and his reactions to the activities of high-ranking politicians were to have important consequences for his future. Deakin's Protectionist Government resigned in April when the Labor Party had a majority for amendments which he was not prepared to accept.

Part Four

Watson was commissioned to form a ministry. He chose seven colleagues according to his personal inclinations, and without first consulting caucus as to who should be selected. Frazer got very worked up about these methods. Senator Dawson, who was often drunk and who died as an alcoholic six years later, was preferred to Pearce as Minister of Defence. Frazer thought that Watson was passing over obvious ability in favour of the prestige of Dawson's leadership of the one-week Labor ministry in Queensland of December 1899. Even worse, Mahon of Coolgardie was installed at home affairs, which would make it difficult for another West Australian Labor MHR to reach cabinet rank in the future. Frazer was convinced that neither Dawson nor Mahon would have had a chance had caucus chosen the ministers. Therefore he became a leading proponent for this to be made official Labor policy, although he conceded the right of the Prime Minister to allocate the portfolios. He waited until October, two months after Labor had lost office, before giving notice of a motion in caucus to give the assembled party members the right of choice.[404] But he found that the numbers were against him, so for nearly a year he made no follow-up move.

Such truculent behaviour on Frazer's part brought the other Labor representatives for Western Australia to understand that he would have to be tamed so that his zeal and spirit could be brought to serve the party and their State better. The four senators and the four MHRs met regularly but informally on behalf of their common interests. Mahon naturally was distant and touchy. He saw in his young colleague an upstart rival for popularity on the goldfields. He tended to snap at him, for instance over Home Rule for Ireland, even though the object of his sarcasm was well in with the Irish groups.[405] But Frazer had no problems with the others. He already knew and liked Senators de Largie and Croft, and he developed quickly a genuine friendship with Senator Pearce, who had worked on the goldfields in 1894-1895. By July he and Pearce had established a working relationship in caucus of proposing or seconding each other's motions.[406] They later travelled by choice together on the ships to and from Western Australia, and made election speeches to help each other. It was Pearce who suggested that Frazer, despite his lack of schooling, had the ability and was still of an age to study. He might well follow the example of W. M. Hughes, who had learnt law in his spare time and had recently been admitted to the bar.

This advice seemed to Frazer to be sound. Good lawyers were at an advantage in many debates, and Hughes was the only qualified one in the federal party. Frazer felt that here was the appropriate direction for his ambitions. He borrowed some law books from Crouch and began a course. He became famous for reading his books in the chamber during dull debates. He was encouraged by the party leaders, and a swift result was that his speeches became better ordered, more factual and therefore more effective. In November 1904 he introduced into the House a resolution which had first been moved by Pearce in the Senate on 17th March, as to the desirability of the government growing and selling tobacco, with the profits to be used to pay for old age pensions.[407] He was a credit to his friend and mentor. He quoted all kinds of references, and put on a thoroughly legal style. This won him commendation, and also fan

Part Four

post from a Victorian grower of thirty years on his 'manly and well-informed statements ... on the whole tobacco question'.[408]

Despite his determination to polish his parliamentary manners and performance, Frazer remained at all times on the critical left wing of his party. On the big issue of conciliation and arbitration, he wanted its widest possible application to include shearers and farm labourers.[409] He was one of the first of his party to speak out for unconditional preference to unionists in government employment. He continued to demand tight immigration controls, whose absence would 'have the effect of swelling the ranks of the unemployed', and he informed Parliament heatedly that Western Australia would be 'flooded with foreigners' if they did not enforce the severest restrictions. His method of solving the problems of the workless was to break up the big estates by means of a heavy land tax, with the closer settlement he had grown up with and run away from as a boy as the happy answer.

Frazer also took the radical side in an internal conflict within the Labor Party. When Watson took office in April 1904, half the Protectionist Party under the leadership of Isaac Isaacs supported him. There was much talk of an alliance or even a coalition. From the first Frazer was outspoken in caucus on behalf of the complete independence of Labor. He considered Isaacs to be 'the slyest man' he had ever met in his attempts to ingratiate himself with Watson and the other party leaders who favoured his proposals, and thus dilute the pure Labor ideology.[410] At the end of April and in May, Frazer was one of the prominent speakers in caucus on behalf of his point of view, and on 17th May he was the proposer of the successful motion that, 'Labor's policy should be announced to the country untrammelled by any Coalition'.[411] But a week later a formal alliance with Isaacs' group was proposed. After a hectic session of two days, this policy was approved by twenty-four votes to eight, with Frazer as one of the growling minority.[412]

During the next few months no formal progress on the matter of the alliance was made. In August the Labor Government fell, once again on the scope of the Arbitration Bill. The Free Trade leader, George Reid, took office with the support of those protectionists who were apprehensive of what a Labor government might do if really given the chance. Deakin gave Reid his full support, having joined him in his praise of liberalism and condemnation of Labor:

> Instead of taking the downward path which will lead to political servitude and perhaps to social slavery, we want to rally to our flag those in favour of responsible government, to restore majority rule, and to maintain that priceless heritage which our forefathers have handed down to us and which we should preserve or perish.[413]

Reid became prime minister with a shaky majority of two in each House. He was supported by all the right-wing forces in Parliament, and at once informed Australia in a public letter that his main concern would be to oppose Labor policies and that 'attempts would be made to give the new departure a conservative aspect'.[414] As far as he

Part Four

and his ministry were concerned, the main political issue was to be that of the deadening and dreadful socialism as demanded by his devious opponents, against the anti-socialism of freedom and enlightenment as proclaimed by himself and his colleagues.

This initiative caused many waves of indignation both in the Labor Party and among Isaacs' group. In September Isaacs set out in writing his conditions for the alliance, which was 'to be for the life of this and the next Parliament'.[415] Labor was deeply divided, and a series of inelegant caucus discussions heated the emotions of the protagonists. Watson and the majority were in favour of Isaacs' proposal. The minority, including Frazer and Pearce, knew well how to delay any final decision. After the conditions of alliance had been approved by eighteen votes to eight, Frazer moved that Watson should not 'have permission to sign on behalf of the Party, but those favourable to the Alliance to sign agreement individually'.[416] He drew the issue out as long as possible, but on 21st September went down in a final vote with only two other members still on his side and even his organisation in Boulder against him.[417] The alliance thereupon formed the policy of the opposition to Reid of both Labor and Isaacs' men.

Although Frazer, due to his uncompromising outspokenness, was getting on the nerves of many of his seniors, his obvious sincerity and desire to learn from experience could not be ignored. Important parliamentarians thought of a way of giving him something responsible to do, which might both curb and direct his scratchy energy. His interest in old age pensions dated from his work for the friendly societies in

Kalgoorlie, when he had seen the hopelessness of the worn-out and destitute miners. In Parliament he had, from the first, shown a real concern in his demands that the pensions should be paid as soon as possible on a national basis.[418] On 20th October, 1904, a committee of nine was appointed by Reid to enquire into the matter, under the chairmanship of the protectionist Austin Chapman. Pearce's recommendation for Frazer to be one of the three Labor representatives was accepted. There were seven committee meetings between 28th October and 1st December. They resulted in a Royal Commission being set up with eleven commissioners, including Pearce, Frazer, Bamford and O'Malley from the Labor Party.

The resultant work took up much of Frazer's time between April 1905 and February 1906. The commissioners travelled to all the State capitals and asked an enormous number of questions of scores of people, which resulted in a volume of redoubtable size because everything was printed. The work was far more restricted than that of party or Parliament, because everyone was working towards a common aim. There was nothing for Frazer to get excited about or to lead any opposition to. He only attended twenty-two of the thirty-five sessions, but did his fair share of the work when he was there. He observed how his older colleagues handled the business and manipulated the questioning, and he learned quickly how to do so himself. For example, of destitute married people, he asked, 'Have the old couples to be separated?' to the pathetic reply that of course they did.[419] Or, more to the point concerning his own electorate, he carefully set the stage.

Part Four

> In the case of miners, there are any number of men who, before reaching fifty, are simply worn out as a result of bad air, hard work, long hours, and not too much food, and who have perhaps been employed by dozens of mine-owners. How would you make provision for them?[420]

The man he was asking, J. B. Trivett, the secretary of the New South Wales friendly societies, gave the expected answer. But when someone failed to do so, Frazer was able to give a cross-examination. When T. H. Lovegrove, the principal Western Australian Medical Officer for Health, showed little understanding, Frazer hammered him into conceding that the conditions in a normal goldmine were dreadful, with the unspoken conclusion that the demand for pensions was without reasonable opposition.

Despite the occasional success, Frazer's main contribution to the work was to give a back-up to his older colleagues. Only once was he allowed to start procedures, when his former working partner, James Braydon, the representative of the goldfields T&LC, was invited to attend and give evidence. Frazer's questioning of him showed his deep understanding, both humane and political, of the problems of the ageing miners.[421] Such sympathies were very widespread, and as a result the members of the commission prepared the expected report. This recommended pensions of 10/- a week from the age of sixty-five, but with a number of conditions such as a means test and that the pensioner should not be a drunkard.[422]

Through such work with experienced politicians,

together with his attendance in the House, Frazer was beginning to learn how to refine his parliamentary style. He deliberately observed the characters and abilities of those men who had achieved the greatest success. He saw how Alfred Deakin was the most approachable and well-liked of men, and grafted some of his geniality on to his own sociableness. He was himself a born organiser and intriguer, but he learnt the tactical procedures of how to hint and elbow-jog from Austin Chapman, the master of the art. Frazer acquired 'the art of appearing to be honest, of making a profession out of honesty' from Sir John Forrest.[423] He improved his own way of attacking political opponents from two experts – Hughes with his barbed taunts and lively, wicked images, and Joseph Cook with his knowledge of parliamentary procedure and tactics, and powers of destructive interjection. After eighteen months of working on himself, the changes in him were clear to political commentators. One of them, remembering him in 1904 as 'a very rough nugget', wrote in August 1905 that he had 'improved out of sight and general knowledge since he bounded into Parliament'.[424]

The syncretic politician who was emerging from this process was one whom the men on his own side were learning to treat with wary respect. Away from Parliament he became known for never saying an unpleasant word. He could switch on and exude charm and friendliness, and much of it was genuine. During the long terminal illness of his friend, Donald Macdonell, of the AWU, he attended his bedside 'with all the love and devotion of a cherished brother'.[425] But Frazer was a politician all the time, and much of his pleasant exterior was the mask of the ambitious man whose skills were to influence and manipulate. Yet he managed to integrate his personal ambition with being a Labor man first and always, and his intrigues were without exception designed to further the interests of the party and cause which he represented.

The necessary corollary to working within the rules of the Labor Party was to attack his opponents, and in this art Frazer from the first showed a purposeful political fearlessness. He went straight for the leading members of the parties he opposed. He did not have Hughes' gift of instant, vivid repartee, but he became a critic with 'a caustic, bitter tongue and a knack of finding out just those things which his opponents do not wish him to say'.[426] He disliked Sir John Forrest intensely, regarding him as a reactionary opponent of the twentieth century in Western Australia, and he never lost an opportunity of sniping at him. In 1907 Forrest was reported as approving of the chaining of aboriginal captives by the neck. Frazer used the chance to quote the report at length in Parliament and also to give the House a moral lecture to discomfit Forrest and to show his own humanitarian concern for the unfortunates in his electorate.[427] Forrest, who understandably detested Frazer in return, was wise enough to make no public reply.

By watching, learning, and then doing, Frazer was making himself into a redoubtable politician in Melbourne. But he never lost contact with his base among the workers and unionists in Kalgoorlie. He spent as much time of the parliamentary recesses there as he could, and when he had to stay away he gave good reasons for his absence. In 1905 he was in Queensland with a committee to check that the kanakas were being repatriated swiftly enough. His wife went along with him, and had to have an emergency operation for some internal trouble.[428] Frazer wrote a series of three articles for a Kalgoorlie paper to show his constituents what he had been doing when he had not been among them, typically without mentioning his personal worries.[429]

When he was in his electorate, no one had cause for complaint that he was not doing enough. He made regular and rousing speeches as to the achievements and hopes of himself and his party in Parliament. He had an eye for the gesture which would bring instant publicity and endear him to the voters. He made it known that he wore clothes stamped with the manufacturing label of the 'Goldfields Tailors and Tailoresses Society'.[430] In Bulong he made a promise before all the important citizens to resolve the long-standing problem that the public telephone was open to the weather and far from private.[431] He made tours of up to a month, mostly alone, but sometimes Pearce went with him to share the platform. He was never in a hurry while visiting even the most remote towns and shanties, and he did this not only during election campaigns. He was punctilious at sending grievances to the right addresses. His speciality was the improvement of postal and telephone services, vital forms of communication in the vast distances of Western Australia.[432] It was no wonder that he became ever more 'trusted and popular' among the people of his electorate, since they could 'appreciate his youth, admire his keenness, and recognise his ability ...'[433]

All this activity, both in Melbourne and in Kalgoorlie, was done with the legitimate ambition of making a swift and fine career for himself in politics. He saw himself as

Part Four

the first of the younger men who would take over the leadership of the party in the next generation. His work in Parliament was to win a reputation as the coming man for, what all his feelings and intuition told him, would be the winning side, that of complete Labor independence and tight caucus control. His work in his constituency was to ensure his re-election as long as Kalgoorlie should go on producing gold. But whereas on the goldfields he had the safe policy of doing what the majority of his electors expected and desired, in Parliament he was prepared to take calculated risks to make a name for himself. Being the man he was, he had a fine instinct for getting in at the beginning of a minority cause and ending up on top.

It was Prime Minister Reid, his greatest political opponent, who was to give him in 1905 such an opportunity. Reid's avowedly anti-socialist and anti-Labor Government in December 1904 staggered into the Christmas recess mainly by doing nothing which might offend its supporters. He devoted the first six months of the new year to organising and publicising his newly formed Australian Liberal League whose main activity was to attack the Labor Party and its supposedly destructive socialist doctrines.[434] He intended to polarise politics and he was ready to fight an early election which he hoped would return his anti-socialists with an Australian-wide majority, thus burying the fiscal issue and the independent Protectionist Party forever.

Frazer was in instant agreement with this attempt to reduce the number of parties in Commonwealth politics to two. He had observed with contempt the party manoeuvrings of 1904 and the wretched legislative records of the governments of alliance. As an eager reformer, he was derisive of the liberal politicians who had been instrumental in the intriguing for place and position. With his large majority in Kalgoorlie, he had no fear of losing his seat in a new general election, and he was, in any case, convinced that the dynamic and reformist policy of the Labor Party would be more attractive than what he saw as Reid's continual blasts of hot air. He had no time for Deakin and his liberal protectionists with their policy of slow reform. He was thus quite prepared to accept any attempt by Reid to force a premature election on the issue of socialism against the reaction to it.

A speech by Deakin and its consequences were to destroy such prospects. On 24th June, 1905, at Ballarat, Deakin thought he was saying that Reid should add a policy of constructive legislation to his anti-socialist cries if he wished to retain protectionist support. Other opinion thought that Deakin was giving Reid 'a notice to quit'.[435] Reid used the opportunity to try to force a dissolution and a new election in which he, as prime minister, would be able to proclaim the issue as being his own anti-socialism against Labor. Deakin and Watson hastily had a meeting which resulted in a proposal for Labor to support a protectionist government in return for legislative concessions for the rest of the Parliament. The matter was considered in a caucus meeting held on 5th July.

Frazer, the young radical, attended this meeting incensed by these reactions to political pressures. His deep distrust of Deakin predated his entry into Parliament. In October 1903 he had sent a letter to caucus, to the colleagues of his hopes, accusing Deakin of

Part Four

'treachery' in abandoning the Conciliation and Arbitration Bill.[436] In August 1904 he had seen how Deakin had allied himself unequivocally with Reid against Labor, now he wished to return to office by opportunistically relying upon the votes of those whom he had, eleven months before, so harshly condemned. The events of June and July 1905 caused, in Frazer, a lasting contempt of Deakin as a man whose word and support could never be relied upon. With a return to his earlier goldfields style, Frazer called him 'a political mongrel', and had great difficulty in making people believe that he had in fact said 'a political rotter'.[437] His grudge against Watson was given appropriate fuel by his leader setting the way for Labor to give support to such a man as Deakin, although he was wise enough to make no unpleasant personal remarks against him. He also thought that Deakin's policy of gradual liberal reform was one of tinkering about with lukewarm legislation, and that those Labor men who supported it were wasting everybody's time. Frazer was one of the very first to set himself in opposition to the proposed course of action. The delaying tactics in caucus were introduced by Hughes and McDonald. Frazer was to the fore in the hard discussion, seconding one amending motion and supporting the other, but at the end there were only six other men on his side.[438]

Frazer was bound by his pledge to respect this majority decision to support Deakin for the rest of the Parliament. He had no thought of disobeying caucus, however much he disliked having to give in to the majority. He chose another method of attack to set about undermining the arrangement. Later in July the third Interstate Labor Party

Conference was held in Melbourne. Frazer attended as Pearce's sidekick, one of six members of the federal Parliament from Western Australia.[439] He took an active role which was calculated to cause Watson the maximum amount of annoyance. He was important in securing majority consent that under no circumstances would the arrangement to support Deakin be prolonged after the end of the Parliament, and that there should be no immunity of election for protectionists. As a blow to Watson's prestige, he was instrumental in reviving and getting passed his relapsed caucus motion that any future Labor ministry should be 'recommended' by caucus and not by the party leader. He also seconded Pearce's successful motion that a land tax should be made a fighting plank on the party platform. He failed only in trying to make New Protection an item of party policy, whereby the increased profits brought about by a higher tariff should be used to raise the wages of the workers. The majority was nervous that the tariff issue might cause a party split as it had done in New South Wales a decade before.

The passage of the motions restricting the alliance and recommending caucus to choose ministers hit Watson hard. On 27th July, he wrote a long letter to the party explaining his reasons for wishing to resign the leadership.[440] Caucus in two meetings on 2nd and 9th August persuaded him to rethink his decision. As a stimulus for him to change his mind, the party voted unanimously to give him Andrew Fisher as deputy-leader.[441] It was hoped and intended that Fisher, with his known qualities of finding a consensus of opinion combined with extreme loyalty to Labor, would be able to restrain and control the activities of the wild men of the party.

This move of the party leaders was successful. Because the conference had made its decisions as they had wanted, Frazer and his cronies had no reason to go on making Watson's life uncomfortable. Fisher had been on their side in Melbourne, so they felt obliged to follow him when he proved to be a loyal deputy to Watson after his appointment. If Watson were to go, there was a good chance that Fisher would be his successor, so it would be counterproductive for them to keep niggling against the combined leadership. Frazer stopped making trouble and waited to see what the next elections would bring. It redounded to Fisher's credit that he had apparently brought peace to the party. The smoother relations were demonstrated by Watson visiting the goldfields in May 1906.[442] Here he could see for himself what kind of place had produced such an importunate representative. Possibly wryly, he was also able to confirm that Frazer would go on being with him after the elections.

The tacit acceptance of the arrangement he disliked caused Frazer to become more positive to legislation. In caucus he joined Pearce in an attempt to make the proposed land tax as stiff as possible, later to make a tariff referendum party policy, and in 1906 he spoke out for an immediate old age pensions act.[443] But this was pressure, not destructive tactics. And in Parliament he stopped making root and branch criticism. He worked to strengthen bills according to his own point of view. In September 1906 Deakin introduced a bill to grant preferential duties to British goods imported into Australia. Frazer proposed an amendment that the privilege should only be given to goods which had been proved to have been made by white British workmen.[444] On its rejection, he proposed that it should only be for goods brought in British ships 'manned exclusively by white British seamen'. When this failed too, his third amendment omitted the word 'British'. This was passed by seventeen votes to sixteen. Deakin did not wish to risk a recommittal, so the bill went through all stages in the House of Representatives.

In other matters, he was equally as penetrating if not quite so obscurantist. He denied the need to ratify the £125,000 Orient Line mail contract to Europe which was to cut the time of delivery by sixty hours.[445] The benefits of the little time-saving this would bring would be enjoyed only by bankers and industrialists, so the money would be better spent on internal postal improvements. On another matter, he was deeply antagonistic to the protectionist proposal to introduce preferential voting, rightly seeing this as an attempt to strengthen their party of the middle. More according to his personal tastes, he scornfully opposed as giving in to the wowsers a bill to allow the postmaster-general to cut off telephone services to those places of immoral purpose, the race courses.

On the positive side, Frazer was beginning to learn how to take his own initiative in Parliament. He received caucus assent in July 1905 to introduce a bill to regulate fire insurance. This had been of long-standing importance to him since the time of some distant swindle in Kalgoorlie.[446] In his hot and arid electorate the insurance companies were happy to take the premiums, but less delighted to pay promptly and in full when it came to claims. The law, 'rotten' according to Frazer, was full of

Part Four

loopholes which helped to bring about delay and part-payment. His first bill was concerned to compel the insurance companies to fulfil their contracts quickly and honestly. On 9th August, 1906, he made his second reading speech.[447] It was well organised, well researched and well delivered. But Deakin's Government had many other matters to attend to at the tail-end of a Parliament, and Frazer's bill lapsed. His frustration was expressed in the following Parliament when he demanded more time for private members' bills, and in a later attempt to pressure Deakin's cabinet to discuss fire insurance as a ministerial matter.[448] When he again met with a lack of interest, he introduced his bill a second time, but it again failed to capture the interest of a majority.

Despite such setbacks, Frazer's confidence was justly complete that he would be successful in the general elections to take place on 12th December, 1906. Only Labor had a functioning party and electoral organisation in Kalgoorlie. The miners, the other workers and the press were almost solid behind their young, energetic and outspoken MHR. In the smaller centres, nobody gave any opponent of his 'the ghost of a chance'.[449] For a long time there seemed to be no issue which could even begin to divide the electors, and that he might well have no opponent to face. And although Kalgoorlie was extreme, there was a recognisably similar situation in much of the rest of the State, where the forces in opposition to Labor were in hopeless disarray, the single exception being in Sir John Forrest's electorate. In Western Australia there was nothing to compare with the three-cornered fight elsewhere between the anti-socialists, the protectionists, and Labor. As late as 12th September, a liberal meeting in

Perth 'to consider matters of importance in connection with the federal elections' was met with public apathy, and the organiser, Dr Thurstan, had little hope that the vote against Labor would be any greater than in 1903.[450]

Such was the situation when, on 21st September, the Senate rejected, on the third reading, a bill to authorise the survey of the transcontinental railway. A wave of anti-federal feeling swept the west, where both Houses of Parliament passed a resolution that the State should secede from the Commonwealth. The leading Liberals thought that they had found their much needed election issue. Forrest was induced to accept the leadership of what was hurriedly called the Western Australian Party. This proceeded to endorse candidates who would apparently defend the interests of their State up to and including their dying breath. With Forrest to the fore, these men attacked Labor for allegedly ignoring the needs of the west on behalf of their own sectional interests. This propaganda backfired. Frazer was typical of the Labor members in castigating the secession idea as 'a childish and foolish resolution', then in showing how he and his colleagues had never subordinated the needs of their State to those of their own party.[451] They all signed a manifesto in which they promised to go on doing so, as well as supporting the national Labor policy. The voters were in sympathy. The press reports show that they virtually ignored all the anti-Labor candidates except Forrest, the meetings of the Labor men 'completely taking all the support'.[452] The opportunist Western Australian Party thereupon disintegrated, each candidate afterwards speaking only for himself.

With the feeble flutterings from the right eliminated,

there could be no real interest in the elections in Kalgoorlie. The Western Australian Party had dug up the mayor of Esperance, W. R. Burton, as an opponent for Frazer. He swiftly repudiated the party label and spoke in favour of radical policies at meetings which, as he had no organisation, hardly anybody attended. The only interesting contribution of the party on the goldfields was when two of its Senate candidates, Sir Edward Wittenoom and C. Clarke, ventured to present themselves to their mining public. Wittenoom was hardly a convincing proposition, since he had 'come forward at great personal inconvenience, purely from a sense of duty and patriotism, to give the people a chance of saying which party should represent them'.[453] The miners had no respect for him. They remembered him as 'Ten-foot Ned', the Minister for Mines who in 1898 had limited alluvial mining to that depth. His audience in 1906 greatly enjoyed making so much noise that his meeting was ruined.[454] Thereafter, Frazer had the electorate virtually to himself.

In his policy speech at the end of October he followed closely the Labor Party line.[455] It was all there, the need for the land tax, old age pensions, an independent Australian navy and the nationalisation of monopolies. He demanded the penny post, and to please the miners he stormed for a stricter immigration control, using his parliamentary amendment against coloured labour to give substance to his words. His organisation flooded the electorate with a very fine floater in praise of his performance in Parliament.[456] He was, as usual, conscientious in visiting the other centres to spread the message, but in the absence of any serious opponent, his campaign was doomed to be without sparkle. The general opinion was that more interest was taken in municipal elections. The only excitement for Frazer was when he visited Forrest's electorate late in November to help the Labor candidate O'Loghlen, and finally had somebody to attack. Then he went back to Kalgoorlie, where he duly won with 7,715 votes to 2,051 for Burton. Only thirty-six per cent of the electors on the rolls voted, but they gave Frazer the biggest majority, measured in percentages, in the whole of Australia. The subsequent Christmas and New Year parties more than made up for the tame events which had preceded them.

Part Four

Chapter III

'The bitterest critic in the Labor ranks.'

In the elections of 12th December, 1906, the Labor Party won one seat in each House to number fifteen senators and twenty-six MHRs. Deakin's Protectionist Party lost heavily to number only five and seventeen. At the first Labor caucus meeting 'a discussion took place on the present political situation, but no decision was arrived at ...'[457] These mild words concealed a scorching debate. Watson's majority held that it was better to go on giving Deakin support for concessions rather than sitting uselessly in opposition. The minority claimed vehemently that it was ignoble for a larger party to yield the making of policy to a miserable rump, and that the electors would later honour a Labor decision to go it alone.

From the start, Frazer took the line that Labor should have neither alliance nor understanding with any other group or party. If the protectionists and the anti-socialists should thereby come together, so be it. In the long run the electorate would reject any opportunist conservative alliance and give the proud and independent Labor Party a chance to fulfil its splendid national programme. When the numbers were against him in February and again in July, his reaction was to begin to organise a so-called 'cave' within caucus to win a majority to his point of view. His actions were in no way in defiance of caucus discipline, since the party conference had limited the agreement to the term of the expired Parliament. All subsequent reports confirmed that he was the leading figure and main manipulator behind the pressure group. In doing this, he was taking a calculated political risk. Watson and other influential party members were greatly irritated by so young a man intriguing against their policy and its majority support. As long as these men continued to direct the party, Frazer would have no chance of advancement. But his instincts told him that the Labor movement would shift to his point of view, so that eventually he would be on the winning side.

He was, of course, not alone, and he knew well how to win the attention of men who had reason for dissatisfaction with Watson's leadership. A close ally was King O'Malley, who thought that his plans for a Commonwealth Bank were not receiving enough attention. W. G. Spence, who had never won the high place in party counsels that he wanted, gave cautious support. Josiah Thomas from Broken Hill had a similar electorate to Frazer and a similar outlook to politics. Needham and Lynch had been elected to the Senate in Western Australia in 1906 with the help of the enormous goldfields vote, and shared Frazer's sentiments. A number of others saw themselves as being the fighting wing of the party and were prepared to make common cause. But Frazer was the man who held them all together, ready to make a serious move when the time was right.

This work was so time-consuming that Frazer finally

Part Four

abandoned his study of the law, which had been dragging on ever more slowly since 1905. He took far more personal satisfaction in every kind of human contact than in poring over past cases and dry theory. His early lack of schooling had begun to tell against him, and the long journeys between Melbourne and Kalgoorlie made it hard for him to concentrate. He let it be known that it was the lack of reciprocity between Western Australian and Victorian law which was the cause of his decision.[458] But the abandonment of his earlier plans was easy for him, because of his fascination in playing the absorbing game of influencing and manipulating men.

His organised needling of Watson achieved its aim on 23rd October, 1907, when the irritated leader announced his irreversible intention of resigning from the position.[459] The official reason was his health; some people whispered that he was under pressure from his wife,[460] but above all he no longer wished to put up with the constant discontent. His successor was to be chosen on 30th October. The main rivals were Fisher and Hughes. For Frazer there was no doubt as to whom he would support. He spent much of his political life in bending men to his own opinions, so he disliked Hughes's impatience with slower-thinking colleagues and his inventive but egocentric way of solving problems by riding over their feelings. Frazer was always given a fair hearing by Fisher, whereas Hughes apparently never really listened to anybody. In addition, Hughes' electorate bordered on Watson's, and there were doubts against establishing a Sydney dynasty. Frazer did everything he could to win votes for Fisher, and this helped him to win by 'a substantial majority'.[461]

Because Fisher owed his success partly to Frazer and his cave, he was far friendlier to him than Watson had ever been. Frazer capitalised on this by making himself a loyal and co-operative assistant to his new leader. He made no difficulties for him when Watson's policy of working with Deakin was continued. Where Frazer had formerly blatantly intrigued, he now stated his opposition openly, and took defeats with good humour. When he sensed that the time for a change of government was nearing, he decided to show Fisher how useful he could be to him. He took the initiative for each Labor member to contribute five shillings a month for Fisher to do what he wanted with.[462] Caucus increased the amount to a pound, and Frazer became its collector and treasurer. Whether he intended it to be a reptile fund for propaganda and payment is not clear, but after Fisher became prime minister and Frazer had failed to join his cabinet, he saw no further use in it and moved for it to be abolished. The party voted for it to continue. The money was used for harmless matters like wreaths and typing accounts until it was finally seen to serve no vital purpose and brought to an end in August 1910.

Frazer supplemented such calculated trimming with ever stronger criticism of Deakin's Government in Parliament. His technique was to support protectionist measures which were accepted by caucus and which were, for him, a step in the right direction, but to pinprick the ministers with harsh criticism on details. Hence he voted for the increase in the tariff as a way of getting a first instalment of New Protection, but he let himself go with fierce attacks on the handling of finances in general.[463] He griped at the delays in providing for old age pensions, until he was able to welcome the Surplus Revenue Bill which promised to provide money to pay for them. He increasingly irritated the government by demanding swifter action on such matters as the establishment of the Federal Capital, the High Commissioner Bill, the penny post, the transcontinental railway, and a comprehensive system of defence. Some of his criticism could be justified, but some was only a lot of noise for its own sake. All the party leaders were in agreement on providing £5,000 to finance Mawson's expedition to the Antarctic. Frazer, for no apparent reason except a desire to take the opposite side to Deakin, carped that the time was not right to do it.[464]

This constant discontent from the party was tiresome in the extreme for Deakin, who was dependent on the votes of men who were satisfied with nothing that he did. Frazer was not admired by him, nor by commentators such as the contemporary historian, H. G. Turner, who described him dismissively as 'a Mr Frazer' whose 'antecedents were unimportant'.[465] But the object of their dislike was growing constantly in the self-confidence and political stature which his successes were giving him. A posed picture of the sitting House of Representatives in 1908 shows this clearly. There he is, completely relaxed on the front bench to the right of the Speaker, next to Deakin's ministers, whose work he professed to despise, obviously comfortable and content and at home in his distinguished surroundings.[466]

It was the matter of New Protection which was to create the tension needed to break Labor's support for Deakin's Government as Frazer wanted. Labor had supported the increased customs duties in return for the

Excise Tariff Act whose purpose was to increase the wages of men working in protected industries. Frazer early sought an assurance that the government would proceed with the policy even if the High Court should declare the act unconstitutional.[467] Two days after Parliament had adjourned in May 1908 the High Court did exactly this. In July, the fourth Interstate Labor Party Conference, which Frazer did not attend, decreed that there would be no alliances of any kind for Labor in the future. When Parliament reassembled on 16th September there was much excitement as to what the new session would bring for the government party and Labor.

Frazer, sensing that his moment was approaching, was active from the start. In caucus he seconded Fisher's motion, which was carried unanimously, that the government should amend the constitution to enable a full New Protection to be carried into law.[468] When Deakin's proposed amendment was made known, it seemed to Frazer that the mountain had not even produced a mouse, since its only intention was to render constitutional a second Excise Tariff Act. He took the lead in a two-day caucus meeting that Deakin's Government should fall. This time he had the numbers. His motion was slightly amended to read,

> that in view of the attitude of the Government in relation to New Protection, Old Age Pensions, Immigration Restriction Act, Finance & other matters, the relations existing between the Party and the Government should not continue.[469]

By nineteen votes to seven with six pairs it was carried.

Part Four

Deakin was voted out of office on 10th November. Fisher was invited to form the second Labor Ministry.

All contemporary reports were unanimous that Frazer had been 'mainly instrumental' in bringing about this development.[470] One well-informed journalist wrote that,

> it was to the persistence with which Frazer fought, the bitter hostility which he displayed to Mr Deakin and some of his colleagues, and the reckless indifference which he showed towards even Ministers with whom he was on friendly term that the eventual reverse of the party's attitude was due.[471]

The conservative *Melbourne Argus*, which approved of Deakin's fall, agreed that it had been done 'mainly through his efforts'.[472] And Frazer himself confirmed in June 1909 that he had taken the leading role and was 'glad' that he had finally persuaded his colleagues to agree with him.[473]

But his work for his cave, despite his sincerity that he was doing the right thing for Labor, had made him many enemies within the party. The requital was immediate. The decision of the party conference, which he had instigated himself, was for caucus to choose the ministers and leave the prime minister the duty of allotting them their portfolios. In the caucus meeting of 12th November, Frazer seconded the motion that this procedure should indeed be adopted.[474] Its success by twenty-four votes to seventeen was to work against him. He was one of twenty-one hopeful candidates, but his reputation for ruthless and covert intrigue weighed heavily against him.

Watson had not forgotten, and persuaded his friends to sabotage his chances. Frazer had the support of Fisher and his own cave, but failed by a single vote.[475] His rival Mahon was once again successful. Frazer was then nominated as whip and secretary, but lost out to David Watkins of Newcastle.

Consequently, for the next five months there was nothing important for him to do in Melbourne. He spent most of the time in Kalgoorlie while Fisher visited all the States in turn to make himself widely known preparatory to giving Labor's policy speech. He delivered this at Gympie on 30th March, 1909. In a number of ways it conflicted with that of Deakin's party, which had given Labor conditional support until the Christmas recess. Fisher advocated a land tax, threatened the nationalisation of monopolies, and refused to give Britain a Dreadnought battleship, preferring to spend the money on building Australian ships. Frazer considered this speech to be the fulfilment of what he had been working towards since he had first begun to intrigue in caucus. As he saw it, before November 1908 Labor had let another party make policy, timetables and tactics, resting content with a few bones of legislation from the master's table. But now Fisher had accepted the full responsibilities and risks for Labor going it alone. There was nothing new in the specific items of policy, yet Frazer felt for the first time that his party was showing itself to be ready and desirous to lead the destinies of the whole country. He responded by calling the speech an expression of 'the true Australian policy'.[476] The enormous coverage given to it by the press showed that the message had been understood, even if commentators then and later were surprised by the lack

Part Four

of any revolutionary message.

The anti-Labor parties in the Federal Parliament were not in agreement that Fisher should lead Australia into the sort of noble and democratic future envisaged by such men as Frazer. At the end of 1908, the conservatives had already tried to detach Deakin from Labor. Fisher's speech was to be instrumental in doing the work for them. In April and May 1909, the three groups under Deakin, Cook and Forrest effected a fusion. They used their majority to eject Fisher ignominiously from office at the first opportunity. Deakin became prime minister again at the beginning of June, having behind him not only his own supporters but also those who had opposed him in a most partisan manner for years.

The Labor Party, now in opposition, resolved on destructive tactics to make it as difficult as possible for the Fusion Ministry to do parliamentary business and pass legislation. Fisher saw clearly how he could make use of Frazer's talents, and he used the caucus meeting of 30th June to appoint him as one of two deputy whips. Frazer leapt at the opportunity and took over the work almost completely from Watkins. He seized on the idea of dividing the Labor members into four committees so that each of them could specialise in one area of opposition and obstruction. He took a leading part in attacking anything to do with the Treasury, where he could offend Sir John Forrest without restraint or remorse. And he revelled in organising his colleagues in each and every debate as to what to do and say, and when to do it. A conservative journalist in 1910 described him as having 'wonderful powers as a tactician, both in caucus and in the House'.[477] The same reporter had earlier written that

Frazer was 'the god in the machine of Labor intrigue. He makes the bomb, he chooses the thrower, and is far away when it's thrown'. Thus he had 'made himself into a power in the party, and a power to be feared'.[478]

With no need to conceal any of his activities, Frazer now led openly, not with hidden manipulation as with the cave. He used his 'great capacity for continuous work' in preparing his party for the debates.[479] He was so successful that for the first time he made headlines in the liberal press, which hastened to inform its readers about this newly risen star in the Labor ranks. The *Melbourne Punch* was one of the first, praising his exceptional tactical abilities and commenting that 'his brain is like lightning' when summing up a political situation. The journalist wrote that Fisher relied heavily upon his advice, and to such an extent that all the tactical coups of the session 'have been worked by Mr Frazer'.[480]

He set an example in his own speeches. As a matter of course he attacked at length everything the Fusion Government was trying to do. It was his manner of speaking, 'didactic and masterful', rather than the content, which gave him a formidable reputation.[481] Of Deakin, a favourite target, he sneered that he was,

> a political fizgig, one of those persons who will sell their friends, and those most closely associated with them, in order to aggrandize themselves and secure their own position.[482]

It was less the insult than the sarcastic tone of the delivery which caused the political wounds. And he picked on the weak points in the personal fate of Samuel Mauger, the reformer of working conditions who had followed Deakin into Fusion and who was now sitting on the same benches as George Fairbairn, the President of the Employers' Federation of Victoria. Frazer drawled that,

> he is in a most unhappy position. He is chairman, or secretary, of the Anti-Sweating League of Victoria, and yet is associated with the biggest sweaters in Australia.[483]

It was true enough, and the truth was enough to hurt.

This destructive opposition, however successful from its own point of view, did not manage to prevent the Fusion Government from passing a considerable amount of useful legislation, including plans for military and naval defence, an agreement to regulate the future finances between the Commonwealth and the States, the High Commissioner Act, and a number of others. The Government rested on its record in the election campaign which began in February 1910, and promised further matters of national interest, such as the transcontinental railway, the takeover of the Northern Territory, and the setting up of an Interstate Commission to regulate industrial relationships. This was far from enough for Labor. Fisher in essentials repeated his Gympie speech, and his policy was condemned in horror by the Fusion Party as being foully socialistic and wishing only by the nasty means of unification to destroy political freedom in Australia and ruin the individuality of the State governments. But it was fully in line with Frazer's long-expressed desire for Labor to go it alone at all costs. The results of the elections would show if his initiatives and intrigues on behalf of his cave had been really in the interests of his party.

These elections were delayed as long as constitutionally possible by Deakin's cabinet, so that the country might have the maximum time to grow used to his government and its policies. The announcement was finally made that they were to be held on 13th April, 1910. Frazer and the Labor Party had become so popular on the goldfields that it was dangerous to oppose them. John Thornett was persuaded to stand as candidate for the Fusion, or Liberal Party as it came to be known. His first meeting was rowdy from the start, turned threatening, and when he tried to defend himself with his water bottle, he was bashed.[484] For some time it was thought he would die, and he made his will on his hospital bed. Neither he nor any other Liberal took a further part in the campaign in Kalgoorlie. Sir John Forrest tried to stir up support for Thornett by writing letters to possible friends, but everybody knew it was a waste of time.[485]

As he was effectively without opposition, Frazer's campaign could not set Kalgoorlie alight. He never deviated from the party line of attacking Deakin for his perfidy and his party for its hopeless conservatism, which in his list notes for his speeches he called 'the dead hand' over Australia.[486] He castigated the Liberals for abandoning New Protection, for their financial agreement with the States, and above all for their miserable characters in joining with their opponents only from a greed for power. He praised Labor's policies, especially the land tax, and the intention to change the constitution by referendum to put the federal government in a

Part Four

position to control industrial relations and monopolies throughout the country. But, as in 1906, the only meetings which provided some excitement were when, late in March, he went to the Swan electorate to give support to O'Loghlen against Forrest.

In the polling, Frazer won 11,162 votes to 2,550 for Thornett, who had recovered but who had gone into hiding. Frazer won 3,447 more votes than in 1906 despite a drop of 6,281 in the rolls. He was the only man in the whole of Australia to poll more than fifty per cent of the registered electors, thereby confirming Kalgoorlie as the safest of all the seats. His victory was part of a great triumph for Labor. Frazer's opinion was that the liberal groups in Fusion had received the quittance for sinking their principles and joining each other with such indecent haste only out of fear and dislike of seeing Labor in office, and a lust for power in themselves. And indeed, Deakin's Protectionists lost eleven per cent of their vote of 1906 in Victoria, and the former anti-Socialists seventeen per cent in New South Wales. In only one electorate in the whole of Australia, Perth, did the anti-Labor candidate make significant gains.[487] In sixty-eight electorates Labor improved its showing, with increased returns of up to thirty per cent of the vote. The party won all eighteen Senate seats, to number twenty-three to twelve with one conservative independent, and forty-two to thirty in the House of Representatives, with three independents, two of whom leaned to Labor. The celebrations on the goldfields were wet and lasted so long that Frazer barely made the caucus meeting in Melbourne which was to choose the ministers for Fisher's new cabinet. He took the last available ship, and had to charter a speedy boat in Port Phillip to get himself more or less on time to Parliament House.[488]

Chapter IV

'More importance attaches to the speech of one associated with the Ministry.'

The caucus meeting which Frazer so nearly missed was held on 29th April, 1910, and was of great importance to him. He had told Crouch that if he were not selected for cabinet he would leave politics, adding that he would do the same if he were not prime minister within ten years.[489] Fifty-eight out of the sixty-five Labor parliamentarians were present. Three senators and six MHRs were to be chosen to join Fisher in his ministry. Senators McGregor, Pearce, and Findley were elected on the first ballot, as were the Representatives Hughes, Batchelor and Tudor. Mahon of Coolgardie had one vote too few. For the second ballot, Frazer's political ally, Josiah Thomas, organised a ticket for both of them and King O'Malley, whereas Mahon made little or no attempt to win more support.[490] Frazer scraped home as the last minister to be elected, two votes ahead of the next man. He had hoped for a full portfolio. With his narrow slide into office he could have no objections when Fisher appointed him to be only an honorary minister.

Frazer's contribution to cabinet was to give enthusiastic support to every measure proposed by the party leaders. He was not an unthinking yes-man in the discussions, for he invariably pressed for the most radical interpretation of every reform. But he always made his arguments openly and never led any intrigue to win waverers on to his side. The effect was that Fisher could rely upon his vote like a rubber stamp. Frazer had more difficulty when Hughes was acting prime minister during Fisher's official trips to South Africa in 1910 and London in 1911. Hughes was impatient with open discussions and saw other opinions as resistance to be squashed. Frazer grumbled about this in a letter to Fisher, while admitting that the second experience had been better than the first.[491] Yet he never made or organised opposition of any kind against Hughes' form of leadership and maintained his position of reliable loyalty despite what he saw as prickly provocation.

Such an attitude was common to cabinet and the Labor backbenchers. The opportunity had been given by the electors, and the Fisher Government was able to pass into law almost its entire electoral programme and also to press on with progressive administration. There were very many measures both in the interests of the workers and of the whole country. The Conciliation and Arbitration Act was widened in its scope, and preference to unionists in government employment was effected by executive order. A land tax was instituted with the intention of bursting up the big estates and thus providing for more closer settlement. Australian banknotes replaced the rickety system of thirty-eight different note issues in the States, and the Commonwealth Bank was established. The transcontinental railway was begun, and the Northern Territory taken over from South

Australia to hasten its development. Defence measures were enthusiastically pressed on with. The plans for Canberra were finalised until O'Malley started to interfere with them. A baby bonus of £5 was paid from 1912. In the three years of office, there was only one great reverse. Two referenda to give the Commonwealth Government power to deal with trusts, monopolies and working conditions throughout Australia were rejected in April 1911. Apart from this setback, all the Labor Party members were able to look with pride upon the record of progressive and dynamic legislation and administration, although it was, of course, in almost everything viewed with horror and attacked by the Liberal opposition.

Frazer was delighted with the achievement of the ministry and his party, and proud to have his say in the making and timing of policy. As a junior member of cabinet, he was determined to do everything he could to be a credit to his colleagues. It was a great advantage to him that he was by far the youngest of them and had no portfolio of his own. He was not under pressure to be an immediate success in the unfamiliar work of administration, but was in the position to learn the best methods and then turn them into good effect when the time came for him to have a ministry of his own. Of great help was Fisher's attitude towards him. Fisher was no more a jealous man than he was an envious one. He knew well of the ambition of the younger man, but his entire political being was for the good of the Labor movement, both in the present which he was privileged to lead, and for the future whatever it might bring. He also realised fully the advantages of having Frazer on his side rather than as a disgruntled accuser. Completely supported by

Pearce, he prepared Frazer for high office and responsibility, possibly even for the highest office itself, a man of the future who could later lead the movement to further action and achievement. Frazer therefore had the best possible teachers. He was expected to work in close contact with Pearce at defence and represent him in the lower House, and also to assist Fisher in routine treasury work. In between he stood in for O'Malley at home affairs and Batchelor at external affairs when they made visits to their electorates in Tasmania and South Australia.

Pearce was indeed a splendid example for him. His later secretary, Peter Heydon, has left an account of his working style.[492] Pearce was prompt and efficient in disposing of ministerial business. He was disciplined in dividing his time between deputations, colleagues and advisers, yet left enough time for relaxation. From both Pearce and Fisher, Frazer learnt to seek and trust the advice of experts, to delegate responsibility, and also to be formally correct but pleasant in his attitudes to the permanent officials as well as to all who worked in the department. As a consequence of making himself into the Patroclus of his two powerful friends, Frazer began to relax his contacts to those radical members whom he had worked closely with in his former cave. In particular he broke his political friendship with O'Malley, who was detested by Fisher and whose incompetent administration did not redound to the glory of the ministry.[493]

Frazer's main public responsibility was to answer, on Pearce's behalf, questions on defence in the House of Representatives. He fulfilled his duties competently. He consulted Pearce regularly, was not obtrusive and handled the business in the House well. He was efficient in lesser matters, as with the organisation of the complimentary luncheon for Fisher before his departure in October 1910 to attend the opening of the Parliament of the South African Union.[494] Because he gave satisfaction, Fisher appointed him to be acting treasurer in his absence. Frazer enjoyed greatly the increased responsibility. As with defence, he handled the routine business efficiently. Whenever important decisions were to be made, he sought the authority of the acting Prime Minister, Hughes. He also showed good nerves with critical presswork, as when he was able to dispel a rumour that a gang of forgers were about to start counterfeiting the new Australian banknotes.[495]

After this term of standing in for Fisher, Frazer visited Kalgoorlie for the first time since the elections. He was given a civic reception and he showed how responsibility had changed him from the fighting Charlie of earlier years. Addressing now the dignitaries rather than the miners, he told them that he would,

> endeavour to make a serious speech, realising that more importance attaches to the speech of one associated with the Ministry than would attach to a member of Parliament simply.[496]

But all that came was praise for the 1910 record of the Government, together with an insider hint that the Northern Territory would soon be taken over by the Commonwealth from South Australia.

The employers of Kalgoorlie were impressed by his new maturity. For years there had been much unrest between the men who cut wood to fuel the mining

Part Four

industry and the owners who used their workers' poor knowledge of English to pay them miserable wages. The issue came to a full-scale strike during Frazer's visit. One of the leading employers was his opponent in Parliament, the Liberal MHR for Fremantle, W. N. Hedges. He was instrumental in asking Frazer, as a man of prestige, to mediate. Frazer was in the difficult position of being a known radical who would be accused of favouritism if he seemed to be on the side of the workers and as a traitor to his principles should he seem to be against them. His method was to listen to both points of view and thereby win the confidence of both sides. For eight days he refereed with such success that a happy compromise could be found, and 'every credit is due to him for the tactful way in which he has brought about the settlement'.[497]

When he returned to Melbourne, Frazer once again served efficiently as acting treasurer when Fisher left Australia in April 1911 to attend George V's Coronation in London and the attendant Imperial Conference. His self-confidence in taking responsibility for, and in managing, Commonwealth finances was shown in two letters he sent to reach Fisher during his return voyage at Colombo. In the second, the close and affectionate relationship between the two men was shown.[498] Addressing his chief as 'My dear Andrew', he gave an informal summary of Australia's finances, a mild warning of future problems, together with the comment that cabinet had been getting along better with Hughes than during Fisher's first trip abroad. It was clearly only a matter of time until Fisher promoted his protégé to a full portfolio. This event came sooner than expected.

The Triumph and the Tragedy

Batchelor died on a walking tour on 8th October, 1911. Frazer and Pearce represented the government at his funeral. Frazer had hoped that Fisher would make him treasurer, 'as he understood' the job.[499] Fisher had no intention of abandoning his personal control of the finances of his government. He gave Batchelor's portfolio to Josiah Thomas, and Frazer became Thomas's successor as postmaster-general. The appointment was well received in high places. The Governor-General, Lord Denman, wrote that Frazer 'impresses me as a shrewd and capable man'.[500]

Being in control of the post office was an ideal way for Frazer to show his worth. Since his entry into Parliament he had interested himself vitally in the extension and improvement of all the services under the control of the department, and not only in his own electorate where efficient communications were so necessary. He had been constantly critical of the methods of his predecessors, so now he had the chance to show that he could do better. A difficult job faced him, involving much hard work and routine administration. There had been nine PMGs in the eleven years since Federation, and this had not contributed to an efficient departmental order. There was never enough money for needed public works and postal developments, although the minister was under constant pressure from all MPs to provide more efficient services in their electorates. Frazer had no doubts of his ability to be a success. By showing progressive Labor dynamism in his administration, he expected to become a credit to himself and thus make a significant contribution to the impressive record of the government and the party. After only two weeks of fact-finding, he announced in

Parliament that he would have the telephone and telegraph systems in the whole country up to date within three years.[501]

The lessons he had learnt from Fisher and Pearce helped him in this grand ambition. He worked hard to gain the respect of his officials, whom he treated with consideration and friendliness. He certainly insisted on making important decisions himself, but he listened carefully to the advice given to him and was always prepared to follow it. He realised that the affairs of the department were too manifold for him to have control of details, so his policy was to delegate as much responsibility as possible to his deputies in each State. In his own words, he instructed them,

> to undertake the construction of all approved telephone lines with the utmost expedition. I have also given them authority to appeal to local municipal councils, trade unions, and any other suitable authority in order to obtain the labour necessary to permit the speedy construction of approved works.[502]

The rapid extension of services was evidence of the success of such delegation.

Nevertheless, Frazer at once met trouble from the opposition. The Report of the Royal Commission on Postal Services had been made public in 1910, and the Liberals were demanding that all the 175 recommendations should be adopted. Most of these on organisation, finance and discipline were generally seen to be reasonable, and were accepted by successive administrations. But one in particular was highly controversial. It recommended that the postmaster-general's responsibilities should be taken over and shared by a three-man board of control of which the PMG himself would be *ex officio* a member. The intention was to avoid the delays and inefficiency which necessarily accompanied the rapid changeover of PMGs. Frazer refused to surrender any of his authority in such a way. To do so, he felt, would be to put shackles on his zeal for expansion. Such resistance ensured that the proposal became an official part of Liberal policy. It was used as a weapon against him by any politician who wanted a quicker extension of postal works in his own electorate.

With his resolve to bear the full responsibility, Frazer put himself under much pressure to deliver. In extending and improving postal services throughout Australia he followed the work of his predecessors of all parties. But the good seasons which accompanied the fortunate Labor Government made it possible to increase expenditure in all areas. With the energy of youth and ambition, Frazer set about doing everything he could to give 'very great and additional facilities' in the bush, and 'a better set of conditions' in the cities.[503] The increase of capital investment was prodigious. Whereas £32,730 had been spent on new works in 1901-1902 and £383,000 in 1908-1909, no less than £907,000 was budgeted for 1911-1912, the bulk of it in Frazer's term of office.

This financial overflow brought about Frazer's speedy approval of the construction of new public facilities. From 1909 until May 1912 there had been 302 new miles of telegraph lines. By the end of the year over 8,000 miles had been authorised or constructed. It was the same with post offices.[504] More than one thousand were opened in the same period, with a building surge during Frazer's term. In 1913 he could point to 98,000 new miles of telephone connections, seventy per cent of them in new areas.[505] He was also swift to understand the need for completely new services, as when he introduced a bill in Parliament to authorise the laying of a cable between Australia and New Zealand.[506]

With so much money available, Frazer was not obsessed with any need to economise at the cost of efficient service. His first ministerial statement declared his intention of giving particular consideration to the outback, which was represented by himself and twelve other Labor MHRs.[507] The need to make a profit was not his foremost consideration. Whereas the policy of Liberal governments had been for the locals to make good any losses, Frazer, while always keeping 'an eye on legitimate expenditure ... never worried very considerably about making the Postal Department a paying proposition'.[508] His predecessor, Thomas, had given the remote areas a subsidy of twenty-five per cent. Frazer increased it to fifty per cent, and was especially generous with making up for losses in telephone services. This caused many anguished cries for economy from the Liberal Party, which had no MHRs at all in the most distant parts of Australia and whose members were dominated by the idea that postal services had to pay for themselves.

The Liberals also found much to complain about in Frazer's policies concerning the working conditions and pay in the postal services. He insisted on day rather than contract labour for all his public works. He was proud of approving pay increases to a total of £260,000 a year, with the conditions being the same in all States. He used the example of telegraphists to show how enlightened he and his party were. The fortunate recipients enjoyed a six and a half hour day, a three weeks' annual holiday, full pay rates (at £193 a year) when they were sick, and six months' paid holiday after twenty years' service.[509]

There was one matter in which Frazer put his completely personal stamp on his administration. The penny post was at last to be introduced. His predecessor, Thomas, had offered a prize for the best stamp design. Masses of entries for the competition came in from all over the world, and it was Frazer's business to make the choice. For years he had been against the King's head as not being a valid symbol of Australia,[510] and in 1912 he saw no reason to agree with the Liberal cry that it was the only appropriate way to show a truly imperialist loyalty. Frazer rejected all the designs. His own idea was the kangaroo on a White Australia which was to become the longest-serving and perhaps the most famous Australian stamp series ever. With the help of the Victorian Artists' Society and especially Blamire Young, the design was made according to his satisfaction, and issued first on 2nd January, 1913. The opposition was appalled. The *Melbourne Argus* mocked Frazer's comment that the stamp was 'simple, yet expressive', commenting that, 'It is to be feared that that phrase may adequately describe the language which all Australians who have any artistic sense will use when they catch sight of the design.'[511]

Such pinpricking left Frazer completely unmoved, and he was adept at finding ways to take the force out of serious opposition. In the matter of wireless stations he showed a capacity for making good and intelligent executive decisions to find a way round obstruction. He had inherited from Thomas the need to construct radio telegraph stations round the coast of Australia.[512] Thomas had arranged for Telefunken to do the work, but the Marconi Company claimed that their patent rights were being infringed. Telefunken suspended negotiations with the Labor Government until the court case had reached a decision, and Thomas had accepted that there would be a long delay. Frazer took office and showed no patience with the warring concerns. He conferred with the newly appointed departmental engineer, J. G. Balsillie, with the result that Balsillie invented and claimed a patent for a third system of radio telegraphy. Frazer authorised it for the Commonwealth installations and kept the building sites closed on security grounds from both Telefunken and Marconi. These agreed to sink their differences and sue the Commonwealth together in order to win the right to investigate the constructions to find out whether Balsillie had stolen ideas from their own patents. W. H. Irvine of the Liberal Party held a brief for Marconi. The Commonwealth first won the case, but on appeal the verdict was reversed. The two companies visited the sites, but could discover no patent infringements. In the meantime Frazer's nineteen stations had advanced almost to completion undisturbed by any delaying tactics that Marconi or Telefunken might have made had they had earlier access.

In all this strenuous work of administration, Frazer never lost his feeling for the interesting act to keep himself in the public eye. He was the first minister to make a flight in an aeroplane. As passenger, he flew for ten minutes at a height of 600 feet at 55 mph over the

Penrith Plains, with his wife going on the second trip.[513] He posed for the press when important post offices or telegraph lines were to be built. He was present, as of right, at the turning of the first sod at the western end of the transcontinental railway, even if the main honours were done by Fisher.[514] The construction gangs took this splendid opportunity to strike for more pay. It was Frazer's job to postpone the problem. He did not solve it, for he followed Fisher back to attend the ceremony of laying the foundation stone at Canberra in March 1913.

All his work for the ministry did not cause Frazer to lose contact with his own electorate. Even at a distance he kept in close touch by post and telephone, and it seemed as if Kalgoorlie would return him for ever. But he certainly lost his closeness to many of the rank and file of the parliamentary party. He did help Fisher by speaking with him during the Queensland State election campaign in 1912, and later he did the same in Tasmania,[515] but he hardly took any initiative in caucus. The quittance came in the meeting of 8th July, 1913, to elect eight members to the party executive. Frazer won only six votes, well behind the eighth man with twenty-two.[516] He was not unduly worried. He had committed himself to Fisher and the leaders of the party, and he would stand or fall by relying on their work together and collective responsibility.

And he had good reason to be proud of his administration of the postal department. His work was subjected to its severest test at the end of the 1912 session of Parliament, when he was attacked for twenty-six hours by Liberals eager to find fault with him. Little was said which deserved the name of constructive criticism. Agar

Wynne, who was to be his successor as PMG, made the absurd suggestion, which he forgot when he was in office, that costs should be reduced by having telephone lines run along hedges rather than on expensive high poles.[517] The Tasmanian McWilliams pontificated that Frazer had 'utterly failed' to improve outback telephone connections. Frazer had the easy counter that he had personally authorised 45,000 miles of them. W. M. Greene could find no greater fault than that Frazer had not constructed three post offices in his electorate where the revenue would be more than £200 a year. In the main, the Liberals kept harping on matters of party policy such as the old demand for a three-man board, and on their insistence that money should be saved while requiring more of it to be spent. Nothing was said which could destroy Frazer's growing reputation as an active and conscientious administrator, and part of the reforming and dynamic Labor Government. He therefore faced the general elections of 31st May, 1913, full of confidence that both he and his party would be confirmed in office.

Chapter V

'I want to go on a trip.'

By the time of the campaign for the general elections, Frazer's political advance seemed to be one of remarkable and swift success and no setbacks. Yet there was a change in him. He had been a member of Tattersall's in Melbourne for years, but towards the end of his term of office he was beginning to visit the club up to three times a week. He regularly played poker, but his opponents were more sophisticated than those of the railway line, and as he was beginning to drink while playing, he started to lose money heavily. According to Crouch, he 'boozed and gambled hard', and as a result 'went to pieces', his life 'spoilt by too quick success and too much leisure'.[518]

This explanation was too simple. Frazer's decline was not due to losing his head because of the elevated circles in which he now moved. It was the subconscious reaction to enormous psychological pressures which were making him regress to the behaviour of his younger years. The worst possible career-smasher had been stealing up on him for over two years. In January 1911 he had for the first time been incapacitated by illness.[519] During the next two years he kept on coming down with heavy colds and

Part Four

influenza. In Perth in April 1913 he had a particularly bad attack which delayed his return to Kalgoorlie for three days. The reason was always given that he had been working too hard. In fact, his health was being undermined and his body was losing its powers of resistance. His increasing weakness from January 1911 might well have been the result of an inborn susceptibility to disease. But if the story about his war service in 1900 is true his slow decline may equally well have been caused by the long-term effects of his wounds.

On 16th April, still not fully fit, he opened his campaign with a speech at Boulder.[520] This caused little excitement. Labor had passed almost all of the programme of 1910 into law, and the leaders had made few plans as to what to do next. Their main effort was to try to secure a majority for the referenda which had been rejected in 1911, but which were again to be submitted to the people at the same time as the election. Frazer spoke intensely on the need for their acceptance, but the theme was not enough for a full performance. He filled up the time with an account of his own accomplishments as postmaster-general. His hearers listened politely, for his popularity was undiminished. The electorate had become even safer for Labor, because in a redistribution it had gained most of the neighbouring electorate of Coolgardie. Kalgoorlie now comprised well over three-quarters of Western Australia, and was by far the biggest democratic electorate in the world. It was recognised that there was no chance of Labor losing it, and nobody wanted to stand for the Liberal Party and risk being hurt as Thornett had been in 1910. Frazer was returned unopposed. He began to make a tour of the smaller towns north-east of

Kalgoorlie to speak on behalf of the Labor Senate candidates and the referenda. His plan was then to visit the centres of the distant north which were new to the electorate. But on 23rd April sickness caught up with him again. He was admitted to Leonora Hospital with a relapse of influenza and pneumonia complications.[521] It was a week before he could move, and another three weeks before he seemed to have recovered. Only in the last days of May did he speak three times for Mahon in the new Dampier electorate, and three times in his own.

This final effort was scarcely necessary, since Kalgoorlie again showed itself to be the safest seat in Australia. An average of eighty-three per cent of formal votes went to the Labor Senate candidates; Pearce topped the poll with 17,548 votes, while the leading Liberal won only 3,994. The referenda were approved by even greater margins of nearly ninety per cent. This enormous majority ensured that Western Australia as a whole voted for the referenda, since otherwise only Fremantle narrowly supported them. But the overall results in Australia were to reject the referenda and to put Labor out of office. The Liberals won thirty-eight seats to thirty-seven, although they had only seven seats to twenty-nine in the Senate. Fisher resigned on 21st June.

The new Liberal Government under Joseph Cook made no attempt to work with Labor under these difficult parliamentary conditions and try to pass non-contentious legislation. From the first the Liberals confronted their opponents directly by enquiring into and changing whatever administrative policies of Labor could be attacked. One of Cook's first actions was to announce the replacement of Frazer's stamp issue with one bearing the

Part Four

King's head. This executive decision was to trumpet to the world the true imperialist attitude of the Liberals and banish the kangaroo to 'become once more a mere oddity of the woods and plains'.[522] Frazer was greatly annoyed. At Boulder and later in Parliament he showed much umbrage at the destruction of his splendid advertisement for Australia which the royal face was not.[523] And the old idea that the post office should be under the supervision of a three-man board remained a vocal part of official Liberal policy.

The Labor Party resolved on tactics of destructive opposition. Frazer did not know that he was dying slowly and talked about going on a world trip in order to restore his health.[524] His weakening condition made it impossible for him to repeat his activities of 1909 against the Government Party, and he made ever fewer contributions to the organisation of his colleagues. His attacks on the Liberals became rare, although he was still able to wind himself up to rasp at Cook's assistant minister, the conceited ex-Etonian Willie Kelly.

> We have heard his inane laugh before. I understand that a portion of a certain tin-mine in New South Wales was devoted to sending this young man to Oxford to cultivate bad manners and a haw-haw.[525]

But he had ever less energy to fuel the final flickers.

His last speech of importance was in September 1913. The Liberal Attorney-General W. H. Irvine had been on Marconi's payroll against the Commonwealth Government in 1912 and still received a retainer fee of five pounds a year. This affair was topical because of a recent serious scandal in England, where four Liberal ministers had bought Marconi shares cheaply shortly before the government announced its intention to surround Britain with a Marconi radio network.[526] Frazer won without difficulty caucus approval to lead a full parliamentary attack on Irvine.[527] He spoke with great heat in his old manner. He asked fiercely whether Irvine could continue to be the chief law adviser in Australia with all his knowledge of Marconi affairs, at the same time as Marconi was suing the Commonwealth. Frazer's authoritative quotes harkened back to the time when he had studied law himself. But Irvine refused to be drawn. He did not treat the matter seriously, and Frazer's motion was lost on party lines.

This was his last significant contribution to parliamentary affairs. His life long, he had always tried to conceal his private feelings. It was the same with his final weakness. He made no complaints, and the press noticed only his general lethargy in the business of attacking the Liberals. The end came quickly. On Friday, 21st November, he spent the whole day in the House. On Saturday he went to the Epsom races, the next morning he felt unwell with a slight cold. To almost everyone's surprise, he was found to be suffering from severe pneumonia in the left lung. He was taken to a private clinic, but at ten o'clock in the morning of Tuesday, 25th November, he died. He was not yet thirty-four years old. Flags flew at half-mast at Parliament House and at the post offices in Melbourne and Kalgoorlie. He was given an impressive funeral, the cortege starting from Parliament House, the pallbearers being Fisher, Pearce and Thomas for the Labor Party, Cook, Forrest and Wynne for the Liberals. He was buried beside his mother in Melbourne. He left only £1,100.[528] Crouch's sisters offered to look after his wife, but she stayed in the hotel, 'Perhaps as well, as in such times as this any strangers are a burden...' Crouch also reported that Pearce saw that she was provided for.

Of all the obituaries, perhaps those of the two federal party leaders were the most pleasingly human. Frazer had been a politician to his fingertips, becoming a master of every kind of intrigue and manipulation possible in the parliamentary process. Cook naturally chose to ignore this and remembered, in all the years they had both had rooms in the White Hart Hotel, only his 'utmost friendship'. And Fisher confirmed that outside his political duties, he 'never spoke an ill word'.[529] His loss to Labor was all the more obvious exactly three years later, when a man of his qualities and abilities was desperately needed by the party to help save it from the process of self-destruction after the conscription referendum of 1916.

PART FIVE

No New Ideas

Percy Coleman and Post-war Labor

"During the last forty years the Labor Party in politics has been the driving force and impulse behind every social advance."

Percy Coleman, 23rd May 1928

Percy Coleman was born on 23rd October 1892 in a working-class area of South Sydney.[530] Both his parents died early, and he was sent to New Zealand. He had to become a ship's boy at thirteen, but the life on board appealed to nothing in his temperament. His empty youth had given him a lasting need for the emotional security which had been denied him, so his desires for a stable existence could not be satisfied by a life at sea which demanded adaptability to unexpected circumstances and the opposite of a staid eight-to-six working day. As soon as he had grown up enough to make his own decisions he abandoned the boats, and became, at sixteen, a junior clerk at the Sydney branch of the Seamen's Union. He had always been extremely conscientious to details, so he found personal satisfaction in the correctness required by the profession, and even more in the praise bestowed on him by his fellow workers for his accuracy and responsible attention to formalities.

In addition, he was able to compensate for his barren childhood in a motherless environment by identifying himself with the trade union and thus with the interests of the other clerks. From the start he won their appreciation for his conscientious work in everything he did on their behalf. He soon gained their trust, and this stimulated him to do ever more for the general welfare.

His good work included the discovery that he was a clear and efficient speaker, and he honed his qualities by meticulous research before he held an oration. He took immense pleasure in receiving the plaudits of enthusiastic audiences, and this encouraged him to take the lead in any form of discussion or debate. As he grew older and more experienced, he pressed himself forward to be the union representative at important conferences, where he invariably spoke according to the wishes of the people who had sent him. He was seen to be so effective in whatever he did that he was made secretary of the United Clerks' Union in New South Wales in 1916 at the age of twenty-three.[531]

All this work and responsibility caused Coleman to join the local branch of the Labor Party, of which he became an absolutely devoted and loyal member. Its policies on behalf of the less privileged people of the world harmonised completely with the subconscious feelings caused by his unhappy youth. He became a constant and acerbic critic of the upper crust and their representatives, and he was totally one-sided in defending everything that Labor had ever done or would ever do. His feelings for the party were fierce and unbreakable, for it was offering him everything which was able to fulfil his deepest needs. He soon made himself into a tireless worker in organisational matters on his home patch.

The respect bestowed upon him by his fellow members, and also by the clerks of his profession, was not enough for Coleman. Because of the deficits in his early years he needed the most widespread recognition, so he suffered during the war from the snubs of people who jeered that he was not fulfilling his duty to his country. He was automatically an anti-conscriptionist, but he volunteered for the Australian Imperial Force in February 1918. He was badly wounded in France, and it took nine months in hospital for him to recover.[532] Such experiences made him into an uncompromising opponent of war in general, and also an implacable defender of the rights of the returned soldiers. After he was able to walk again, his abilities as an orator were made use of, and from July 1919 he was employed by the High Commission in London to speak about the benefits of emigration to Australia. The positive reactions of his audiences went deep into his inner being, and after his honourable discharge in April 1920 he accepted an offer to continue his activities in the United States. He then returned to his homeland, where he went on with his work for as many clerical unions as possible. He celebrated his widespread acceptance by marrying Elsie Prince on 17th December 1921.

Coleman's devotion to the interests of his colleagues in the unions and in the Labor Party had thus been extended by his experiences during the war. He developed ambitions to get into parliament in order to fight on behalf of the returned soldiers and attack the policies of the National Government and its leader W. M. Hughes, that "dangerous political Cerberus".[533] Accordingly, he succeeded in being nominated as the Labor candidate for the new and mainly working-class seat of Reid in the area of his birth for the Federal general elections of December 1922. He won comfortably, and from the first settled happily into the patterns of post-war Labor behaviour. His maiden speech, held early in the first session, showed with great clarity who and what he was.[534] His oration was long but well-delivered, and attacked his National Party opponents with a vigour which was to be one of his hallmarks in the coming years. He was entirely partisan on behalf of Labor, demanding positive reconstruction instead of "increasing armaments", and prophesying that when his party was once again returned to rule Australia as in 1910, its people would "enjoy true national government, true national prosperity, and true national expansion."

Yet it was one thing to speak in the House of Representatives on behalf of his party, and another to take part in its internal matters. Coleman was such a devoted member that from the very first he worked entirely within the established framework of regulations. All his working life he had seen how the decision-making process had to be a co-operative one, and he automatically accepted this for his work in caucus. He was always ready to take the lead in proposing the establishment of a committee on anything whatever and, if necessary, be on it himself. Many of his contributions to caucus discussions concerned his desire for group activity to consider such matters as the proper way to deal with the press, how to administer war service homes, or to ensure the efficient working of the Commonwealth Bank.[535]

The problem with such an attitude to administration or government was that, while it worked well with minor union matters where almost everyone shared the basic tenets, it did not often bring about swift and positive action on issues with which few of the politicians involved had wide experience, and the results were often enough redolent of the old saw that a camel is a horse deigned by a committee. In addition, the Labor leaders outside parliament insisted that the elected members should be under their control and jump as required. This all led to a general absence of independent activity within the House of Representatives. Coleman, as an advocate of correct formalities and procedure, gave no help or encouragement to any process to bring about a positive organisational change.

In addition, he fully accepted the higher authority of the party executive. He was always ready to refer problems great and small to its solemn deliberations, and then give his support to whatever solutions had been arrived at.[536] Thereby he was willing to do more than his fair share of work for any form of collective responsibility which had been delegated, although he was perfectly capable of protesting when the numbers of his co-workers fell below what he felt to be appropriate. The security of the herd mentality and the subconscious pleasures of being accepted also dominated his attitudes to expressing party policy in parliament. He was constantly available to make a speech on any matter required of him, but his orations, however well delivered, were little more than standard remakes of conference decisions, even though he was well able to embarrass or trick up the government.[537] On the rare occasions when he had something original to say, irrespective of what the subject matter was, he carefully secured the agreement of caucus before delivering his opinions, as when he wished to inform the House about the dangers of white lead in paint.[538]

Only once, in fact, during his time in parliament, did

he think of taking an independent stand. In 1926 the National Government desired to hold a referendum "to revolutionise the public borrowing system of the Federal and State governments." Coleman at first wanted to abstain from voting, but such an attitude was anathema to the Labor men outside who insisted on controlling their parliamentary representatives. The State executive demanded that he give in and vote against the bill. Coleman obediently abandoned any sign of individual action, and did what was required of him.[539]

In such a way he showed either that he had not been allowed or that he did not want the young man's privilege of giving fresh impulses to the established generation, even though Labor was in urgent need of being kicked into developing new methods and attitudes. His automatic obedience to the party managers, even though it fulfilled all his needs and gave him strength, was also his greatest weakness. He did indeed win much recognition both from his colleagues and from journalists who had to suffer from the dubious debating techniques of many other representatives, but very little of what he said or did prepared the way for any new course of action. Coleman was widely thought to be a rising Labor star, but his unfriendly tactics of opposition to the government increasingly shrouded the positive qualities which he undoubtedly possessed.

Nevertheless, the fact that Labor politics in the 1920s were not creative did not lead Coleman completely unmoved. The party in parliament was his new haven of security and the main forum for his speeches, but he could well see that it was not enjoying any spectacular success. He made a decision with which he hoped to refine his abilities so that he could have more influence in party counsels, and thus establish a leading position for himself in the future. At the end of 1920s he started to work for a degree in law. Such a fresh course appealed to him greatly, first because of the profession's dependence on formalities, facts and precedents, and also because he felt he would be able to use and sharpen his rhetorical abilities for the good of his party.

At first he was as conscientious in his studies as in all his other activities, but Labor's unexpected victory in the elections of October 1929 slowed his pace. He had hoped to be included in the new ministry, but he was not elected by caucus. The Prime Minister, J. H. Scullin, saw him as a coming man, so as an encouragement for the future he was made Chairman of the Parliamentary Joint Committee of Public Accounts, his main qualification being that he had always attacked the National Government for wasting money. He was later appointed to represent Australia at labour conferences in Europe and England, and also in the Mandates Commission at the League of Nations. Coleman enjoyed intensely the experience of being part of such august assemblies and in speaking to international audiences. He performed his duties to the satisfaction of those who had sent him, and on his return delighted in their appreciation and praise. But it was another performance during his visit which showed better the negative influences which were taking hold of him. He had been instructed in his role as Chairman of the Committee for Public Accounts to prepare a report on Australia House in London and on his country's representation in Europe. He worked immensely hard for six weeks, but his long explanatory speech in Parliament on his return showed that he was anything but positive. He was almost entirely critical of the wastage of money on behalf of the most "pretentious and costly" buildings he had ever seen, and he added that they were in the wrong place as well.[540]

This unhelpful report expressed well his general attitude to administration, and it was typical of the Labor government under Scullin. Its members were so used to opposition that they were not able to take swift and positive decisions which were needed to help Australia recover from the grave consequences of the world depression. The result was pointless bickering and indecision in cabinet and elsewhere, with vacillating politicians waiting to be told what to do by people outside parliament who had not the slightest workable ideas themselves. The constant intrigues caused the party to lose its direction and its purpose, so Scullin was compelled to hold an early election in December 1931. Coleman was viciously attacked by Lang Labor for his refusal to consider new ways to confront the crisis. He did his best, but he was dumped by the voters, as was the government, which won only fourteen seats.

Coleman's reaction was not to make any approaches to Lang Labor which had crushed him, but to increase his activities as a prominent figure in the New South Wales orthodox Labor Party for which, despite his catastrophic defeat, he retained all his deepest feelings and sympathy. He even stood as Lang's opponent for the State elections after the Premier's dismissal by the Governor in 1932. He lost, but this in no way deterred him from his course. He became the president of the anti-Lang organisation, where he showed yet again that he had been little influenced by the need for drastic change. He was, however, able to give more time to his legal studies. He passed all the examinations, and in March 1933 was called to the Bar. Sadly, he started to suffer from heart problems, which were probably a late consequence of his war wounds. His performance on all fronts was swiftly reduced by his poor health. On 25th May 1934 he had an unexpected final seizure and died.[541]

And so the end came early to him, as it had to Charlie Frazer, in both cases after ten years in Federal politics. There was, however, immense differences in the personalities of the two men and in what they had achieved. In this, they reflected the changes between pre-war and post-war Labor. Frazer had been in the vanguard of an active movement for democratic progress, and his ambition and abilities had worked to the advantage both of his party and of himself. Coleman, by contrast, had done almost nothing political on his own initiative, so that he had had little influence on the dreary Labor stumbling through the 1920s. He had shown no desire to do anything outside the limits set for him by small-minded and unbending traditionalists. He thus became no more than one of the politicians who were incapable of learning from defeat and adversity, and who thus failed to bring about a revival of the earlier Labor life-philosophy and attitudes.

PART SIX

Reflection in Writing

Frank Anstey and the Literature
of the Labor Up-and-Down

"Revolution in action and method is the one saving instrumentality, the sole alternative to a long grinding period of absolute slavery."

Anstey: *The Kingdom of Shylock*, Introduction

The Triumph and the Tragedy

The completely different conditions in the Labor Party before and after the war, like everything else in politics, were mirrored in the writings of contemporary participants and observers. As long as Labor was full of self-confidence stemming from its increasing success, so were the newspapers, magazines, essays and books devoted to its hopes and achievements. The series of articles with the title, *The Case for Labour* by W. M. Hughes and the two books by W. G. Spence showed most vividly an unbounded optimism concerning everything that the workers' movement stood for. To read them was to realise why their authors believed that the future first of Australia and then of the entire western world would be completely different from the past, with democracy and social fairness taking the place of the evils of brutal capitalism and class dictatorship.

As soon as the war had started, this flow of positive enthusiasm dried up completely. The new and uncreative content of the local Labor publications during and after the war was well represented by the output of the left-wing Frank Anstey. He had been born in the East London slums in 1865, after the death of his father who had been a docker. His mother left the city, and Anstey had a miserable boyhood in the English countryside. Only a few people managed to escape from such a wretched upbringing, but he was one of them. At the age of eleven he stowed away for Australia, and after jumping ship at Sydney became a bosun's boy for all his teenage years. He married at the age of twenty-two, and landed up in working-class Melbourne. He was able to overcome the unhappy experiences of his early years because he possessed an amazing amount of self-confidence for one so young. This carried him through to manhood without breaking his spirit, and enabled him to become highly literate and an irrepressible fighter for the cause of socialism.

His youth of deprivation and the way he had overcome his disadvantages were to form his character and dominate his working life. He had grown up as one of those who had to suffer under the cruelties of unrestricted capitalism, and nothing could diminish his hatred for the system. He had indeed saved himself from succumbing to the appalling pressure, but most of the people he knew well had not. Wherever he looked he saw worn-out middle-aged figures and the dejected faces of exploited families, all of who had been crushed and defeated so that the men of money would safely float on the sea of human misery. Anstey identified himself with the struggling masses and made it into his life's purpose to fight on behalf of the poor of the world, in the hope of cracking the system and leading towards the revolution.

In this way his socialism was grounded deeply in his own experiences, and it swiftly dominated his personality. He developed into a man of furious and hardly controllable spirit who poured forth his passions at any and every opportunity. It took some time for him to realise that the workers would not rise up as Marx had prophesied, so that the people's revolution was not as pre-ordained as he had believed. In the last years of the nineteenth century he started to accept that the gradualism of the Labor Party was a sensible way to prepare the way for the changes he so desired. He made his way into the Victorian Legislative Assembly in 1902, and then into the House of Representatives in 1910. He was a magnificent orator whose speeches were a massive contrast to the more boring delivery of most of his colleagues. Yet he was so partisan and prejudiced that he had little influence on the men in Parliament, even though the quality of his heartfelt orations could be appreciated and enjoyed by all.

It came as no surprise that in August 1914 Anstey was one of those who instantly opposed the war. He made it his purpose to inform the Australian people about what he saw to be the unquestionable and undivided truth. For months he collected material to condemn the evil warmongers and financiers of every nation for their hellish deeds. The result was a soft-cover book of about one hundred pages, containing a collection of cartoons, quotes and comments. It was published by the left-wing *Labor Call* press in 1915 with the title of *The Kingdom of Shylock*, and it was immediately so popular that an attempt was made by authorities to suppress it.

The content of this compendium showed that the war had made Anstey revert to his earlier beliefs, that only a full revolution could destroy the system he so hated. His attitudes were confirmed by the success of Lenin in Russian in 1917, which caused him to bring out a revised edition in 1921, now entitled, *Money Power*. This booklet, in both its forms, was divided into thirty parts, none of which was more than five pages long. Each part purported to illustrate one aspect of the evil power of international finance, but Anstey's comment in the chapter entitled, *The Clutching Hand*, summarised his whole philosophy. He wrote that the group of greedy money-makers ...

> controls the whole mechanism of exchange, and all undertakings in the field of industry are subject to its will and machinations. It wields an unseen sceptre over thrones and populations, and bloody slaughter is as profitable for its pockets as the most peaceful peculation. No nation can be really free where this financial oligarchy is permitted to hold dominion, and no "democracy" can be aught but a name that does not shake it from its throne.[542]

The rest of the page was given over to a picture of a devastated family and the comment that "war, fathered by greed and hypocrisy, mothered by ignorance and gullibility brings but poverty and misery to the working-class".

The remainder of the booklet hammered home the message of what the "Lords of Lootery" were doing. Anstey carefully collected quotes from serious and distinguished men to support his arguments. He cited William Jennings Bryan who had said in 1906 that:

> The Money Power preys upon the Nation in times of peace, and conspires against it in the hour of its calamity. Conscienceless and compassionless, it enervates its votaries, while it

impoverishes its victims. It can only be overthrown by the awakened conscience of the Nation.

And it was this massive feeling which it was Anstey's purpose to jolt out of the people's lethargy, with his almost endlessly repeated hammer blows concerning the fearful selfishness and immorality of the infinitely greedy rich.

He sought in his publication to improve on this message with a series of splendidly propagandistic cartoons. In one of them, a mourning mother stands at a cross, "To the memory of the brave lads who fell at Gallipoli 1915". At her side stands Mr Fat in his finest clothes, carrying a bag with the script, "Interest on War Loans". With the face of a heartless bird of prey he is made to say: "Poor Soul! Lost your only son at the war, eh? Well, we must all be prepared to make sacrifices. Think of me!" Or, on another page, two of the same sort are standing with huge stomachs, wide grins, laden with enormous money bags, the "spoils of war", and chanting the following ditty:

> Tho' we're far too fat to fight
> We are 'out for blood' all right;
> And we think we've 'done our bit'
> When you come to think of it.
> We have 'charged' and we have won,
> And we're proud of what we've done;
> Never mind a tinker's cuss
> What the country thinks of us!

Part Six

There could be no doubt as to the message which Anstey was so starkly giving to the country. And it can also be read with a certain amount of sardonic humour by those who experienced the financial crisis which started in 2008.

Yet there were problems with Anstey's propaganda and social philosophy. He simplified everything, as if the whole of society was divided into the unbelievably heartless and ugly few and the handsome but relatively brainless many. He naturally had not the slightest idea of what a supposedly socialist revolution, like that in Russia, would do, and he wrote as if the noble workers would immediately be able to bring justice and equality to the world. His utter certainty in the correctness of everything he put down caused his booklet to become monotonous, especially as his short analyses were never thorough and completely one-sided in any case. And his anti-Semitism, although modified in the re-issue of 1921, is hardly pleasing to a later generation.

This expression of Anstey's violent emotions was certainly exceptional, but he was only representing one of the main forces of Labor opinions, which grew the longer the war dragged on. His fury canalised the feelings of many members of the working classes that the government was unable to do anything against price rises and economic imbalance at home, but was slavishly helping profiteers while agreeing to the foulest policies abroad. Why should young men be forced to be sent away to die horribly in foreign lands when the only ones to benefit were those capitalists without conscience who never, under any circumstances, would risk their lives at anything more dangerous than eating too much and becoming Mr Fat?

Despite the intense feelings which inspired his booklet, Anstey lacked completely the positive idealism and political philosophy of the kind so vitally expressed in the pre-war Labor publications. What he was against was abundantly clear, but there was no sound analysis of what could or should be done to change the world and make it a safer and fairer place. Whereas Spence in *Australia's Awakening* had stood for gradualism, Anstey thought that it was enough to focus on the evils, in the conviction that when the workers had been brought to understand the situation they would react accordingly, so that the revolution would automatically bring about justice and peace. *The Kingdom of Shylock* was thus not creative in its content. Anstey had hoped to help in cleansing the world of the parasites of high finance and warmongering, but regrettably he wrote so selectively that he hardly showed more than the drastic change in the attitudes of Labor publications brought about by the war.

Anstey himself would never have paid any attention whatever to such criticism, even if he had listened to it. He was so confident in his ideas and their presentation that nothing could have altered his opinions. In consequence he became a leading figure in that section of the Labor Party which opposed the war in each and every way. As a matter of course the idea of conscription was anathema to him, and he reacted to Hughes' attempts to enforce it with the hatred of a priest forced to sit at a table together with the master of lies. He took an extremely vociferous part in the first referendum campaign, and after the success of the Noes he was one of those who would listen to no argument against throwing his Prime

Part Six

Minister out of the party. His angry denunciations were continued during the second referendum campaign, and in the following years he enjoyed much prestige among the Labor members, even becoming party deputy-leader. Yes his career was to end in disaster. He was made Minister for Health in Scullin's unhappy government at the start of the Great Depression. In this high position he discovered how helpless the politicians were to fight against the collapse of international finance, and he reacted like a punctured tyre until his death in 1940.

Anstey in this way represented both in his publication and in his political work the sudden swing of Labor from pre-war positivism to war-time and post-war disappointment. This sudden swing was even clearer in the books written by visitors from the northern hemisphere in the early years of the century. Before 1914 there was intense curiosity as to what was going on in Australia, because the movement for a full democracy was far ahead of the conditions in Europe, so hidebound by God-given aristocracy. The positive attitudes of the pre-war visitors were best stated by some German academics, who showed in their books how impressed they were by the conditions they had observed and analysed. One of them was Robert Schachner, who became professor of political economy at the University of Jena in July 1908. A few months earlier he had returned from almost two years in Australia, during which time he had researched for a series of three volumes dealing with life on the continent. The first one, published in July 1909, was concerned with politics, economics and culture of every form and kind.[543] The other two detailed all aspects of society and the welfare of the people who lived on the land.

The Triumph and the Tragedy

These three books were the result of diligent research; they were praiseworthy in very many respects, but they were also paradigms of dry and dusty academia. Far more readable was a series of letters he sent home, telling of his own experiences and feelings.[544] In all his works, naturally enough more personally in his letters, he showed his deep and genuine interest in the democratic development represented and headed by the Labor Party. Although he was critical of certain aspects of the system, his opinions could well be summed up in his judgement that in "Australia's socio-political conditions of political and economic duties ... governments care for the well-being of the workforce."[545] His writings demonstrated clearly the conditions which enabled such men as Andrew Fisher and Charlie Frazer to have such momentous careers.

It was completely different when the Great War had put a sudden stop to the positive qualities of Labor. After the party had wrecked itself, the overseas interest in the Labor movement existed no longer. The mostly dull books by European visitors were concerned with other matters than the amazingly advanced form of social democracy which had formerly been found on the continent. There were any number of tourists from abroad who published their experiences, but without exception they either elucidated certain chosen aspects of Australian life in boring detail with the help of dry statistics, or they unburdened themselves of superficial and uninteresting travellers' tales. The Germans were again to the fore, but the title of a 1928 book by one of them, Dr Walter Geisler, revealed how the content was going to be: *Through Australia's Wilderness. Investigative*

Part Six

Travels from Australia's Cultural Centres to the Native Peoples. Geisler indeed tried to personalise his experiences by recording long conversations with locals of every description. One early quote should be enough to dispel any hopes that the reader would be inspired to plough through to the end:

> "Go to Oodnadatta," suggested Professor Woolnough. "The train goes once a fortnight. When you have arrived, I can tell you, you will have also seen enough. The inland is all the same, and it is a dreadful burden to sit day in, day out, on a camel's back without seeing anything except sand dunes covered with Spinifex grass. I have experience in expeditions, and I advise you against them because you do not know the conditions. And it is very exhausting indeed."[546]

The book was fully decorated with such sober titbits, and none of them was concerned with the matters which had so fascinated the academics before the war.

It was no different with Walter Stölting, whose *Australia: the Land of Tomorrow* came out in 1930. His intention was to inform his readers on every interesting aspect of Australian life, but his book could not stand comparison with the works of Robert Schachner. He did no more than graze over matters such as "Australia Today" or "The Fate of Germanness". His tedious accounts were as shallow and as devoid of interest as those of Geisler, even if he mostly managed to avoid the spoken word. His final chapter was indeed entitled, "The Country of the Worker", but it went into no analytic detail, and showed no interest in the politics of the contemporary Labor Party. He was full of such information as that,

> A tram conductor earns more than 475 marks a month, a shoemaker 450, a plumber, longshoreman, bricklayer 550, a baker in Sydney 580, in Melbourne 600 marks – some a little more, others a little less. But no-one under 412 marks, because 412 marks is the lowest lawful amount for an unskilled, unmarried worker in the cities.[547]

But not a word as to how this amazing condition had been achieved, or of what Australian democracy was all about.

Such reflections, indeed, showed only that the continent had been changed by the war. The excitement over the pre-war Labor successes had disappeared, as had the political creativity of men like Charlie Frazer. The end of the careers of Andrew Fisher, W. G. Spence and Frank Tudor were not merely unhappy individual events, they were fully symptomatic of what was happening to the workers' movement. The lives of the Labor men before the war had been full of thrust, achievement and promise for the future. Afterwards, those of Percy Coleman and Frank Anstey were typical – little more than obedience to short-sighted policies, or agreement with outdated theories as to the inevitability and justice of the coming revolution.

PART SEVEN

PHOTOS

How the *Kalgoorlie Sun* saw Frazer's election victory over Kirwan in 1903.

Fisher's second ministry, including Frazer and Tudor. *Left to right (front):* C.E. Frazer, E. Findlay, *(middle):* W. M. Hughes, A. Fisher, G. McGregor, *(back):* J. Thomas, K. O'Malley, G. F. Pearce, E. L. Batchelor, F. G. Tudor.

The official portrait of Frazer for the 1903 election campaign.

The Frazer wedding photograph of 31st August, 1904 (left, Mr and Mrs R. A. Crouch).

Top: The bridge over the Carmel, 1911.
Middle: A typical Ayrshire miner's dwelling.
Bottom: Oakleigh House, East St. Kilda.

East Ayrshire Libraries

Andrew Fisher when he first became Prime Minister.

Australian Archive, ACT CRS A1632/1

Andrew Fisher in 1911 with Robert, Margaret, John, Henry and Peggy.

Australian Archives, ACT CRS A1632/1

Andrew Fisher's one method of relaxation as High Commissioner.

East Ayrshire Libraries

Fraser's design, issued 2nd January, 1913.   The Liberal reply, issued 8th December, 1913.

W. G. Spence

Frank Tudor

TROUBLE IN THE BARNYARD.

For the elections of December 1919 the Labor movement had faith in Ryan, and not in Tudor, to beat Hughes.
(*Labour News* 18th October, 1919)

Frank Anstey

Cartoon of (the Scotsman) Fisher as Prime Minister 1910.

Andrew Fisher at the time of his greatest achievements.

REFERENCES

1 Murdoch, J. *Fortune, Folly, Fate.* Melbourne 2009 I, Section Five, Part Three gives a detailed analysis of this matter.
2 Fitzhardinge, L. F., *William Morris Hughes,* II, Sydney 1979, p. 233.
3 Murdoch, op.cit., II, Preface, makes this point clearly.
4 Some examples: Fitzhardinge: op.ci., I,p.171 that he was dominated by Hughes; A. R. Hoyle: *King O'Malley, The American Bounder,* Melbourne 1981, pp.100-132, that he was financially naive, unimaginative, dour, pedestrian, ignorant, and that he could not add up correctly; G. F. Pearce: *Carpenter to Cabinet,* London 1951, p.69, that of the early Prime Ministers he was "the least equipped for the task"; H. V. Evatt: *Australian Labour Leader,* Sydney 1945, p243, 262, that he was "easily manageable" and "far inferior" to Deakin. The present study regards all such comments (up to 1914) as either highly subjective or nonsense.
5 Turner, I. *Industrial Labour and Politics in Eastern Australia 1900-1921,* Canberra 1965. Chapter One shows the complexity with great clarity. Many modern historians seem to underestimate the strength of idealism in their diligent and detailed factual analyses. The representatives of our less hopeful age readily understand the strivings for laws which have long become integrated in our own political and social system, but tend to discount the often inchoate dreams which accompanied them. As examples, R. Gollan, *Radical and Working Class Politics in Eastern Australia 1850-1910,* Melbourne, 1960, especially p.208; D. J. Murphy, *Labor in Politics,* St Lucia, 1975, especially the introduction (but see pp.54-5); N. B. Nairn, *Civilising Capitalism,* Canberra, 1973. Yet to contemporaries, the widespread and genuine idealism was all new and vivid, full of threatening vigour from the conservative point of view, and humanity from Labor's. Consider H. G. Turner, *The First Decade of the Australian Commonwealth,* Melbourne, 1911, p.252, which gives the assessment of a contemporary who did not base his judgement on archival documents and reports of party meetings. He shows the Labor hopes as they appeared to him, strong, dynamic and binding, if also simplistic, naive, and absurd.
6 Arnot, especially Chapter One, for the background.
7 Malkin, p.6.
8 ibid, p.5.
9 Shepherd, p.295.
10 Shepherd, p.289. Fitzhardinge, op.cit., p.252 tells the story differently. The conservative *Melbourne Argus* mocked a Labor Prime Minister who bought such a mansion. Fisher described the paper as 'inexpressibly mean... a paper without scruples or manners and run by cads.' (*Crouch Memoirs*).

References

[11] *Crouch Memoirs*
[12] Malkin, p.7.
[13] A good example of Fisher's mature style is his introduction to Ambrose Pratt's book on South Africa, written in 1911 after they had visited the Union together for the ceremonies attending the opening of its Parliament.
[14] Shepherd, p.268.
[15] Dougan, p.4.
[16] G. F. Pearce: op.cit., p.69. Examples of such phrases in this portrait are 'Get right up against a man', 'The speculating and the labouring classes', 'The triumphant plutocracy', 'We are all socialists now', 'To the last man and the last shilling', 'The Empire is a family of nations'.
[17] Dougan, p.4.
[18] Malkin, p.8.
[19] Dougan, p.4.
[20] MS of an interview of Andrew Fisher by A. G. Stephens, corrected and initialled by Fisher, 1909 (MLA 1494).
[21] The *Gympie Times*, 6th May 1893.
[22] The *Gympie Truth* 1899, quoted by Marginson p.23
[23] The *Gympie Times* 6th May 1893.
[24] The letters are in the *Fisher Papers*. A selection of them is referred to in Marginson pp.37f and 191.
[25] Marginson, pp42-44.
[26] Spence, p.175.
[27] Gollan, p.145f; Murphy, *Labor in Politics* p.129f.
[28] The *Gympie Times*, 6th May, 1893.
[29] The *Gympie Times* July 1893, quoted by Marginson, p.52.
[30] Murphy, *Labor in Politics*, pp.140-1.
[31] *Fisher Papers* MS 949/344.
[32] The *Gympie Times*, 30th March, 1893.
[33] The *Gympie Times*, 2nd May, 1893.
[34] Spence, p.174.
[35] Murphy, *Labor in Politics*, pp.156, 225.
[36] C. A. Bernays, *Queensland Politics During Sixty Years*, 1859-1919, Brisbane, p.139.
[37] QPD 70: 22-25, May, 1893
[38] Murphy, *Prelude to Power*. P.187. The quote is from Marginson's essay. In full, it reads, defining the 'speculating classes' as 'the systematic swindlers, who promote land booms and mortgage banks, water the capital in prosperous times by multiplying it on paper by two or three, call it prosperity then rob the poor to pay interest thereon... the commercial men who in this commercial age do things they would revolt from in another

age... the squatters and western landlords who exploit and manipulate the nomad western labourer.'
[39] Shepherd, p.101.
[40] CPD 6:6909, 6th November, 1901.
[41] Marginson, p.77.
[42] The *Gympie Times*, 14th March, 1896; 24th March, 1896.
[43] Marginson, p.119-124.
[44] Murphy, *Labor in Politics*. pp.160-2.
[45] Marginson, pp.106-7.
[46] ibid, p.188.
[47] The *Brisbane Courier* 12th March 1901; 28th March 1901. On his colleagues, 30th March 1901.
[48] CPD 6:6914-5, 6th November, 1901.
[49] Marginson, pp.191-3 gives details of the accidents, and of his marriage.
[50] Robert was born in Edinburgh. The others were all born in Melbourne, Margaret in 1904, Henry in 1906 (named after his mother's father), Andrew in 1908, John in 1910, and James Garven in 1912.
[51] This is mentioned in several sources, e.g. Pearce, p.59.
[52] Weller, p.44 (7th May, 1901), pp.46-7 (20th May, 1901); p.55 (17th July, 1901); p.68 (30th October, 1901).
[53] CPD 3: 3548-9, 8th August, 1901; 7:7415, 19th November, 1901.
[54] CPD 47:130, 17th September, 1908.
[55] CPD 6:6906-17, 6th November, 1901; 8:11136-8, 20th March, 1902.
[56] CPD 9:11646, 10th April, 1902.
[57] Weller, p.96 (27th May, 1903); p.101 (1st July, 1903).
[58] ibid, p.112 (21st October, 1903).
[59] ibid, p.123 (14th April, 1904); p.124 (20th April, 1904); La Nauze, pp.301, 365-6.
[60] *Crouch Memoirs*.
[61] These facts are taken from the *Age*. Availability 3rd May, 1904; unloading 8th May, 1904; hallmarks 12th May, 1904; jam 3rd August, 1904; promotion 13th June, 1904; customs officials 17th June, 1904 and 20th June, 1904 — the three were given a reprimand.
[62] J. Murdoch, *Principle or Expediency? Liberalism in Australian Federal Politics 1901-1917*, London, 1997, Chapters Two and Three give an analysis of Reid's motives and his anti−socialist campaigns.
[63] The *Worker*, 8th April, 1905. Watson made socialistic remarks two months later: 'The Socialism of the Labor Party is this — we look forward to the ideal when collectivism takes the place of competition in this world, when production will be for use, and not for profit.' The *Worker*, 1st July, 1905. See also CPD 31:683, 22nd June, 1906.

References

⁶⁴ Weller, p.482-4 prints Watson's long letter to the members of caucus of 27th July, 1905.
⁶⁵ ibid p.161 (9th August, 1905).
⁶⁶ The *Brisbane Courier*, 28th November, 1906.
⁶⁷ Weller, p.189 (19th February, 1907).
⁶⁸ Some historians accept Watson's public explanation that he retired because of health reasons, and because his wife did not like his long absences from Sydney in Melbourne. But see J. Murdoch: *The Vision and the Void*, London 1999, Part One, for the political reasons.
⁶⁹ The *Age*, 24th October 1907.
⁷⁰ Turner, p.117.
⁷¹ Fisher to A. G. Stephens 30th November, 1908 (ML).
⁷² CPD 47:129, 17th September, 1908.
⁷³ Weller, p.202 (30th October 1907). Fitzhardinge, p.170, wrongly puts the incident of the cup of tea into 1905.
⁷⁴ The *Age*, 31st October 1907.
⁷⁵ The *Age*, 2nd November 1907. The definition reaffirmed the existing policy, but with greater firmness. A. Fisher to J. W. Kirwan, 31st October 1907 (Kirwan Papers ANL).
⁷⁶ CPD 41:6134f, 19th November, 1907.
⁷⁷ CPD 44:9303, 19th March, 1908.
⁷⁸ CPD 44:9020, 13th March, 1908.
⁷⁹ Fisher to Alfred Deakin 24th June, 1908 (Deakin Papers).
⁸⁰ DT 9th September, 1908.
⁸¹ Report of the Fourth Commonwealth Labor Conference in Brisbane, July 1908, p.14. Fisher's often repeated remark that 'We are all Socialists now' was a play on Joseph Chamberlain's 'We are all Imperialists now' of a decade previously.
⁸² Dudley to the Secretary of State for the Colonies 11th November, 1908 (CO 418/61).
⁸³ H. G. Turner: op. cit., p.198 rings true. But see also P. Heydon: *Quiet Decision*, Melbourne, 1965, p.22; DT 14th November, 1908 and Weller, pp.224-5.
⁸⁴ Fisher's speech was reported in great detail by all the dailies on 31st March, 1909. For the Labor development in Australian defence ideas, Meaney, Chapter 6. See also Appendix A(b).
⁸⁵ CPD 51:3100, 7th September, 1909.
⁸⁶ Shepherd, pp.96, 121, 268.
⁸⁷ Weller, p.237 (11th August, 1909), and pp.477-8.
⁸⁸ E. Scott, *Australia During the War*, Sydney, 1936, p.43. For good examples of such Fisher speeches see CPD 49:115f, 27th May, 1909, and 54:6539f, 30th

November, 1909.
[89] For Fisher's attack on Cook, DT 11th February, 1910. The story stuck, and was repeated by Pearce, p.70, as if Cook was indeed an idiot.
[90] Scott: op. cit., p.44.
[91] Shepherd, pp.67, 100, 121, 136, 169-70, 223.
[92] These two quotes come from *Crouch Memoirs*.
[93] Shepherd, p.256.
[94] Turner, Chapter 15, has carefully thought-out criticisms which represent those of the Liberal opposition.
[95] Shepherd, pp.94, 134-5.
[96] Munro Ferguson to the Secretary of State for the Colonies 21st October, 1914 (CO 418/133).
[97] For these measures, Kewley, Chapters 4, 5 and 6.
[98] CPD 66:3322-3, 24th September, 1912.
[99] Gollan: *The Commonwealth Bank*, Chapter 7, summarises the arguments.
[100] Fitzhardinge, p.252.
[101] Shepherd, p.129.
[102] CPD 64:105, 21st June, 1912. See also Murphy, *Prelude to Power*. Chapter 8.
[103] Murdoch, *The Vision and the Void*, Chapters 3 and 4, shows their relationship in detail.
[104] Pearce, p.109. He relates some stories of how O'Malley got on Fisher's nerves. See also p.62.
[105] e.g. Weller, p.299 (14th June, 1912). On p.29 is a discussion of the way Fisher handled caucus.
[106] Shepherd, pp.154-6, 158, 278.
[107] ibid, pp. 133-5, 94-5.
[108] The *Melbourne Punch*, 6th July, 1911.
[109] Shepherd, p.209.
[110] ibid, pp.142, 172. Fisher cannot be said to have had 'a naive pleasure in the trappings of office' as told by Fitzhardinge, p.252.
[111] Shepherd, p.228.
[112] DT 13th June, 1910.
[113] Shepherd, pp.123, 147f. (Letter from Lord Dudley to Fisher, April 1909).
[114] ibid, p.280. (Letter from Lord Denman to Fisher — undated).
[115] Munro Ferguson to the Secretary of State for the Colonies 9th June, 1914 (CO 418/123); 18th November, 1915 (CO 418/134).
[116] ibid, 26th October, 1914 (CO 418/133).
[117] Munro Ferguson to Bonar Law 8th November, 1915 (Novar Papers ANL) Quoted also by Scott: op. cit., p.171-2, and Fitzhardinge, Vol. II, p.47.
[118] The following account is taken from Shepherd, p.165f.
[119] DT 14th August, 1911.

References

[120] Meaney, Chapter 7 gives an excellent account of Fisher and Pearce at the Conference.
[121] ibid, p.223.
[122] DT 21st June, 1911.
[123] Press cuttings, East Ayrshire libraries, Kilmarnock.
[124] ibid.
[125] The *Melbourne Punch*, 6th May, 1910, p.623; 26th May, 1910, p.719; 27th July, 1910, p.119.
[126] CPD 49:45, 26th May, 1909.
[127] DT 25th July, 1911; Meaney, pp.226-7.
[128] Denman to the Secretary of State for the Colonies 18th September, 1911 (CO 418/89).
[129] DT 14th August, 1911.
[130] Denman to the Secretary of State for the Colonies 1st April, 1913 (CO 418/110). For Fisher's speech: DT, 1st April, 1913.
[131] e.g. CPD 73:73f, 16th April, 1914.
[132] DT 17th March, 1914.
[133] DT 1st August, 1914; CPD 75:175, 14th October, 1914. For Cook, NSWPD 100:1456, 18th October, 1899.
[134] e.g. DT 31st January, 1911 (a speech to the Australian Natives Association).
[135] Munro Ferguson to the Secretary of State for the Colonies 9th October, 1914 (CO 418/123). Weller pp.376-7 for the election of Ministers.
[136] CPD 76:2135, 17th December, 1914.
[137] Munro Ferguson to the Secretary of State for the Colonies 13th May, 1915 (CO 418/133); CPD76:2135, 17th December, 1914. See also Scott, p.485f.
[138] Fisher: CPD 75:144, 14th October, 1914; Anstey: ibid p.146f. This furious speech, even in the dry pages of Hansard, still has the power to prickle the reader.
[139] Munro Ferguson to the Secretary of State for the Colonies 21st October, 1914 (CO 418/133).
[140] DT 24th December, 1914.
[141] Hughes to Fisher 11th January, 1915 (Fisher Papers). Quoted in Fitzhardinge, Vol. II, p.39.
[142] Munro Ferguson to Bonar Law 8th November, 1915 (Novar Papers). The letter goes on: 'In fact no man's constitution could stand up to the strain put on an Australian Prime Minister.' Shepherd, p.289, wrote that much of his time was taken up with bringing papers to Fisher's mansion.
[143] Pearce: op. cit., pp.126-7.
[144] DT 25th September, 1915. See also Scott, op. cit., pp.291f, 342.
[145] Munro Ferguson to the Secretary of State for the Colonies 13th May, 1915

(CO 418/133).
[146] CPD 76:2369f 15th April, 1915.
[147] Munro Ferguson to the Secretary of State for the Colonies 11th October, 1915 (CO 418/133).
[148] Pearce, pp. 126-7.
[149] DT 27th October, 1915. Weller pp. 426-7 gives the details, and the date strangely as 30th October, 1915.
[150] Fitzhardinge, Vol. II, pp.74, 91-3. Cook had to suffer the same fate in 1918-1919, but at least Hughes had recommended him beforehand for a G.C.M.G., which he loved.
[151] W. H. Demaine to Fisher 25th December, 1915. There are many other letters sent about this time in the Fisher Papers, expressing dislike of Hughes. This one and others are referred to in Fitzhardinge, op. cit., 234; and Weller p.34.
[152] Heydon, op. cit., pp. 105, 24.
[153] Shepherd, p.381.
[154] SMH, 8th August, 1921, 10th August, 1921. For A. Gardiner's explanation of the executive's decision, SMH, 11th August, 1921.
[155] CPD 6:8353, 5th December, 1901.
[156] The dates were provided by Alison Pilger of the Australian National University.
[157] The *Melbourne Punch*, 15th March, 1917.
[158] J. McCalman, *Struggletown, Public and Private Life in Richmond 1900 – 1965*, Melbourne, 1984, pp.7-12. Improvements to the drains and the hovels were first undertaken at the end of the century. This splendid book gives a most vivid picture of Richmond and its people. The author also wrote the article on Tudor for the *ADB*.
[159] ibid., p.72f. The description of the school system is of the early years of this century. It is made clear that it is applicable to late Victorian times.
[160] The *Age*, 11th January, 1922.
[161] The *Melbourne Punch*, 15th March, 1917.
[162] CPD 88:11888, 22nd August, 1919.
[163] The *Melbourne Punch*, 15th March, 1917.
[164] ibid. and CPD 6:8352-3, 5th December, 1901.
[165] CPD 88:11185, 22nd August, 1919. He had to go as an immigrant, although because of his engagement he had no intention of remaining long. Ibid., p.11888.
[166] CPD 30:6029, 5th December, 1905.
[167] "Weller, op. cit., I, p.159 (7th July, 1905).
[168] CPD 6:8352, 5th December, 1901; the *Age*, 11th January, 1922.
[169] CPD 25:764, 9th August, 1905.

References

[170] CPD 13:272, 28th May, 1903; and the *Melbourne Punch* 15th March, 1917.
[171] The children were Ellen Edith, born in 1898; [Frank] Gwynne, in 1899; Susie Elizabeth, in 1900; Llewellyn Christian, who was crippled, in 1904; Bernice May, in 1906; and Wilfred Herbert, who died young, in 1908.
[172] Turner, p.8, details the work of the T. H. C. Tudor did his best to be impartial, but some people in smaller hat factories accused him of favouring Denton. See the letter from Paul Chabert, the *Age*, 15th March, 1901.
[173] CPD 49:1168, 14th July, 1909.
[174] The *Age*, 19th February, 1901.
[175] ibid.
[176] The *Age* 7th March, 1901; 11th March, 1901; 15th March, 1901.
[177] CPD 49:1168, 14th July, 1909.
[178] 'Ted Sullivan' (pseudonym), quoted in McCalman, p.39
[179] CPD 91:469-70, 17th March, 1920.
[180] The *Age*, 11th January, 1922.
[181] *OBU* (One Big Union) *Herald*, 1st February, 1922.
[182] CPD 91:470, 17th March, 1920.
[183] Crouch Memoirs.
[184] Weller, op. cit., I, p.51 (12th June, 1901). The first executive consisted of the leaders in both Houses and the two secretaries.
[185] ibid., p.59 (7th August, 1901); p.93 (10th September, 1902).
[186] ibid., p.86 (4th June, 1902).
[187] CPD 2:1818, 26th June, 1901 and 14:1568, 30th June, 1903 (wages); 21:4253-5, 12th August, 1904 (C and A); 12:1564-5, 2nd September, 1902 (bonuses).
[188] CPD 6:8353, 5th December, 1901 (hat tariff); 13:266f, 28th May, 1903 (hatters).
[189] Crouch Memoirs.
[190] CPD 4:4830-1, 12th September, 1901.
[191] For example, CPD 21:4253-5, 12th August, 1904 for his becoming heated; 22:5290, 6th October, 1904, for his becoming confused.
[192] Munro Ferguson to the Secretary of State for the Colonies, 15th January, 1918 (CO 418/169). The occasion was Tudor's speech on his own Motion of Confidence after Hughes's Government had taken office again after promising not to.
[193] Fitzhardinge, I, p.159f, recounts the process well.
[194] Weller, op. cit., I, p.156 (27th June, 1905).
[195] ibid., p.238 (12th August, 1909); p.247 (27th October, 1909).
[196] CPD 49:1166f, 14th July, 1909.
[197] Weller, op. cit., I, p.256 (29th April, 1910).
[198] Telegram, Tudor to Andrew Fisher, 14th May, 1913 (Fisher Papers ANL).
[199] Tudor to Hugo Wertheim, 12th March, 1911 (Fisher Papers).

[200] CPD 64:801f, 16th July, 1912. The quote is from p.806. Crimping was inducing a seaman to desert so as not to have to pay his wages and then making him fork out a pound to be allowed to enlist on another ship. Shanghai-ing was getting a man drunk (mostly with 'bad whisky') and making him work on ships bound for places he didn't want to go to (p.811). The bill had been prepared two years before: Weller, I, p.261 (24th June, 1910).

[201] The *Melbourne Punch*, 15th March, 1917.

[202] Munro Ferguson to the Secretary of State for the Colonies, 3rd November, 1916 (CO 418/146); 18th March, 1917 (CO 418/157).

[203] Weller, I, pp.376-7 (17th September, 1914).

[204] I. Turner, p.81, in summing up an excellent analysis of the problems which developed during the first months of the war.

[205] Tudor to Andrew Fisher, 27th November, 1916 (Fisher Papers).

[206] CPD 80:8606, 14th September, 1916.

[207] Evatt, p.373, quotes Tudor fairly, and then gives an excellent leftist analysis on the soundness of his opinions and on the worthlessness of those of the Liberals concerning borrowing and taxation. For his conscriptionist speech, see H. McQueen, *Labour History*, no.16, May 1969, p.44.

[208] CPD 79:7770, 10th May, 1916. Cook conveniently forgot this utterance when Hughes announced the referendum, saying that he was 'profoundly disappointed' that conscription would not be directly introduced. But here, too, he was being a politician, since Hughes had visited him at his home on 20th August, and had obtained Cook's guarantee of Liberal Party support for a referendum, four days before he faced caucus. See J. Murdoch, *Sir Joe*, London, 1996, p.113.

[209] For the pressure on Hughes in favour of conscription, see I. Turner, p.105; and Fitzhardinge, II, p.174f.

[210] For the early opposition of the Labor movement, Evatt, p.396f and I. Turner, p.97f. See *DT*, 12th May, 1916, as to a trade union ballot of 258,018 against conscription, and only 753 for it.

[211] McCalman, p.98.

[212] CPD 80:9962, 15th December, 1916.

[213] Weller, I, pp.434-5 (24th-28th August, 1916); Fitzhardinge, II, pp.185—

[214] CPD 80:8606, 14th September, 1916. Only nine members of caucus approved of his resignation: Weller, I, p.437 (14th September, 1916).

[215] I. Turner, p.110. Hughes had made a list of four ministers and seventeen Labor Party members who were for conscription. Tudor replied with a list of zero ministers and thirty-four members who were against it. See the *Age*, 29th September, 1916 for the 'No' Manifesto.

[216] The 'Yes' Manifesto, *DT*, 18th September, 1916; Hughes in Sydney, *DT*, 19th

References

September, 1916.
[217] Fitzhardinge, II, p.196.
[218] Plus one senator and two MHRs who were on active service. See Weller, I, p.442, for the lists. For the tears, M. L. Shepherd, *Memoirs*, MS A 1632 (ANL), p.318.
[219] J. E. West to A. Fisher, 24th November, 1916 (Fisher Papers, ANL). The contested leadership vote was reported in all the newspapers (e.g. the *Age* 16th November, 1916). It was snowed over in the caucus minutes, where Tudor was said to have been unanimously elected – which did indeed happen in a final formal vote after McDonald had lost. But see Weller, I, pp.439-440, for the version based on the minutes, and p.488, that Tudor thought Hughes to be a discredited dictator.
[220] Tudor to A. Fisher, 27th November, 1916 (Fisher Papers ANL). See the quote on p.136.
[221] DT, 11th November, 1916; 15th November, 1916; 27th November, 1916.
[222] Weller, I. p.441 (15-16th November, 1916).
[223] CPD 80:9243f, 29th November, 1916.
[224] I. Turner, p.117.
[225] Weller, I. p.447 (7th December, 1916); *see* also *DT*, 16th December, 1916. For A. Gardiner's explanation about the double dissolution, *DT*, 27th December, 1916.
[226] For the negotiations which led to the coalition of 17th February, 1917, see Fitzhardinge, II, Chapter 11 from Hughes's point of view; Murdoch, *Sir Joe*, Chapter 8 from Cook's.
[227] The *Age*, 10th January, 1917.
[228] *DT*, 23rd January, 1918. Tudor repeated that the only reasonable and honourable solution would be to hold a new general election. See CPD 81:11005-6, 6th March, 1917, for the correspondence between Hughes and Tudor.
[229] Munro Ferguson to the Secretary of State for the Colonies, 18th March, 1917 (CO 418/157). He thereby quoted approvingly Tudor's former colleague, W. O. Archibald.
[230] The *Age*, 30th March, 1917. The assessment of Tudor and the Labor Party in general as 'feeble' also comes from this source, but all the main dailies agreed. Tudor also spoke in favour of generous repatriation schemes and for help for the man on the land. He was against profiteers, and for borrowing within Australia.
[231] Munro Ferguson to the Secretary of State for the Colonies, 28th November, 1916 (CO 418/146); G. F. Pearce, *Carpenter to Cabinet*, London, 1951, p.140.
[232] Tudor to Andrew Fisher, 1st August, 1919 (Fisher Papers).
[233] ibid., for the quotations in this paragraph.

[234] The caucus minutes contain many detailed proposals: Weller, II, pp.35, 42 (10th July, 1917-19th July, 1917); pp.56-7 (11th April, 1918); pp.63 – 5, (16th May, 1918-23rd May, 1918) gives examples.
[235] I. Turner, pp. 134,159, for Labor's weak attitudes.
[236] For example, CPD 86:129, 12th July, 1917, when Tudor said he would not debate the Address-in-Reply, on the grounds that the Government should make its proposals known, and caught out Hughes who had nothing ready. DT, 13th July, 1917 for a fine comment.
[237] DT, 14th November, 1917.
[238] Munro Ferguson to the Secretary of State for the Colonies, 15th January, 1918 (CO 418/169).
[239] Munro Ferguson's dispatches are full of anti-Labor sentiments: 'No one looks back upon the period of Mr Fisher's rule with any particular pleasure... [because of its] extravagance, bad laws, and maladministration...' (20th June, 1917, CO 418/158); or 'Tudor will leave no stone unturned to prepare the way to re-establishing the ascendancy of the Union-ridden caucus...' (3rd January, 1917, CO 418/157).
[240] Freeman's Journal (Sydney), 21st March, 1918 (quoted Murphy, p.371).
[241] Tudor to Andrew Fisher, 1st August, 1919 (Fisher Papers).
[242] Murphy, p.357.
[243] CPP, 1917, 1918, 1919, IV, (12th April, 1918-19 April, 1918). Tudor's conditions are on p.660f.
[244] Murphy, pp.360-5.
[245] Report of the Seventh Commonwealth Labor Conference, p.23f; and I. Turner, p.177.
[246] K. O'Malley to Andrew Fisher, 5th May, 1919 (O'Malley Papers, quoted by Murphy, p.421); see also L. Noye, *O'Malley MHR*, Geelong, 1985, p.248.
[247] Murphy, pp.454-463. The conference lasted three days.
[248] Weller, II, p.15.
[249] Murphy, p.472.
[250] Munro Ferguson to the Secretary of State for the Colonies, 27th November, 1919 (CO 418/178).
[251] 'Manifesto of the Australian Labor Party to the People of Australia', Hobart, 1919; and Murphy, p.467f.
[252] Tudor to Andrew Fisher, 1st August, 1919 (Fisher Papers).
[253] DT, 5th November, 1919. Murphy, Chapter 17, gives a fine account of Ryan's electoral campaign with all its difficulties.
[254] DT, 21st January, 1920 (expulsion); CPD 93:4633, 16th September, 1920, (joined the National Party).
[255] CPD 94:6382-6472, 9th November, 1920-11th November, 1920; Fitzhardinge, II, pp.452-6.

References

[256] There were censure motions in March *(DT,* 4th March, 1920), July *(DT,* 9th July, 1920), and October *(DT,* 22nd October, 1920). That of July is best for showing Tudor's ineffectiveness, and how Hughes got the better of him in debate (CPD 92:2684f, 14th July, 1920).
[257] Murphy, p.487, for a good example of Labor's unintelligent tactics in debate.
[258] Weller, II, p.118f (August 1920). For comments, Murphy, p.490.
[259] The *Age,* 16th March, 1921. He was elected deputy on 9th September, 1920 *(DT,* 10th September, 1920).
[260] Weller, II, p.138 (5th May, 1921). *SMH,* 1st June, 1921 for his departure.
[261] Weller, II, p.145 (29th September, 1921).
[262] *ADB,* see also the *Age,* 15th November, 1916.
[263] *AA,* p.15.
[264] *ADB.*
[265] *ADB.*
[266] *AA,* p.20. See also his evidence to the Victorian Royal Commission on Goldmining in September 1890.
[267] *ADB.*
[268] *AA,* pp.20-23.
[269] *AA,* p.36; Creswick branch secretary, p.21.
[270] *AA,* p.337.
[271] *AA,* p.338.
[272] *AA* p.357.
[273] *AA,* p.61.
[274] *AWU,* p.27.
[275] *AWU,* p.73; also *AA,* pp.56, 134, 142; *AWU,* Chapter Seven.
[276] *AA,* p.34.
[277] *AA,* p.281.
[278] ibid.
[279] *AA,* p.18.
[280] ibid.
[281] Weller, op. cit., I: section on first Parliament.
[282] *AWU* , Chapter Nine.
[283] E. Scott, *Australia During the War,* Sydney, 1936, p.51.
[284] *AA,* p.97.
[285] *AA,* p.11.
[286] *AA,* pp.277, 281.
[287] *AA,* p.146.
[288] *AA,* pp.16-17, 325.
[289] *AWU,* pp.23-4; *AA,* p. 44.
[290] *AA,* p.72.

[291] *AA*, Chapter 15 (the press); p.114 (the medal).
[292] *AA*, p.106f.
[293] *AA*, p.73.
[294] *AA*, p.285.
[295] *AWU*, pp.6-8.
[296] *AA*, pp.64-5.
[297] *AA*, p.145.
[298] *AA*, pp.216-7.
[299] *AA*, p.217.
[300] *AA*, p.49.
[301] *AA*, pp.101, 313.
[302] *AWU*, p.78.
[303] *AA*, p.60.
[304] *AA*, pp.53-4.
[305] *AA*, pp.37, 124, 135.
[306] *AA*, p.13. For an earlier paean of praise of himself and his co-workers, CPD 15:3490, 12th August, 1903.
[307] *AA*, p.59; *AWU*, p.106.
[308] *AA*, p.115.
[309] *AA*, p.148.
[310] *AA*, pp. 133-5; G. O'Collins, *P.M. Glynn*, Melbourne, 1965, pp.90-92.
[311] *AA*, p.279.
[312] *AA*, p.336; smallpox, p.113.
[313] *AA*, p.336.
[314] *AA*, p.334. A cynic might note that mighty bulls are killed by far weaker matadors.
[315] *AA*, p.24.
[316] *AWU*, pp.121-2.
[317] *AA*, p.347.
[318] *AA*, p.27.
[319] *AA*, pp.77f; 287.
[320] *AA*, pp.320, 351. Some historians deny such a causal connection as made by Spence, e.g. Murphy, *Labor in Politics*, pp.3-4.
[321] *AA*, p.280.
[322] *AA*, p.283.
[323] *AA*, Chapter 28.
[324] *AA*, p.217.
[325] *AA*, p.352.
[326] *AA*, p.51.
[327] *AA*, p.277.
[328] *AA*, p.53.

References

[329] *AA*, p.332.
[330] *AA*, p.110.
[331] *AA*, p.381.
[332] *AA*, p.273.
[333] *AA*, p.336
[334] *AA*, p.382.
[335] *AA*, p.139.
[336] J. Murdoch, *Principle or Expediency: Liberalism in Commonwealth Politics 1901-1917*, London, 1997. Chapter Nine, discusses this development. See also Part Two of this book.
[337] The Governor-General to the Secretary of State for the Colonies, 18th November, 1915 (CO 418/134).
[338] L. C. Jauncey, *The Story of Conscription in Australia*, Melbourne, new edition 1968, pp.12, 22, 212; and the *Age*, 3rd October, 1916.
[339] Meanjin, Nr 25 (1966) argues for Lamond having influenced Spence. The interpretation here is that he made his own decision.
[340] CPD 85:5561, 5th June, 1918.
[341] J. Symes and J. Chamstrom, *Wilby Walkabout 1873-1933*, Benalla, 1993, p.60. The reference is to a report of James' death on 16th February 1906 at his home near Mulwala. He was given a Presbyterian funeral. The *Wilby Walkabout* is a series of press cuttings and photographs, together with lists of names of settlers. It gives a fine idea of the difficulties of the growth of the young community.
[342] Information on births obtained from the Genealogical Society of Victoria.
[343] *Wilby Walkabout*, op. cit., p.161.
[344] These details come from A. J. Dunlop, *Wide Horizons. The Story of Yarrawonga, Tungamah and Cobran Shires*, Bentleigh, 1978, pp.13-48,134; and J. M. Holmes, *The Murray Valley*, Sydney, 1948, pp.141,209.
[345] Closer settlement was the usual term used for putting farmers on the land after breaking up the big sheep runs.
[346] Dunlop, *Wide Horizons*, op. cit., pp.47-8.
[347] *Wilby Walkabout*, op. cit., p.5.
[348] ibid., p.130 for the overcrowding. One batch of prizes is given in *The Yarrawonga Mercury*, 7th November, 1883, when Adeliza and John won fifth places, and William a seventh. The teachers in the school during Charlie's time there were Will Henry Kaigan (1884-1888), Miss M. McDonald (1888), Annie M. Earles (1888-1890), Elizabeth Armour (1890), James Sharp (1890-1900). *Wilby Walkabout*, p.132.
[349] Information from Jennifer Gowland of the Family History Centre in Wangaratta.
[350] ibid.

[351] Ibid.
[352] *Wilby Walkabout*, p.161.
[353] A. S. McClintock, *The West Australian Goldfields and Some of the Pioneers in Mining, Commerce, Politics etc.*, Kalgoorlie, 1912, p.5.
[354] The *Kalgoorlie Sun*, October 1913, (in Frazer's Scrapbook) and the *Age*, 30th April, 1910.
[355] The *Age*, 30th April, 1910.
[356] Frazer's Scrapbook, probably from the *Kalgoorlie Sun*.
[357] e.g. CPD, 18:212, 8th March, 1904.
[358] The *Age*, 30th April, 1910.
[359] *The Melbourne Punch*, 2nd September, 1909.
[360] Frazer's Scrapbook.
[361] D. J. Murphy (ed.), *Labor in Politics*, Brisbane, 1975. Chapter 6 gives the background to the situation in Western Australia. Details of the 1901 election are on p.351. See also the *Western Argus*, 5th March, 1901.
[362] A. Reid, *Those Were the Days*, Perth, (new ed.) 1986, p.265 gives the details.
[363] The *Westralian Worker*, 10th January, 1902.
[364] ibid., 25th July, 1902.
[365] The *Kalgoorlie Miner*, 15th April, 1903.
[366] The *Western Argus*, 31st August, 1904. The *Kalgoorlie Sun*, 13th May, 1906.
[367] Reid, op. cit., p.281, gives the results. Also the *Westralian Worker*, 21st November, 1902.
[368] The Minutes of the Kalgoorlie Town Council, 3rd December, 1902 (Battye Library).
[369] Frazer's Scrapbook.
[370] J. W. Kirwan, *My Life's Adventure*, London, 1936, p.65.
[371] W. Redmond, *Through the New Commonwealth*, Dublin, 1906, p.125, pp.141-4. The classic book on Kalgoorlie is G. Casey and T. Mayman, *The Mile that Midas Touched*, Adelaide, 1964. There are splendid photographs in I. Templeman and B. McDonald, *The Fields*, Fremantle, 1988. Reid, op. cit., gives, through contemporary newspaper extracts, a plastic account of the first ten years, with many details of the human side.
[372] The Minutes of the Kalgoorlie Municipal Council, 10th June, 1903.
[373] ibid., 31st July, 1903.
[374] The *Kalgoorlie Sun* (cutout in Frazer's Scrapbook), undated.
[375] *The Goldfields T&LC Minutes Book*, 9th February, 1903 (Battye Library).
[376] CPD 19:2220, 9th June, 1904.
[377] The *Kalgoorlie Sun* (in Frazer's Scrapbook); the *Age*, 30th August, 1910.
[378] P. Weller (ed.), *Caucus Minutes of the Federal Labor Party (Vol.1) 1901 – 1917*, Melbourne, 1975, p.102. The copy of this letter is in the *Goldfields T&LC Letter*

References

Book in the Battye Library. Dated 3rd July, 1903, it informs Tudor that 572 Asiatics arrived in Western Australia in four months, while only 188 left in three – 'a serious influx'.
[379] Crouch Memoirs.
[380] ibid.
[381] The *Westralian Worker*, 25th September 1903.
[382] Ibid. Frazer's Scrapbook.
[383] Kirwan, op. cit., p.212.
[384] ibid.
[385] The following details from the *Westralian Worker*, 3rd November, 1903 and 10th November, 1903.
[386] From the *Kalgoorlie Sun*, in Frazer's Scrapbook.
[387] Kirwan, op. cit., pp.212-3.
[388] From the *Kalgoorlie Sun*, October 1903, in Frazer's Scrapbook.
[389] The *Western Argus*, 3rd November, 1903 and 10th November, 1903.
[390] The *Morning Herald* (Perth), 26th October, 1903; the *Kalgoorlie Sun*, 13th December, 1903.
[391] Kirwan, op. cit., p.213. At least Kirwan, years afterwards, was able to pay a handsome tribute to Frazer, who 'proved himself remarkably well adapted to political life. Parliament acts as a university for bright young men such as he'. Op. cit., pp.213-4.
[392] The *Western Argus*, 12th January, 1904.
[393] G. Black, *A History of the Labor Party in New South Wales*, Sydney, 1926, pp.6-7. Black quotes from his own speech in Parliament in 1891.
[394] A fine example of this idealistic vision is in Part Two of this book.
[395] Consider, for instance, the testimony of Robert Harper that he had supported all the ministries of 1901-1906 except Watson's, but had never once been consulted on matters of policy. CPD 31:677, 22nd June, 1906.
[396] M. and A. Webb, *Golden Destiny*, Kalgoorlie, 1993, p.386. See also Casey and Mayman, pp.130-1.
[397] *Table Talk* (Frazer's Scrapbook).
[398] The *Western Argus*, 31st August, 1904; the *Bulletin*, 8th September, 1904; Crouch Memoirs.
[399] The *Moira Independent*, 27th November, 1913.
[400] Weller, op. cit., p.118 (1st March, 1904).
[401] CPD 18:208-12, 8th March, 1904.
[402] The *Melbourne Punch*, 2nd September, 1909.
[403] Crouch Memoirs.
[404] Weller, op. cit., p.146 (5th October, 1904).
[405] M. A. Blaulow (Secretary of the Irish National Foresters' Society) to Frazer 8th November, 1905, thanking him for supporting the 'Home Rule for

Ireland' resolution in the House of Representatives (Frazer's Scrapbook). For an example of Mahon snapping at him, CPD 38:2800-1, 4th September, 1907.
[406] Weller, op. cit., pp.136, 138, 142 (27th July, 1904, 10th August, 1904, 14th September, 1904).
[407] CPD 23:6833f, 10th November, 1904. See also H. G. Turner: *The First Decade of the Australian Commonwealth*, Melbourne, 1911, p.80.
[408] A. W. Byrne to Frazer, 17th November, 1904 (Frazer's Scrapbook).
[409] Shearers and farm labourers: CPD 19:1993-4, 3rd June, 1904; preference to unionists: CPD 21:4166, 11th August, 1904; immigration control and land tax: 20:2601, 26th June, 1904; 'flooded with foreigners': CPD 23:6762, 9th November, 1904.
[410] Crouch Memoirs.
[411] Weller, op. cit., p.127 (17th May, 1904).
[412] ibid., p.129 (26th May, 1904).
[413] *DT*, 2nd August, 1904.
[414] ibid., 22nd August, 1904.
[415] Weller, op. cit., pp.468-70, agreed to by caucus on 14th September, 1904.
[416] ibid., p.143 (15th September, 1904).
[417] ibid., p.144 (21st September, 1904). The other two were Brown and Pearce. The Boulder AWA wired on 28th September, 1904, that it supported Watson.
[418] CDP 18.211, 8th March, 1904.
[419] Report of the Royal Commission on old age pensions, in CPP, 1906, Vol. 3, p.1637, 21st August, 1905.
[420] ibid., p.1705, 9th January, 1906. For Lovegrove, ibid., p.1586, 3rd May, 1905.
[421] ibid., p.1587f, 4th May, 1905.
[422] Given in the report, and also in A. R. Hoyle, *King O'Malley, The American Bounder'*, Melbourne, 1981, p.91.
[423] The *Melbourne Punch*, 2nd September, 1909, makes these references.
[424] The *Sunday Times (WA)*, 27th August, 1905.
[425] The *Australian Worker*, 27th November, 1913.
[426] The *Melbourne Punch*, 2nd September, 1909.
[427] CPD 36:471-2, 11th July, 1907. Also in D. M. Catts, *King O'Malley, Man and Statesman*, Sydney, 1957, p.118.
[428] Crouch Memoirs.
[429] The *Kalgoorlie Sun*, 9th June, 16th June, 30th June, 1905.
[430] CPD 25:769, 9th August, 1905.
[431] The *Westralian Worker*, 16th May, 1906.
[432] For example, CPD 31:591f, 21st June, 1906; 46:11281, 20th May, 1908; 47:200, 22nd September, 1908.

References

[433] The *Western Argus*, 14th February, 1905; the *Melbourne Punch*, 19th May, 1910.

[434] J. Murdoch, *Principle or Expediency: Liberalism in Commonwealth Politics 1901-1917*, London, 1997, Chapters 2 and 3 give a full account of these developments.

[435] See La Nauze, op.cit., Chapter 17, and H. G. Turner, op.cit., pp.97-101 for analyses of these events.

[436] Weller, op. cit., pp.111-2 (21st October, 1903).

[437] Frazer's Scrapbook.

[438] Weller, op. cit., p.158 (5th July, 1905).

[439] Report of the Federal Labor Party Conference 1905, esp. p.18; the *Melbourne Argus*, 11th and 12th July, 1905; R. N. Ebbels, (ed.) *The Australian Labor Movement*, Melbourne, 1960, p.237.

[440] Weller, op.cit., pp.482-4: Watson to Members of Caucus 27th July, 1905.

[441] ibid., p.161 (9th July, 1905).

[442] The *Western Argus*, 15th May, 1906.

[443] Weller, op. cit., pp.176-181 (27th June, 1906 – 5th September, 1906),

[444] CPD 35:5303-21, 25th September, 1906. See also H. G. Turner, op.cit., p.128.

[445] Orient Line: CPD 32:1781-3, 25th July, 1906; preferential voting: CPD 33:3865, 4th September, 1906; race courses: CPD 35:6001, 3rd October, 1906.

[446] Weller, op. cit., p.159 (7th July, 1905). The background to his initiative is given in Crouch Memoirs; the *Kalgoorlie Sun*, 12th March, 1905; and the *Age*, 27th July, 1906.

[447] CPD 32:2592f, 9th August, 1906.

[448] CPD 38:2797f, 4th September, 1907; 47:340, 350, 24th September, 1908.

[449] The *Kookynie Press*, 24th November, 1906.

[450] The *West Australian*, 13th September, 1906. A fuller account of the election in Western Australia is given in J. R. M. Murdoch, 'The Western Australian Party in the 1906 Federal Elections', in *The Australian Journal of Politics and History*, August 1967, pp.247-50.

[451] The *West Australian*, 18th October, 1906; 29th October, 1906; 9th November, 1906.

[452] ibid., 3rd December, 1906.

[453] ibid., 26th November, 1906.

[454] ibid., 21st November, 1906. See Casey and Mayman, p.102f for 'Ten- foot Ned'.

[455] The *Western Argus*, 30th October, 1906.

[456] Frazer's Scrapbook.

[457] Weller, op. cit., p.189 (19th February, 1907).

458 The *Melbourne Punch*, 2nd September, 1909.
459 Weller, op. cit., p.201 (23rd October, 1907).
460 La Nauze, op. cit., p.428.
461 The *Age*, 31st October, 1907. See also Weller, op. cit., p.202 (30th October, 1907).
462 Weller, op. cit., p.217 (15th September, 1908); pp.221-2 (21st October, 1908); p.227 (2nd December, 1908); the accounts are on pp.479-80.
463 Tariff: CPD 38:3512, 29th August, 1907; pensions 36:161, 5th July, 1907; Federal Capital etc. 46:11798f, 2nd June, 1908 and 47:193f, 22nd September, 1908.
464 CPD 42:7492-3, 13th December, 1907. Also La Nauze, op. cit., p.433.
465 H. G. Turner, op. cit., pp.128, 165, 262.
466 D. M. Catts, *James Howard Catts MHR*, Sydney, 1953, p.40.
467 CPD 45:10132, 3rd April, 1908; the *Westralian Worker*, 12th June, 1908.
468 Weller, op. cit., p.216 (15th September, 1908).
469 ibid., p.223 (4th November, 1908). The vote was taken on the following day.
470 The *Southern Sphere*, 1st July, 1910.
471 The *Australian Magazine*, 1st July, 1910, p.580.
472 The *Melbourne Argus*, 30th April, 1910.
473 CPD 49:453, 25th June, 1909.
474 Weller, op. cit., p.224 (12th November, 1908).
475 ibid., p.225; the *Melbourne Punch*, 2nd September, 1909.
476 The *Kalgoorlie Miner*, 2nd April, 1909. For Fisher's speech and editorials on it, any Australian newspaper, 31st March, 1909. H. G. Turner, op. cit., pp.207-11 gives a good summary with interesting conservative comments.
477 The *Melbourne Punch*, 19th May, 1910.
478 ibid., 2nd September, 1909.
479 The *Melbourne Argus*, 26th November, 1913.
480 The *Melbourne Punch*, 2nd September, 1909.
481 ibid.
482 CPD 49:179, 28th May, 1909.
483 CPD 51:2489, 13th August, 1909.
484 Frazer's Scrapbook.
485 Forrest to an unknown correspondent, 1st March, 1910 (Frazer's Scrapbook).
486 Frazer's Scrapbook; The *Kalgoorlie Miner*, 16th February, 1910.
487 This successful Liberal candidate, strangely enough, was J. M. Fowler, the only Labor man during Fisher's term of leadership to leave the party and join its opponents (on 8th November, 1908). The Labor comment was that many Labor voters had not realised his switch. Fowler's main reason was anger

References

and frustration that he had not won office in Fisher's ministry, and that Mahon and even Frazer had been preferred to him.
[488] The *Melbourne Argus*, 26th November, 1913.
[489] Crouch Memoirs.
[490] *DT*, 30th April, 1910; The *Age*, 30th April, 1910; Weller, op. cit., p.256n (29th April, 1910).
[491] Frazer to Fisher, 19th July, 1911 (Fisher Papers).
[492] P. Heydon, *Quiet Decision*, Melbourne, 1965, pp.46-9. Heydon was Pearce's secretary in 1936-7.
[493] Hoyle, op. cit., tries to show how O'Malley did good work, but he succeeds only in demonstrating how he led his Department of Home Affairs into chaos and disorder. (Chapter 8).
[494] Weller, op. cit., p.270 (21st September, 1910).
[495] The *Melbourne Leader*, 22nd October, 1910, p.37.
[496] The *Western Argus*, 24th January, 1911.
[497] ibid., the *Kalgoorlie Sun* in Frazer's Scrapbook; Casey and Mayman, op. cit. p.131.
[498] Frazer to Fisher, 19th July, 1911 (Fisher Papers).
[499] Crouch Memoirs.
[500] Denman to the Secretary of State for the Colonies, 20th October, 1911 (co 418/89).
[501] CPD 61:2094-5, 1st November, 1911.
[502] CPD 69:7670, 20th December, 1912.
[503] CPD 64:581, 10th July, 1912. The graphs and statistics are given in full in the Annual Reports of the Postmaster-General's Department. CPP 1912, Vol. 3, p.899f, and 1913, Vol. 3, p.961f.
[504] CPD 64:581, 10th July, 1912.
[505] CPD 70:342f, 21st August, 1913.
[506] CPD 63:4601, 8th December, 1911.
[507] CPD 61:2094, 1st November, 1911.
[508] CPD 70:343-4, 21st August, 1913.
[509] CPD 64:582-4, 10th July, 1912.
[510] For example, CPD 40:4957-8, 22nd October, 1907.
[511] The *Melbourne Argus*, 4th April, 1912. The rest of the series came in batches, the last one being the £2 stamp on 8th April, 1913.
[512] For Frazer's account of the business, CPD 70:350f, 21st August, 1913. See also the *Western Argus*, 5th and 12th March, 1913.
[513] The *Melbourne Herald*, 4th January, 1912.
[514] The *Kalgoorlie Miner*, 14th February, 1913.
[515] *DT:* for Queensland, 15th and 24th April, 1912, for Tasmania, 29th April, 1912.

516 Weller, op. cit., p.324 (8th July, 1913).
517 Wynne, CPD 69:7473; McWilliams, 69:7438; Greene, 69:7447, all 18th December, 1912.
518 Crouch Memoirs.
519 The *Western Argus,* 24th January, 1911.
520 The *Kalgoorlie Miner,* 17th April, 1913.
521 ibid., 24th April, 1913.
522 The *Melbourne Argus,* 14th July, 1913. The Cook Government's issue was released on 8th December, 1913.
523 The *Western Argus,* 5th August, 1913. CPD 70:345-6, 21st August, 1913.
524 Cook in CPD 72:3436, 25th November, 1913.
525 CPD 70:353, 21st August, 1913.
526 R. Blake, *The Unknown Prime Minister,* London, 1955, p.140f.
527 Weller, op. cit., pp.331-2 (2nd September, 1913); CPD 70:944f, 9th September, 1913.
528 Crouch Memoirs.
529 CPD 72:3436-39, 25th November, 1913.
530 ADB for his background and newspaper references.
531 For his wide experiences in the clerks' union, CPD 112:930, 1926.
532 CPD 104:1075, 12th July 1923, and 106:217, 2nd April 1924.
533 CPD 104:837, 10th July 1923.
534 CPD 103: 162f, 7th March 1923.
535 Weller, II, has many examples of his committee approach to everything. In the cases mentioned: press p.191-2, 21st June 1923; homes p.241, 20th August 1925 and p.340, 29th August 1929; bank p.241, 27th August 1925.
536 Some examples, ibid p.217, 10th July 1924; p.259, 26th May 1926; p.301, 3rd May 1928.
537 CPD 103:162f is an early but typical example of his complete support for whatever his party was doing. There are many others.
538 Weller, II, p.207, 8th May 1924. Also CPD 106:786, 21st May 1924 and 108:3572, 26th August 1924.
539 ibid, p.269 and note. See also G. Sawer *Australian Federal Politics and Law,* I, Melbourne 1956, p.262.
540 CPD 125:999f, 17th April 1931 is his long, detailed and mostly critical report.
541 The *Melbourne Argus* 26th May 1934.
542 The references to *The Kingdom of Shylock* are on pages 5, 7, 8, 13, 30 and 47.
543 Schachner, R. *Australien in Politik, Wirtschaft und Kultur,* Jena 1909
544 Lack, J. (ed), *The Workers' Paradise?* Letters written by Robert Schachner from Australia 1906-7. See also J. Murdoch, *Folly, Fortune, Fate,* I, Melbourne

References

2009, parts 4 and 6 for a more detailed analysis of the Germans and their writing.
[545] Lack. Op.cit., quoted on p.10.
[546] Title as in text, p.9.
[547] Title as in text, p.241.

www.ingramcontent.com/pod-product-compliance
Lightning Source LLC
Chambersburg PA
CBHW050616300426
44112CB00012B/1526